BREVIARY
LIVES OF THE SAINTS

BREVIARY LIVES

OF THE

SAINTS

FEBRUARY – MAY

Latin Selections with
Commentary and a Vocabulary

by

Rev. Frederick J. Murphy, M.A.,S.T.L.

CARDINAL O'CONNELL SEMINARY
BOSTON, MASSACHUSETTS

Wipf and Stock Publishers
EUGENE, OREGON

NIHIL OBSTAT:

JOHN WALSH, S.J.
Diocesan Censor

IMPRIMATUR:

✠ RICHARD CARDINAL CUSHING
Archbishop of Boston

July 1, 1964

Wipf and Stock Publishers
199 West 8th Avenue, Suite 3
Eugene, Oregon 97401

Breviary Lives of the Saints: February - May
Latin Selections with Commentary and a Vocabulary
By Murphy, Fr. Frederick J.
Copyright© January, 1965 by Murphy, Fr. Frederick J.
ISBN: 1-59244-281-1
Publication date: July, 2003
Previously published by Daughters of St. Paul, January, 1965

Parentibus

CONTENTS

Preface	13
St. Ignatius of Antioch	15
St. Blaise	21
St. Agatha	24
St. Cyril of Alexandria	29
The Apparitions at Lourdes	35
St. Peter Damian	44
Sts. Perpetua and Felicitas	53
St. Thomas Aquinas	57
St. Gregory I the Great	65
St. Patrick	73
St. Cyril of Jerusalem	79
St. Joseph	86
St. Benedict	90
St. John Damascene	96
St. John Capistrano	104
St. Isidore of Seville	111
St. Leo I the Great	118
St. Justin Martyr	124
St. Anselm	131
St. Mark	139

St. Peter Canisius	143
St. Paul of the Cross	151
St. Catherine of Siena	158
St. Athanasius	165
St. Monica	172
St. Pius V	177
St. Gregory of Nazianzus	183
Sts. Philip and James	189
St. Robert Bellarmine	195
St. John Baptiste de la Salle	201
St. Gregory VII	208
St. Philip Neri	217
St. Bede the Venerable	223
St. Augustine of Canterbury	230
The Queenship of Mary	237
MAPS	241
INDEX TO THE NOTES	246
VOCABULARY OF PROPER NAMES AND PLACES	252
GENERAL VOCABULARY	260

Preface

This book intends to set before the student a semester text of intermediate Latin which will fulfill his language requirement in Latin and at the same time introduce him to some prominent figures in Church History. Since the saints selected for this text cover the last twenty centuries and span Europe and the Near East from Ireland to the Holy Land, it is hoped that there will emerge for the student an awareness of the history and tradition of the Church, her glories and her sorrows, her failures and her triumphs. At the same time, as he studies the many different ways in which these saints served God and the Church, there should emerge an awareness of the one thing they all had in common: personal lives of great holiness.

The commentary for each selection has been written to help the student in the reading and translation of the Latin and also to give him a fairly complete historical and biographical picture of each saint and his times. It is hoped that many ideas will occur to both teacher and student which will provide opportunity for further independent research.

The Latin text is based on the second nocturn readings of the Matins of the Roman Breviary. No change was made in the text save in a few instances where a different word-order seemed helpful for the student. In three instances, sentence structure was altered for reasons of grammar and sense.

No attempt has been made to give the student a bibliography for each saint. For further reference he should consult the works which were most helpful to the author in the preparation of the commentary, viz., the *Acta Sanctorum,* the *Catholic Encyclopedia, Butler's Lives of the Saints,* edd. Thurston and Attwater (New York 1956), *The Saints, A Concise Biographical Dictionary,* ed. John Coulson (New York 1960).

Finally the author is happy to express his appreciation to his colleagues in the seminary for their interest and encouragement, particularly the Rector, the Rt. Rev. William A. Granville, and the Rev. Gerard L. Dorgan, whose assistance and criticism was especially valued in the selection of the illustrations. The many helpful suggestions and enthusiasm of the Daughters of St. Paul are also acknowledged with gratitude.

F.J.M.

1. ST. IGNATIUS OF ANTIOCH

February 1 † c. 107

Ignatius, Antiochenae ecclesiae tertius post Petrum Apostolum episcopus, commovente persecutionem Traiano, damnatus ad bestias, Romam vinctus mittitur. Cumque navigans Smyrnam venisset, ubi

> This biography is taken from St. Jerome's *De Viris Illustribus*, a valuable work which contains biographies of all outstanding Christians from the Apostles down to Jerome's own day. (cf. St. Mark, 20)
> 1. **Antiochenae**: Antioch in Syria, the greatest city of the ancient world after Rome and Alexandria. Here the followers of Christ were first called Christians (*Acts* 11), and from here St. Paul started his first and third missionary journeys (*Acts* 13; 18,23)
> **tertius ... episcopus**. Evodius was the second, of whom nothing further is known. (Eusebius, *H.E.* 3, 22) Antioch was St. Peter's first see before he moved at uncertain date to Rome.
> 3. **Traiano.** Trajan (98-117) persecuted the Christians for refusing to worship the gods, to whom he attributed his famous victory over the Dacians on the Danube frontier. There is an account of a personal meeting between Trajan and St. Ignatius at this time, but it is legendary. (cf. *Acta Sanctorum*, February vol. 1, pp. 29-33.) Five years later, in correspondence with Pliny the Younger, the governor of Bithynia, Trajan determined the policy of the Empire for the next century: Christians were not to be sought out, but if detected, they were to be prosecuted. (Pliny, *Ep.* 97) cf. 7.ln.

5   Polycarpus, auditor Ioannis, episcopus erat, scripsit
unam epistulam ad Ephesios, alteram ad Magnesia-
nos, tertiam ad Trallenses, quartam ad Romanos. Et
inde egrediens scripsit ad Philadelphios et ad
Smyrnaeos et propriam ad Polycarpum, commen-
10 dans illi Antiochensem ecclesiam; in qua et de
Evangelio, quod nuper a me translatum est, super
persona Christi ponit testimonium, dicens: "Ego
vero et post resurrectionem in carne eum vidi et
credo quia sit. Et quando venit ad Petrum et ad eos
15 qui cum Petro erant, dixit eis: 'Ecce palpate me et

    5. **Polycarpus.** Polycarp (c. 69-157) was a disciple of St. John the Evangelist, by whom he was appointed bishop of Smyrna. Both he and Ignatius are called Apostolic Fathers, the name given to a number of writers who lived in the late first century and early second century and who are supposed to have known the Apostles. Polycarp is the earliest witness to the authenticity of Ignatius' letters. Soon after Ignatius' death, he wrote to the Philippians: "We send you as requested the Epistles of Ignatius which were sent to us by him."

    6. **epistulam.** These seven epistles are of great importance as they are the main source of information about their author, and because they illustrate the character of early Christianity. Ignatius insists among other things that the people remain close to their bishops and clergy and beware of schism and heresy.

    10. **in qua.** Jerome is mistaken, for it is the epistle to Smyrna, ch. 3, that contains this reference to the physical state of the risen body of Christ.

    11. **Evangelio**; actually the apocryphal Gospel of the Nazarenes, believed by Jerome to be the Aramaic original of the Gospel of St. Matthew. cf. *Lk.* 24,39.

    13. **vidi.** As Ignatius used οἶδα - I know, the Latin rendition should be *scio*, not *vidi*. Ignatius' meaning: "I know and believe that He was in the flesh even after the resurrection."

THE MARTYRDOM OF ST. IGNATIUS. Miniature from the Menology of Basil II (tenth century). **Vatican Library**

videte quia non sum daemonium incorporale.' Et statim tetigerunt eum et crediderunt."

Dignum autem videtur, quia tanti viri fecimus mentionem, et de epistula eius, quam ad Romanos scripsit, pauca ponere: "De Syria usque ad Romam pugno ad bestias in mari et in terra, nocte dieque ligatus cum decem leopardis, hoc est militibus, qui me custodiunt; quibus et cum benefeceris, peiores fiunt. Iniquitas autem eorum mea doctrina est; sed non idcirco iustificatus sum. Utinam fruar bestiis, quae mihi sunt praeparatae; quas et oro mihi veloces esse ad interitum, et alliciam eas ad comeden-

21. **in mari et in terra.** After leaving Smyrna, Ignatius was taken to Troas, where he wrote the letters mentioned in 1. 7; from there he sailed to Neapolis, then travelled overland to Dyrrachium on the Adriatic; from there he sailed to Brundisium; then overland to Rome. This was the usual route of travel.

22. **hoc est**, 'that is to say'. ($=$ *id est*)

23. **quibus ... benefeceris.** The relative pronoun or adverb beginning a new thought after a period or semi-colon should be translated by *and* and a *demonstrative;* 'and even when you do *them* a kindness'. This use of the relative is extremely common in these lives.

24. **doctrina**, 'schooling'.

sed ... iustificatus sum. cf. 1 *Cor.* 4,4. Ignatius means that his endurance of the soldiers will not of itself 'justify' or 'save' him; he wants nothing less than martyrdom, and martyrdom from the wild beasts.

26. **quas ... esse;** quas is the subject accusative of **esse;** 'I pray that they may be swift. . . .'

27. **ad interitum**; ad to express purpose, depending on **velox.**

dum me, ne sicut aliorum martyrum, non audeant corpus attingere. Quod si venire noluerint, ego vim faciam, ego me ingeram ut devorer. Ignoscite mihi, filioli; quid mihi prosit, ego scio.

"Nunc incipio Christi esse discipulus, nihil de his quae videntur desiderans, ut Iesum Christum inveniam. Ignis, crux, bestiae, confractio ossium, membrorum divisio, et totius corporis contritio et tota tormenta diaboli in me veniant; tantum ut Christo fruar." Cumque iam damnatus esset ad bestias, et ardore patiendi rugientes audiret leones, ait: "Frumentum Christi sum; dentibus bestiarum molar, ut panis mundus inveniar." Passus est anno undecimo Traiani. Reliquiae corporis eius Antiochiae iacent extra portam Daphniticam in coemeterio.

28. **sicut aliorum martyrum**; elliptical: 'Just as they have not ventured to touch the bodies of other martyrs. . . .'

32. **nihil ... desiderans.** The original Greek expresses the idea: "Let no visible or invisible thing envy me my finding of Jesus Christ."

36. **tantum ut Christo fruar**, 'only may I enjoy Christ'. While *utinam* is far more common, *ut* is also used with the subjunctive to express a wish.

40. **mundus**, 'fine', 'not coarse'. cf. the Communion prayer of Ignatius' Mass; from *Ep. ad Romanos* 4.

anno undecimo, i.e., 109. The Acts of his martyrdom, however, indicate the ninth year, 107. cf. *Acta Sanctorum*, p. 19

41. **Reliquiae corporis.** Ignatius' remains were removed in the sixth century to the Church of St. Clement in Rome where they are preserved today. (cf. *Acta Sanctorum*, p. 35.)

42. **Daphniticam.** The gate led to the park of Daphne five miles south of the city. (cf. Ovid, *Met.* 1,451 sqq.)

Oratio

Infirmitatem nostram respice, omnipotens Deus, et quia pondus propriae actionis gravat, beati
45 Ignatii Martyris tui .atque Pontificis intercessio gloriosa nos protegat. Per Dominum nostrum.

2. ST. BLAISE

February 3 † 316?

Blasius Sebaste in Armenia cum virtutum laude floreret, eiusdem civitatis episcopus eligitur. Qui, quo tempore Diocletianus insatiabilem crudelitatem in Christianos exercebat, se in speluncam abdidit
5 montis Argaei; ubi tamdiu latuit, dum ab Agricolai

Devotion to this oriental saint was introduced into the West (France, Germany) in the ninth century, for then his name begins to be found in martyrologies. Beyond the fact that he was a bishop and martyred early in the fourth century, other incidents related about him depend upon legendary Acts of his life. cf. *Acta Sanctorum*, February vol 1, pp. 340-357.

1. **Sebaste** was of considerable importance. Following the division of the Roman Empire in 305, it was made the capital of Armenia Minor.

cum, 'since'. Conjunctions are often found postponed as here; in translating they should be placed first.

2. **episcopus eligitur**. According to legend, Blaise had previously been a physician.

3. **quo tempore**, 'at the time when'.

Diocletianus, Emperor 284-305, but most accounts place Blaise's martyrdom a decade later in the reign of Licinius who ruled as colleague of Constantine in the East 313-324. (cf. *Acta Sanctorum*, p. 334.)

5. **Argaei**; Mt. Argaeus in central Cappadocia, the highest mountain in Asia Minor.

dum, 'until'.

Agricolai. Agricolaus was the governor of Cappadocia and Armenia Minor.

ST. BLAISE. A panal by Rossello di Jacopo Franchi (1377-1456). **Cathedral, Florence. Courtesy, Alinari**

St. Blaise

praesidis militibus venantibus deprehensus et ad
praesidem ductus, eius iussu coniectus est in vincula.
Quo in loco multos aegrotos sanavit, qui ad Blasium,
eius fama sanctitatis adducti, deferebantur. In illis
puer fuit, qui desperata a medicis salute, transversa
spina faucibus inhaerente, animam agebat. Productus autem ad praesidem Blasius semel et iterum,
cum nec blanditiis nec minis adduci posset ut diis
sacrificaret, primum virgis caesus, deinde in eculeo
ferreis pectinibus dilaniatus est. Postremo dempto
capite illustre fidei testimonium Christo Domino
dedit tertio Nonas Februarii.

Oratio

Deus, qui nos beati Blasii Martyris tui atque
Pontificis annua solemnitate laetificas, concede propitius ut cuius natalitia colimus, de eiusdem etiam
protectione gaudeamus. Per Dominum nostrum.

6. **militibus venantibus**, 'hunters'; lit., 'soldiers hunting'. Sent into the mountains after wild beasts for the amphitheatre, they are supposed to have found Blaise surrounded by animals over which his healing powers were said to extend.

10. **transversa ... inhaerente**, 'because a fish-bone was stuck crosswise in his throat'; **transversa** should be translated as an adverb. Because of this miracle St. Blaise is invoked as patron saint to protect against afflictions of the throat, and on his feast throats are blessed by a priest with the prayer: *Per intercessionem sancti Blasii episcopi et martyris liberet te Deus a malo gutturis et a quolibet alio malo, in nomine Patris*, etc.

17. **tertio Nonas Februarii**, i.e., *die* tertio *ante* Nonas: 'on the third day before the Nones of February'; *die* and *ante* are omitted as usual. The name of the month should be in the form of an adjective. cf. 32.44n.

3. ST. AGATHA

February 5 † c. 250

    Agatha virgo in Sicilia nobilibus parentibus
nata, quam Panormitani et Catanenses civem suam
esse dicunt, in persecutione Decii imperatoris Cata-
nae gloriosi martyrii coronam consecuta est. Nam
5 cum pari pulchritudinis et castitatis laude commen-
daretur, Quintianus, Siciliae praetor, eius amore

    2. **civem suam.** Both Palermo and Catania claim St. Agatha, since it is not known in which of the two cities she was born.
    3. **persecutione Decii.** Decius (250-253) decided to revive the old paganism in order to solve the problems facing the Empire. His orders that Christians renounce their faith and worship the pagan gods led to a persecution more violent than any the Church had yet experienced. For an earlier emperor with a similar regard for the gods, see Trajan, 1.3n. That Agatha died in the Decian persecution is attested to only by the legendary Acts of her maryrdom, which are no older than the sixth century and have little claim to historical reliability. cf. *Acta Sanctorum*, February vol. 1, p. 621-624. Their content indicates the hagiographer was more interested in elaborating an edifying account than in transmitting bare historical facts.
    Catanae. This much only can be accepted as history, and the fact that her cult is found very early, for her name appears in the so-called *Martyrologium Hieronymianum* and in the *Martyrologium Carthaginiense* of c. 530. Further, St. Gregory the Great (see 9) dedicated to her a church in Rome which was in existence as early as the fifth century (the present St. Agatha dei Goti).

captus est. Sed cum tentata modis omnibus eius pudicitia Agatham in suam sententiam perducere non posset, christianae superstitionis nomine comprehensam, Aphrodisiae cuidam mulieri depravandam tradit. Quae cum de constantia colendae christianae fidei et servandae virginitatis removeri non posset, nuntiat Aphrodisia Quintiano se in Agatha operam perdere. Quare ille ad se virginem adduci iubet et, "Nonne," inquit, "te pudet nobili genere natam, humilem et servilem Christianorum vitam agere?" Cui Agatha: "Multo praestantior est christiana humilitas et servitus regum opibus ac superbia."

Quam ob rem iratus praetor hanc ei optionem dat, velitne potius venerari deos an vim tormentorum subire. At illa constans in fide, primum colaphis caesa mittitur in carcerem, unde postridie educta, cum in sententia permaneret, admotis

8. **in suam sententiam...**, 'since he could not bring her over to his own attitude'. Like Maria Goretti, Agatha was a martyr for her chastity.

9. **comprehensam ... depravandam;** the words agree with *eam* understood: 'handed her over, after she had been arrested ... to be corrupted'.

11. **colendae christianae fidei,** 'of practising the Christian faith'; lit., 'of the faith to be practised'. This gerundive construction is very common.

20. **velitne ... an ...;** a double indirect question introduced by **optionem,** 'choice, whether she would wish to ... or ...'

23. **admotis candentibus laminis,** 'by the application of hot plates'; lit., 'after hot plates had been applied'. The ablative absolute frequently offers the opportunity to express the meaning in various other ways in English.

ST. AGATHA. Mosaic (twelfth century) in the **Capella Palatina Palermo**. Courtesy, Alinari

St. Agatha

candentibus laminis in eculeo torquetur; tum ei
mamilla abscinditur. Quo in vulnere Quintianum
appellans virgo, "Crudelis," inquit, "tyranne, non te
pudet amputare in femina, quod ipse in matre
suxisti?" Mox coniecta in vincula, sequenti nocte a
sene quodam, qui se Christi Apostolum esse dicebat,
sanata est. Rursum evocata a praetore et in Christi
confessione perseverans, in acutis testulis et
candentibus carbonibus ei subiectis volutatur.

Quo tempore ingenti terraemotu urbs tota
contremuit, ac duo parietes corruentes Silvinum et
Falconium intimos praetoris familiares oppresserunt.
Quare vehementer commota civitate, veritus populi
tumultum Quintianus Agatham semimortuam clam
reduci imperat in carcerem. Quae sic Deum precata:
"Domine, qui me custodisti ab infantia, qui abstulisti
a me amorem saeculi, qui me carnificum tormentis
superiorem praestitisti, accipe animam meam." Ea
in oratione migravit in caelum Nonis Februarii;
cuius corpus a Christianis sepelitur.

24. **ei**, 'from her'; a dative of separation; verbs of *taking away*, especially compounds of *ab, ex, de,* govern a dative of the person affected.

25. **mamilla abscinditur.** This particular torture became the peculiar attribute of Agatha in medieval art.

29. **Christi Apostolum**; St. Peter—so the legendary Acts, whose narrative of this visitation and cure provides the proper antiphons of the Matins, Lauds, and Vespers of this feast. (cf. *Acta Sanctorum*, p. 623.)

Oratio

Deus, qui inter cetera potentiae tuae miracula
etiam in sexu fragili victoriam martyrii contulisti,
concede propitius ut qui beatae Agathae Virginis et
Martyris tuae natalitia colimus, per eius ad te exempla gradiamur. Per Dominum nostrum.

4. ST. CYRIL OF ALEXANDRIA

February 9   c. 375-444

Cyrillus Alexandrinus, cuius praeconia non unius tantum vel alterius sunt comprobata testimonio, sed etiam oecumenicorum conciliorum Ephesini et Chalcedonensis actis celebrata, claris
5 ortus parentibus ac Theophili episcopi Alexandrini nepos, adhuc adulescens praecellentis ingenii clara specimina dedit. Litteris ac scientiis egregie imbutus, ad Ioannem episcopum Hierosolymitanum se contulit, ut in christiana fide perficeretur. Alexandriam
10 deinde cum rediisset, Theophilo vita functo, ad illius sedem evectus est; quo in munere ita optimi

    1. **cuius praeconia ... celebrata,** 'whose praises have been attested to, not by the testimony of just one or two, but also celebrated by the acts of the councils. . . .' For Ephesus, see below 35n.; for Chalcedon, see 17,23n.

    5. **Theophili,** bishop of Alexandria 385-421, some of whose writings are extant.

    7. **Litteris ac scientiis,** 'in literature and other subjects' (not 'sciences'). Cyril's fine classical education is especially apparent in his apologetical work against Julian the Apostate (for whom see 11.29n.).

    8. **Ioannem,** bishop of Jerusalem 386-417, noted for his eloquence and virtue, whose life was troubled by controversies.

    11. **evectus est,** October 18, 412, and not without strong opposition in favor of a rival candidate.

pastoris formam ab Apostolo definitam constanter prae se tulit, ut sanctissimi praesulis gloriam merito sit adeptus.

¹⁵ Salutis animarum zelo incensus, curas omnes intendit ut sibi commissum gregem in fidei et morum integritate servaret atque a venenatis infidelium et haereticorum pascuis defenderet. Hinc tum Novati asseclas e civitate expelli, tum Iudaeos, qui furore ²⁰ acti in caedem Christianorum conspiraverant, iuxta leges puniri sategit. Singulare vero Cyrilli studium pro catholicae fidei incolumitate enituit contra

12. **pastoris formam ... definita**: 1 *Pet.* 5, 1-4.

15. **zelo incensus**. In addition to drive and zeal, Cyril was also characterized by an obstinate and domineering personality, which made him a forceful and respected leader but brought him into conflict with many groups.

18. **Novati**. When Cornelius was chosen in 251 to succeed the martyred Pope Fabian, Novatian, an ordained priest in Rome, had himself elected Pope by three Italian bishops. Excommunicated, he set up a schismatic church, which even two hundred years later was still curiously flourishing in the East.

19. **expelli**. Cyril had their churches closed and sacred vessels confiscated. The Patriarch of Alexandria had by the fifth century become one of the most powerful politically in the Empire.

Iudaeos. The most important Jewish center outside of Palestine was in Alexandria, and was known for its size, wealth and intellectual activity. From the beginning, the Jewish colony had its own quarter in the city and had received special privileges, but relations between Jew and Gentile were never amicable. On this occasion the Jews were held responsible for riots in which Christians had been massacred.

ST. CYRIL OF ALEXANDRIA. Fresco by Domenichino (1581-1641). **Abbey of Grottaferrata, Italy**

Nestorium Constantinopolitanum episcopum, as-
serentem Iesum Christum ex Maria Virgine
25 hominem tantum et non Deum natum, eique
divinitatem pro meritis esse collatam, cuius emenda-
tionem cum frustra tentasset, eum Caelestino
Pontifici maximo denuntiavit.

Caelestini delegata auctoritate concilio Ephesi-
30 no praefuit, in quo haeresis Nestoriana penitus
proscripta est, damnatus Nestorius et a sua Sede
deiectus, ac dogma catholicum, de una in Christo
eaque divina persona et divina gloriosae Virginis
Mariae maternitate, assertum; plaudente populo
35 universo, qui incredibili gaudio gestiens collucenti-

23. **Nestorius** had been a monk in a monastery near Antioch before being called in 428 to be Patriarch of Constantinople.

25. **hominem tantum et non Deum,** 'as man only and not as God'. Catholic theology teaches that there are two natures in Christ, one divine and one human, but only one Person, that of the God-Man Jesus Christ, who is the Second Person of the Trinity. Since Mary is the mother of Jesus, and since Jesus is a divine Person, Mary is truly the Mother of God. Nestorius maintained that there were two persons in Christ, which were only morally united, and that Mary was the mother of Christ as man only. In effect, Nestorius denied the Incarnation, that God was made man, and as a corollary denied the divine maternity of Mary. The chief debt the Church owes Cyril is for the firm stand he took in dealing with Nestorius' heretical teaching.

26. **pro meritis,** 'in keeping with his merits', 'in proportion to his merits'.

27. **Caelestino.** In addition to the condemnation of Nestorius at the Council of Ephesus, Pope St. Celestine (422-432) is remembered for sending St. Patrick to Ireland. cf. 10.16n.

35. **gaudio gestiens.** Ephesus had been famous for its devotion to the goddess Artemis, whose temple in the city was to

bus facibus domum deduxit episcopos. Sed hac de causa Cyrillus calumniis, iniuriis et persecutionibus plurimis a Nestorio eiusque fautoribus impetitus fuit; quas ipse patientissime tulit, ita ut de sola fide
40 sollicitus, quidquid adversus eum effutiebant ac moliebantur haeretici, pro nihilo haberet. Tandem pro Ecclesia Dei maximis perfunctus laboribus, plurimisque scriptis editis tum ad ethnicos et haereticos confutandos tum ad sacras Scripturas et
45 catholica explananda dogmata, sancto fine quievit anno quadringentesimo quadragesimo quarto, episcopatus tricesimo secundo. Leo decimus tertius Pontifex maximus Officium et Missam praeclarissimi

---

the ancients one of the Seven Wonders of the World. With Christianity devotion to Mary, the Mother of God, *Theotokos*, replaced devotion to this pagan goddess. By denying the validity of this popular title, Nestorius had violently disturbed the East. Its confirmation by the Council was thus responsible for the tremendous outburst of enthusiasm by the people.

38. **fautoribus.** The condemnation of Nestorius was not accepted by his many supporters, even among the hierarchy, among them the influential Archbishop of Antioch, who, with forty-three other supporters, arrived late for the Council. Cyril was unable at first to overcome the archbishop's resistance, but two years later, in 433, a reconciliation was brought about, though Antioch was still radically hostile. In spite of all the difficulties Cyril encountered, the statement here is excessive and exaggerated.

43. **plurimis scriptis editis.** After St. John Chrysostom, Cyril was the most prolific writer among the Greek Fathers. Besides many exegetical works, homilies and letters, his tracts on the Incarnation, Trinity and Eucharist are especially important.

huius fidei catholicae propugnatoris et Orientalis
50 ecclesiae luminis ad Ecclesiam universam extendit.

Oratio

Deus, qui beatum Cyrillum Confessorem tuum atque Pontificem divinae maternitatis beatissimae Virginis Mariae assertorem invictum effecisti, concede ipso intercedente ut qui vere eam Genetricem
55 Dei credimus, materna eiusdem protectione salvemur. Per eumdem Dominum nostrum.

---

49. **Orientalis ecclesiae luminis.** Though imprecise in his terminology, in an age when terminology was not yet determined, Cyril has been recognized as the foremost theologian among all the Greek Fathers and as second only to his contemporary (d. 431) St. Augustine among the Latins. In 1882 Cyril was officially declared a Doctor of the Church by Leo XIII, and Pius XII in 1944 issued an Encyclical honoring the fifteenth centenary of his death.

5. THE APPARITIONS AT LOURDES

February 11　　　　　　　　　　　　1858

Anno quarto a dogmatica definitione de immaculato beatae Virginis Conceptu, ad Gavi fluminis oram prope oppidum Lourdes dioecesis Tarbiensis in Gallia, ipsa Virgo in rupis sinu super
5　specum Massabielle puellae cuidam, vernacula lingua Bernadette nuncupatae, pauperrimae quidem

1. **a definitione.** On December 8, 1854, Pius IX solemnly defined the doctrine that Mary was conceived without stain of original sin in her mother's womb. Certain events in the earlier part of the century had prepared the way for this Papal definition of the doctrine: Pius VII (1800-1823) had authorized a Mass in honor of the Immaculate Conception, and in 1830 Mary appeared to St. Catherine Labouré of the Sisters of Charity and showed her a medal (the Miraculous Medal) inscribed with the words, "O Mary, conceived without sin, pray for us who have recourse to thee."

4. **Virgo ... puellae ... obtulit,** 'The Virgin many times offered herself to be seen by the girl'. **Puellae** is perhaps best translated as a dative of agency with **conspiciendam.**

6. **Bernadette** Soubirous was fourteen at the time of the apparitions. Two years later she entered the Convent of the Sisters of Charity at Nevers, where she remained as a boarder for eight years. In 1886 she took the habit as Marie Bernard and spent seven of her eight remaining years as a nurse in the infirmary. She died in 1878 at thirty-six and was buried in the convent chapel, where her body lies exposed to view. She was canonized in 1933 by Pius XI.

sed ingenuae ac piae, pluries se conspiciendam obtulit. Immaculata Virgo iuvenili benigno videbatur aspectu, nivea veste niveoque pallio contecta ac
10 zona caerulea succincta; nudos pedes aurea rosa ornabat. Primo apparitionis die, qui fuit undecimus Februarii anno millesimo octingentesimo quinquagesimo octavo, puellam signum crucis rite pieque faciendum edocuit, atque ad sacri rosarii recita-
15 tionem exemplo suo excitavit, coronam, quae prius ex bracchio demissa pendebat, manu advolvens; quod in ceteris etiam apparitionibus praestitit. Altero autem apparitionis die puella in simplicitate cordis sui, diabolicam fraudem timens, lustralem
20 aquam in Virginem effudit; sed beata Virgo, leniter arridens, benigniorem illi vultum ostendit. Cum vero tertio apparuisset, puellam ad specum per

    8. **iuvenili**. According to Bernadette, Mary had the appearance of a girl of sixteen or seventeen. The description given here is Bernardette's own and one she always clung to.

    9. **aspectu**, an ablative of quality, 'she seemed of . . . kindly appearance'.

    10. **aurea;** there were yellow roses on her feet.

    11. **undecimus**, or *tertio Idus Februarii;* notice the modern notation.

    13. **puellam . . . edocuit,** 'taught her to make the sign of the cross correctly and devoutly'; lit., 'taught her the sign of the cross to be made. . .'

    16. **manu advolvens**, 'turning over in her hand', 'moving through her fingers'.

    17. **praestitit,** 'performed', 'continued to do'. The recitation of the rosary was a prominent feature of the apparitions.

    22. **tertio**, Thursday, February 18.

THE IMMACULATE CONCEPTION. Painting by Bartolomè Murillo (1617-1682). **Prado Museum, Madrid**

quindecim dies invitavit. Exinde eam saepius est allocuta, ac pro peccatoribus orare, terram deosculari, paenitentiamque agere est hortata. Deinde imperavit ut sacerdotibus ediceret aedificandum ibi esse sacellum, solemnisque supplicationis more illo accedendum. Mandavit insuper ut e fonte, qui sub harena adhuc latebat sed mox erat erupturus, aquam biberet eaque se abstergeret. Denique die festo Annuntiationis, percontanti enixe puellae illius nomen, cuius aspectu toties dignata fuerat, Virgo

per quindecim dies, i.e., for two weeks, from February 19 to March 4. Mary did not appear on February 22 or 26.

24. **pro peccatoribus orare**. This request was made during the sixth apparition on February 21.

terram deosculari. On February 23, the Virgin said to Bernadette, "You will kiss the earth for sinners." Having done so herself, Bernadette had the crowd do the same.

25. **paenitentiam agere**, the eighth apparition, February 24.

26. **aedificandum ... sacellum**, the eleventh apparition, February 27, though there is some dispute about this, which Bernadette herself could not settle, but could only say that Mary often made this request of her.

28. **accedendum**, sc. *esse*; the impersonal construction; lit., 'it must be approached'; translate: 'men must approach....'

fonte. The spring appeared above ground during the ninth apparition on February 25 and flowed in greater strength as the day progressed.

31. **percontanti enixe**. Three times Bernadette repeated her question until she received her reply. (**nomen** is the object of **percontanti** which agrees with **puellae**; **puellae** is dative after **respondit**.)

illius, 'of her'. The demonstrative is often used where English uses the personal pronoun.

admotis pectori manibus elatisque in caelum oculis respondit: "Immaculata Conceptio ego sum."

Percrebrescente fama beneficiorum quae in sacro specu recepisse fideles dicebantur, augebatur in dies hominum concursus, quos loci religio ad specum advocabat. Itaque prodigiorum fama puellaeque candore motus, Tarbiensis episcopus quarto ab enarratis anno post iuridicam factorum inquisitionem supernaturales esse apparitionis notas sua sententia probavit, cultumque Virginis immaculatae in eodem specu permisit. Mox aedificatum sacellum: ex illa die paene innumerae fidelium turbae, voti ac supplicationis causa, ex Gallia, Belgio, Italia, Hispania ceterisque Europae provinciis necnon ex longinquis Americae regionibus quovis anno illuc adveniunt, nomenque Immaculatae de Lourdes ubique terrarum inclarescit. Fontis aqua, in cunctas orbis partes delata, aegris sanitatem restituit. Orbis vero catholicus, tantorum memor benefactorum,

34. **Immaculata**...In the local patois the words of Mary were, "Que soy er' Immaculada Councepsion", words which Bernadette always had great difficulty pronouncing and whose significance she did not then comprehend.
37. **loci religio**, 'respect' or 'reverence for the place'.
39. **Tarbiensis Episcopus**. Bishop Bertrand-Sévère Laurence on July 28, 1858, appointed a commission to investigate the visions, the requests of the person seen in the visions, the spring and the cures already being claimed. On January 18, 1862, the bishop gave his formal approbation.
40. **ab enarratis**, 'from the events just narrated'.
41. **supernaturales**..., 'he declared that in his opinion the marks of the apparition were supernatural'.
43. **aedificatum**, sc. *est*.

aedes sacras mirabili opere ibi exstruxit. Vexilla
innumera, acceptorum beneficiorum veluti monu-
menta, illuc a civitatibus ac gentibus missa, aedem
55 Virginis miro ornatu decorant. In hac sua veluti
sede immaculata Virgo iugiter colitur, interdiu
quidem precibus, religioso cantu solemnibusque
aliis caerimoniis, noctu vero sacris illis supplica-
tionibus, quibus infinitae propemodum peregrinan-
60 tium turbae cereis facibusque accensis procedunt
et laudes beatae Virginis concinunt.

Peregrinationes huiusmodi fidem frigescente
saeculo excitasse, animum ad christianam legem
profitendam addidisse, cultumque Virginis imma-
65 culatae mirum in modum auxisse, omnibus compertum est. In qua mirabili fidei professione christianus
populus sacerdotes veluti duces habet, qui illuc
suas plebes adducunt. Ipsi etiam Sacrorum antistites sanctum locum frequenter adeunt, peregrina-
70 tionibus praesunt, solemnioribusque festis intersunt.
Nec adeo rarum est ipsos Romanae Ecclesiae pur-

52. **mirabili opere**, 'with marvelous workmanship'.

59. **quibus...concinunt**, 'in the course of which they move in procession ... and sing ...' The famous Lourdes hymn is *Immaculate Mary*.

65. **omnibus compertum** est; impersonal construction; lit., 'it has been found by all ...'; translate: 'All have found out ...' **Peregrinationes** is subject accusative of **excitasse, addidisse, auxisse.**

68. **Sacrorum antistites**, lit., 'overseers of sacred things'; i.e., bishops.

71. **purpuratos patres**, the Cardinals, so called because their robes are of dark red, symbolic of the martyrdom they must be ready to suffer as princes of the Church.

puratos patres humili peregrinorum more accedentes conspicere. Ipsi quoque Romani Pontifices pro sua erga Immaculatam de Lourdes pietate sacram aedem donis nobilissimis cumularunt. Pius nonus sacris indulgentiis, archiconfraternitatis privilegio ac minoris Basilicae titulo ipsam insignivit, ac Deiparae imaginem ibidem cultam solemni ritu per legatum suum apostolicum in Gallia diademate distinctam voluit. Leo vero decimus tertius innumera etiam contulit beneficia, indulgentias ad modum iubilaei

    73. **pro sua ... pietate**, 'in keeping with their devotion', 'because of ...'

    76. **archiconfraternitatis**; a confraternity which possesses the power to affiliate other confraternities and impart to them its own privileges and indulgences.

    77. **minoris Basilicae titulo.** A Basilica (βασιλικη - a royal hall) in its origins was a public building, rectangular in shape, divided lengthwise into three or five areas by colonnades. By the time of Constantine this style of architecture was in common use in church construction. As a canonical term, *basilica* designates a specially privileged church. There are four major or patriarchal basilicas in Rome: St. Peter's, St. Paul's Outside the Walls, St. Mary Major, and St. John Lateran. There are also many minor basilicas, a title which the Pope can bestow on a particularly prominent church. The title was bestowed on Lourdes in 1874.

    78. **imaginem ... distinctam**; *esse* understood, as often; 'wished that the statue be adorned....' In 1876 the Archbishop of Paris was delegated to consecrate the Basilica, and an Apostolic Nuncio was sent to crown the statue.

    81. **ad modum iubilaei**. In its Old Testament (*Lev.* 25) origins, the Jubilee sanctified every fiftieth year and proclaimed remission to the people. Boniface VIII (1294-1300) was the first Pope whom history records as having decreed, in 1300, a

vigesimo quinto Apparitionis anno vertente concessit, peregrinationes sua auctoritate verboque provexit, ac solemnem Ecclesiae sub titulo Rosarii
85 dedicationem suo nomine peragi curavit. Quorum beneficiorum amplitudinem cumulavit, cum plurium episcoporum rogatu solemne festum sub titulo Apparitionis beatae Marie Virginis immaculate proprio Officio et propria Missa celebrandum benigne
90 concessit. Tandem Pius decimus Pontifex maximus pro sua erga Deiparam pietate, ac plurimorum votis annuens Sacrorum antistitum, idem festum ad Ecclesiam universam extendit.

Jubilee Year, and as having granted special indulgences during its observance. The solemnity, which is distinguished by the opening and closing of the 'holy doors' of the four major basilicas in Rome, has generally been observed every twenty-five years, and at times the special faculties and indulgences of the jubilee have been granted to the faithful on certain important occasions and anniversaries.

82. **vigesimo quinto**, 1883. In the same year the Archbishop of Toulouse laid the cornerstone of the Church of the Rosary, which was blessed by the Legate of the Pope, the Archbishop of Paris, in 1889 and consecrated in 1901 by the Archbishop of Rheims.

87. **festum ... celebrandum ... concessit**, 'permitted the celebration of the feast with its own Office and its own Mass'; lit., 'permitted the feast to be celebrated. ...' This was in 1890.

93. **extendit**, in 1907.

Oratio

95 Deus, qui per immaculatam Virginis Conceptionem dignum Filio tuo habitaculum praeparasti, supplices a te quaesumus ut eiusdem Virginis Apparitionem celebrantes, salutem mentis et corporis consequamur. Per eumdem Dominum nostrum.

6. ST. PETER DAMIAN

February 23   988-1072

Petrus, Ravennae honestis parentibus natus, adhuc lactens a matre, numerosae prolis pertaesa, abicitur; sed domesticae mulieris opera semivivus exceptus ac recreatus, genetrici, ad humanitatis sen-
5 sum revocatae, redditur. Utroque orbatus parente, tamquam vile mancipium sub aspera fratris tutela duram servitutem exercuit. Religionis in Deum ac pietatis erga patrem tunc specimen dedit. Inventum siquidem forte nummum non propriae inediae suble-
10 vandae sed sacerdoti, qui divinum sacrificium ad

    1. **Ravennae**. Famous for its Roman and Byzantine architecture and art of the fifth to the eighth centuries, especially mosaics, Ravenna had been the residence of many Emperors, among them the Ostrogoth Theodoric (493-526). Justinian (527-565) made the city the residence of the exarchs of the Byzantine Roman Empire.
        honestis parentibus; his parents, though poor, were of the nobility; 'honorable'; never 'honest.'
    3. **abicitur**. Peter nearly died from his mother's refusal to nurse him, but a domestic servant-cook took and fed him, and by her example brought the mother to her senses.
    8. **patrem**, i.e. his brother, *in loco parentis*.
    9. **propriae inediae** . . . , 'to relieve his own hunger'. **inediae** is dative after **erogavit**, balancing **sacerdoti**; lit., 'to his own hunger to be relieved'.
    10. **qui** . . . **offerret**; relative clause of purpose, 'to offer'.

illius expiationem offerret, erogavit. A Damiano fratre, a quo uti fertur cognomentum accepit, benigne receptus, eius cura litteris eruditur, in quibus brevi tantum profecit, ut magistris admirationi esset. Cum autem liberalibus scientiis floreret et nomine, eas cum laude docuit. Interim ut corpus rationi subderet, sub mollibus vestibus cilicium adhibuit, ieiuniis, vigiliis et orationibus solerter insistens. Calente iuventa cum carnis stimulis acriter urgeretur, insultantium libidinum faces rigentibus fluvii mersus aquis noctu exstinguebat. Tum venerabilia quaeque loca obire totumque Psalterium recitare consueverat. Ope assidua pauperes levabat, quibus frequenter pastis convivio propriis ipse manibus ministrabat.

    Perficiendae magis vitae causa in Avellanensi

13. **litteris**; almost like our own *ABC's*.
14. **tantum profecit**, 'he made such progress'.
    magistris admirationi, a double dative (a dative of purpose and a dative of reference); lit., 'for an admiration to his teachers'. Peter had an outstanding record at the University of Parma where he taught when twenty-five.
15. **liberalibus scientiis**, cf. 4.7n.; 'literary studies', 'cultural subjects'.
    nomine, 'reputation'.
18. **Calente ... consueverat**. The authority for this statement is the *Vita* (ch. 2) written by St. John of Lodi, a disciple of Peter's who says that he wrote down the things that were either told him by Peter or described by witnesses or seen by himself. cf. *Acta Sanctorum*, March vol. 3, p. 424.
23. **quibus**, dative governed by **ministrabat**;
24. **pastis**, perf. pass. part. of *pasco* agreeing with **quibus**.
26. **perficiendae ... causa**, 'to make his life more perfect'.

Eugubinae dioecesis coenobio, ordini monachorum sanctae Crucis Fontis Avellanae, a beato Ludulpho, sancti Romualdi discipulo, fundato, nomen dedit.
30 Non ita multo post in monasterium Pomposianum, mox in coenobium sancti Vincentii Petrae Pertusae ab abbate suo missus, utrumque asceterium verbo sacro, praeclaris institutionibus et moribus excoluit. Ad suos revocatus, post praesidis obitum Avellani-
35 tarum familiae praeficitur, quam novis variis in locis exstructis domiciliis et sanctissimis institutis

27. **coenobio**; κοινος βιος, common life.
ordini; dative with **nomen dedit**; (in 1035)
28. **sanctae Crucis Fontis Avellanae**. Fonte Avellana was known by the title of Holy Cross of Fonte Avellana only after 1050; it owed the name to its special observance of Friday as a commemoration of the Holy Cross. (cf. line 70)
29. **Romualdi**. One time abbot of the Benedictine Monastery of St. Apollinare near Ravenna, Romuald (c. 950-1027) travelled for thirty years in Italy reforming monasteries and establishing hermitages, the chief of which was that at Camaldoli near Arezzo in Tuscany, from which his order received its name. St. Romuald's object was to introduce into the West the eremitical life led by monks in the East in imitation of the Fathers of the Desert.
fundato; agrees with **coenobio**.
30. **Pomposianum**. Pomposa Abbey at this time rivalled Monte Cassino in scholarship and virtue. Its library was famous for its treasures of ancient literature. Guido d'Arezzo, a contemporary of Peter's, who became famous as the inventor of the modern musical scale and system of musical notation, was a monk here.
32. **asceterium**, ἀσκητερια, an abode for ascetics.
34. **suos**, i.e., the monks at Fonte Avellana.
35. **praeficitur**, in 1043.

ST. PETER DAMIAN. Fresco by Antonio da Fabriano (fl. 1450-1485). **Accademia di Belle Arti, Ravenna**

ita auxit, ut alter eius ordinis parens ac praecipuum ornamentum iure sit habitus. Salutarem Petri sollicitudinem alia quoque diversi instituti coenobia, canonicorum conventus, et populi sunt experti. Urbinati dioecesi non uno nomine profuit; Theuzoni episcopo in causa gravissima assedit ipsumque in recte administrando episcopatu consilio et opera iuvit. Divinorum contemplatione, corporis macerationibus, ceterisque spectatae sanctimoniae exemplis excelluit. His motus Stephanus nonus Pontifex maximus eum, licet invitum et reluctantem, sanctae Romanae Ecclesiae cardinalem creavit et Ostiensem episcopum. Quas Petrus dignitates splendidissimis virtutibus et consentaneis episcopali ministerio operibus gessit.

37. **alter parens** with Ludolph, who had established the community at Fonte Avellana in 977 and had received a rule from St. Romuald in 989. The order continued in existence until 1570 when it became a Camaldolese possession.

39. **diversi instituti**, 'of different constitution', i.e., belonging to other Orders.

40. **canonicorum conventus**, 'chapters of canons', groups of clerics attached usually to a Cathedral, who are governed by their own statutes and whose duties are to pray the office in choir and assist the bishop in administration. Such chapters are not found in America.

46. **Stephanus nonus**. A former abbot of Monte Cassino, Stephen carried on during his short pontificate (1057-1058) the work of reform in the Church with the help of Peter and Hildebrand, the future Gregory VII. (cf. 31)

48. **Ostiensem**. Ostia was the ancient port of Rome. Since the eighth century the bishops of Ostia were called upon by the Popes for extraordinary ecclesiastical business.

Difficillimo tempore, Romanae Ecclesiae summisque Pontificibus doctrina, legationibus, aliisque susceptis laboribus mirifice adfuit. Adversus Nicolai-
55 tarum et simoniacam haereses ad mortem strenue decertavit; huiusmodi depulsis malis, Mediolanensem Ecclesiae Romanae conciliavit. Benedicto et Cadaloo

53. **Pontificibus adfuit,** 'helped'; similarly **assedit** 1. 35.
susceptis, 'which he undertook'.

54. **Nicolaitarum.** *Apoc.* 2.6,15 mentions a sect of Nicolaites in Asia Minor, but its character remains very obscure, despite references to it in several ecclesiastical writers. But because Ireneus (*Adv. Haer.* 1,26,3) says that they led lives of unrestrained indulgence, antinomianism was regarded as the characteristic of the sect, and the scandalous lives of the clergy of Damian's time occasioned the reuse of the term. Peter's biographer, John of Lodi (cf. above, 18n) describes this and simony as *gemina pestis exsecrabilis* which had befouled with impunity almost the entire church, but which was eliminated by the efforts of St. Peter. cf. *Acta Sanctorum,* Feb. vol. 3, p. 429.

55. **simoniacam,** the sacrilegious selling or buying of spiritual things, here specifically ecclesiastical offices or benefices. Much of the abuse of the time stemmed actually from lay investiture. The name *simony* is derived from Simon Magus, the magician who tried to buy from St. Peter the power to confer the Holy Spirit. (*Acts* 8)

56. **Mediolanensem.** In 1059 Peter was sent by Nicholas II to support the reformers in that city. By the force of his eloquence he secured from the clergy a solemn promise that they would cease their simony and reform their lives.

57. **Benedicto.** When Stephen IX died in 1058 the Roman nobility and some of the clergy elected the bishop of Velletri who took the name Benedict X. In the regular election, which had to be held at Siena, the bishop of Florence was chosen, who as Nicholas II succeeded in deposing the anti-pope. His edict

falsis pontificibus fortiter restitit; Henricum quartum Germaniae regem ab iniquo uxoris divortio
60 deterruit; Ravennates, ad debita Romano Pontifici obsequia revocatos, sacris restituit; canonicos Veliternos ad sanctioris vitae leges composuit. In provincia praesertim Urbinate vix ulla fuit episcopalis ecclesia, de qua Petrus non sit bene meritus; Eugu-

of 1059 determined once for all the manner of Papal elections and ended the interference, not only of the Roman nobility, but also of Germany and the Holy Roman Emperor.

Cadaloo. The death of Nicholas II in 1061 was followed by another schism. The bishop of Lucca was elected Pope, the first to be chosen by the College of Cardinals, and chose the name Alexander II. But German interests supported the rival election of Pietro Cadalous, bishop of Parma. As Honorius II, Cadalous was finally deposed in 1064.

58. **Henricum.** Two years after his marriage to the daughter of an Italian marquis, the young king of Germany (1050-1108), destined to have further quarrels with Gregory VII (cf. 31.46n), sought an annulment and found support in the archbishop of Mainz. In 1069 Peter as legate of Alexander II succeeded in persuading Henry to drop the proceedings.

60. **Ravennates.** The archbishop and people of Ravenna had been excommunicated by Alexander II for supporting the antipope Honorius II (Cadalous). In 1072 Peter was sent as legate to reconcile the city to the Holy See.

61. **sacris**, lit., 'to sacred things,' i.e. to the Sacraments.

canonicos Veliternos. In a letter to an archbishop-friend of his Peter mentions that 'our' canons (Velletri was part of the see of Ostia) have within the past month returned to an exemplary life, distinguished by fasting, silence and daily praying of the psalter. cf. Migne, *P.L.* 145, 599.

64. **Eugubinam**, sc. *ecclesiam;* so also **alias**, 1. 55: sc. *ecclesias.*

65 binam, quam aliquando creditam habuit, multis
levavit incommodis; alias alibi, quando oportuit, perinde curavit ac suae essent tutelae commissae.
Cardinalatu et episcopali dignitate depositis, nihil
de pristina iuvandi proximos sedulitate remisit.
70 Ieiunium sextae feriae in honorem sanctae Crucis
Iesu Christi, horarias beatae Dei Genetricis preces
eiusque die Sabbato cultum propagavit. Inferendae
quoque sibi verberationis morem ad patratorum
scelerum expiationem provexit. Demum sanctitate,
75 doctrina, miraculis et praeclare actis illustris, dum e
Ravennate legatione rediret, Faventiae octavo Kalendas Martii migravit ad Christum. Eius corpus
ibidem apud Cistercienses, multis miraculis clarum,
frequenti populorum veneratione colitur. Ipsum
80 Faventini, non semel in praesenti discrimine propi-
tium experti, patronum apud Deum delegerunt. Leo
vero duodecimus Pontifex maximus Officium Mis-
samque in eius honorem tamquam Confessoris
Pontificis, quae aliquibus in dioecesibus atque in
85 ordine Camaldulensium iam celebrabantur, ex sac-

65. **aliquando.** In 1057 Peter, in addition to Ostia, had been appointed administrator of the diocese of Gubbio.

68. **episcopali dignitate** ... Peter remained of course a consecrated bishop, but was finally allowed by Alexander II to resign in 1061 the see of Ostia. He lived as a simple monk, although he was obliged to spend much time away from Fonte Avellana on papal missions.

73. **verberationis morem.** The penitential use of the "discipline", a scourge for self-flagellation, was introduced by Peter despite much opposition. At his suggestion it was also introduced at Monte Cassino.

rorum Rituum Congregationis consulto addita Doctoris qualitate ad universam extendit Ecclesiam.

Oratio

Concede nos, quaesumus, omnipotens Deus, beati Petri Confessoris tui atque Pontificis monita et exempla sectari, ut per terrestrium rerum contemptum aeterna gaudia consequamur. Per Dominum nostrum.

---

87. **Doctoris qualitate** by Leo XII (1823-1829) in 1823.

7. STS. PERPETUA AND FELICITAS

March 6 † 203

Perpetua et Felicitas in persecutione Severi imperatoris in Africa una cum Revocato, Saturnino et Secundulo comprehensae sunt et in tenebricosum carcerem detrusae; quibus ultra adiunctus est

1. **Perpetua.** Vibia Perpetua was 22, of distinguished family and the wife of a man of good position; Felicitas was her slave. Their names appear consistently in all the early martyrologies, e.g., the Philocalian calendar at Rome of 354. The record of their martyrdom is based on an authentic and detailed account, of which the largest part is Perpetua's own diary which was finished by an eye-witness who many believe to have been Tertullian (c. 160-c. 240.) (cf. *Acta Sanctorum*, March vol. 1., p. 632-636.) A treasure of ancient Christian literature, the account was publicly read in the African churches in the fourth century and St. Augustine had to warn against its being placed on a level with the Bible.

      Severi. Under Septimius Severus (193-211) a new edict was issued in 202 prohibiting all conversions to Christianity. Directed against catechumens and neophytes, it annulled the rescript of Trajan (cf. 1.3n.) which had proscribed Christianity and ordered the punishment of all Christians brought to justice, but had laid it down that they were not to be sought out.

2. **in Africa:** in Carthage, the ancient city founded c. 850 B.C. by Phoenicians, destroyed by Rome in 146 B.C., and rebuilt by Augustus in 29 B.C. From an early date the city had a flourishing Christian community. Excavations begun at the end of the last century uncovered an abundance of the oldest remains of

54 BREVIARY LIVES OF THE SAINTS

5 Satyrus. Erant adhuc catechumenae sed paulo post baptizatae sunt. Paucis diebus interiectis e carcere ad forum deductae cum sociis, post gloriosam confessionem ab Hilarione procuratore damnantur ad bestias. Inde hilares descendunt ad carcerem, ubi
10 variis visionibus recreantur et ad martyrii palmam accenduntur. Perpetuam nec patris, senio confecti, iteratae preces et lacrimae nec erga filium infantem pendentem ad ubera maternus amor nec supplicii atrocitas a Christi fide dimovere umquam potuerunt.
15   Felicitas vero instante spectaculi die, cum octo iam menses praegnans esset, in magno erat luctu ne differretur; leges quippe vetabant praegnantes supplicio affici. At precibus commartyrum accelerato partu, enixa est filiam. Cumque in partu laborans

---

Christian edifices, and in 1907 the Basilica Maiorum where Perpetua and her companions were buried yielded an ancient inscription bearing their names and the date of their martyrdom.

5. **Satyrus**, the instructor in the faith of those arrested, who surrendered voluntarily. Part of the authentic document was written by him.—**catechumenae**; from the Greek κατηχουμενος —one receiving elementary instruction.

10. **visionibus**. The visions were recorded by Perpetua herself and are of great importance in showing the eschatalogical beliefs of the early Christians. In one of them, Perpetua saw her younger brother, who had died a pagan when seven years old, coming out of a dark place, hot and thirsty. But after praying for him (which she knew could help him), she saw the place now luminous and her brother clean and refreshed.

17. **ne differetur**, 'that *the day of her martyrdom* would not be put off'.

STS. PERPETUA and FELICITAS. Mosaic (sixth century) in the **Archbishop's Palace, Ravenna. Courtesy, Alinari**

20 doleret, ait illi quidam de custodibus: "Quae sic modo doles, quid facies obiecta bestiis?" Cui illa: "Modo ego patior. Illic autem alius erit in me, qui patietur pro me, quia et ego pro illo passura sum."

In amphitheatrum toto inspectante populo pro-
25 ducuntur tandem generosae mulieres Nonis Martii, ac primum flagellis caeduntur. Tunc a ferocissima vacca aliquamdiu iactatae, plagis concisae et in terram elisae sunt. Demum cum sociis, qui a variis bestiis vexati fuerant, gladiorum ictibus conficiun-
30 tur. Harum sanctarum Martyrum festum Pius decimus Pontifex maximus ad ritum duplicem pro universa Ecclesia evexit ac diei sextae Martii assignari mandavit.

Oratio

Da nobis, quaesumus, Domine Deus noster,
35 sanctarum Martyrum tuarum Perpetuae et Felicitatis palmas incessabili devotione venerari, ut quas digna mente non possumus celebrare, humilibus saltem frequentemus obsequiis. Per Dominum nostrum.

    20. **illi**, 'to her'; cf. 5.31n.
        Quae ... doles, 'You who now groan in such pain. . . .'
    21. **obiecta**, 'when you are thrown. . . .'
        Cui illa, sc. *ait*.
    32. **diei sextae Martii**. Pius X (1903-1914) ordered the feast to be anticipated on March 6 and left March 7 to St. Thomas Aquinas. (Notice the two methods of indicating date, *diei sextae Martii* and *Nonis Martii*, 1.22.)
    36. **quas**; the object of **frequentemus** is to be supplied from **quas**: 'that we may observe the feast of *those women* whom. . . .'

8. ST. THOMAS AQUINAS

March 7   c. 1225-1274

Praeclarum christiani orbis decus et Ecclesiae lumen, beatissimus vir Thomas, Landulpho comite Aquinate et Theodora Neapolitana nobilibus parentibus natus, futurae in Deiparam devotionis affectum
5 adhuc infantulus ostendit. Nam chartulam ab eo inventam, in qua salutatio angelica scripta erat, frustra adnitente nutrice, compressa manu valide retinuit, et a matre per vim abreptam ploratu et gestu repetiit, ac mox redditam deglutivit. Quintum

2. **Landulpho ... Theodora.** His mother was of Norman descent; his father, head of one of the few noble families in Italy at the time, was related to the kings of Aragon, Castile and France, and was a nephew of the late Emperor Frederick Barbarossa and a cousin of the reigning Frederick II. At the time of Thomas' birth, Landulf was away fighting with Frederick, who was warring with the Papacy by extending his authority through central and northern Italy.

4. **affectum ... ostendit.** The story that demonstrates this fanciful assertion is found in the earliest biographies, and while it certainly is typical of a child, its genuineness is not demonstrable. cf. *Acta Sanctorum*, March vol. 1, p. 658.

6. **salutatio angelica**, i.e., *Hail Mary*, the words of the Angel Gabriel at the Annunciation (*Lk.* 1,28).

9. **Quintum annum agens.** It was the custom of the times to send children even at such a young age to a monastery for their schooling. Thomas' uncle was the abbot of Monte Cassino

annum agens, monachis sancti Benedicti Cassinati-
bus custodiendus traditur. Inde Neapolim studiorum
causa missus, iam adulescens Fratrum Praedicatorum
ordinem suscepit. Sed matre ac fratribus id indigne
ferentibus, Lutetiam Parisiorum mittitur. Quem
fratres in itinere per vim raptum, in arcem castri
sancti Ioannis perducunt; ubi varie exagitatus ut

and Thomas' parents had ambitions that their youngest son
would enter the monastery and someday be its abbot.

11. **Neapolim.** Thomas' stay at Monte Cassino perhaps
ended when the monastery was seized and closed by Frederick II (1220-1250). In 1236 or 1239 (the chronology is not
certain), Thomas was sent to the new University of Naples.

12. **iam adulescens.** Thomas had applied for admission in
1242 when he was seventeen, but had been advised to wait.
Two years later he was accepted.

Fratrum Praedicatorum. The Friars Preachers or Dominicans had been founded less than thirty years before at
Toulouse by Dominic Guzman to combat the Albigensian heresy.
Devoting themselves to study, teaching and preaching, the friars
soon found themselves occupying important positions in the
new universities.

13. **matre ... indigne ferentibus.** Not only had Thomas not
followed their ambition that he become a Benedictine, but he
had joined an unknown mendicant order.

14. **Lutetiam Parisiorum.** Fearing that his mother would
take him away, the Dominicans had sent him first to Rome and
then, when his mother sought him there, to Paris.

15. **fratres. . . .** His two older brothers were at this time in
Tuscany with the army of Frederick, which was ravaging northern Italy and the Papal States. His brothers captured him near
Siena.

arcem. . . . in the tower of the castle of San Giovanni,
a family possession near Rocca Secca, Thomas' birthplace overlooking the town of Aquino.

ST. THOMAS AQUINAS. Fresco by Taddeo Gaddi
(c. 1300-1366). **Santa Maria Novella, Florence.
Courtesy, Alinari**

sanctum propositum mutaret, mulierem etiam, quae
ad labefactandam eius constantiam introducta fuerat, titione fugavit. Mox beatus iuvenis, flexis genibus ante signum crucis orans, ibique somno correptus, per quietem sentire visus est sibi ab Angelis con-
stringi lumbos; quo ex tempore omni postea libidinis
sensu caruit. Sororibus, quae ut eum a pio consilio
removerent in castrum venerant, persuasit ut con-
temptis curis saecularibus ad exercitationem caelestis vitae se conferrent.

Emissus e castro per fenestram, Neapolim re-
ducitur; unde Romam, postea Parisium a Fratre
Ioanne Theutonico, ordinis Praedicatorum generali
magistro, ductus, Alberto Magno doctore philo-

---

21. **sentire visus est.** . . . Thomas on his death-bed revealed all this to his friend and confessor Brother Reginald of Piperno (who later testified before the canonization commission), and gave him the cord which today is kept in the Dominican Priory in Piedmont. cf. *Acta Sanctorum*, p. 660.

23. **Sororibus.** One of the sisters became a Benedictine nun, the other married and remained devoted to her brother all her life.

27. **Emissus** . . . In 1245 Thomas was allowed to escape—in a manner reminiscent of St. Paul from Damascus (*Acts* 9,25)—after the intervention of Pope Innocent IV forced the family to relent.

29. **Ioanne Theutonico.** Bishop John the Teutonic was the fourth Master General of the Order (1241–1252).

30. **Alberto Magno.** St. Albert the Great (c.1206–1280) was the most renowned teacher of his time. He pioneered the introduction of Aristotle into scholastic philosophy and theology, and by his keen sense of accurate scientific observation was a forerunner in the development of the natural sciences. His most

sophiae ac theologiae operam dedit. Viginti quinque annos natus, magister est appellatus publiceque philosophos ac theologos summa cum laude est interpretatus. Numquam se lectioni aut scriptioni de-
35 dit nisi post orationem. In difficultatibus locorum sacrae Scripturae ad orationem ieiunium adhibebat. Quin etiam sodali suo Fratri Reginaldo dicere solebat, quidquid sciret non tam studio aut labore suo peperisse, quam divinitus traditum accepisse. Neapo-
40 li cum ad imaginem Crucifixi vehementius oraret, hanc vocem audivit: "Bene scripsisti de me, Thoma. Quam ergo mercedem accipies?" Cui ille: "Non aliam, Domine, nisi teipsum." Collationes Patrum assidue pervolutabat; et nullum fuit scriptorum genus
45 in quo non esset diligentissime versatus. Scripta eius et multitudine et varietate et facilitate explicandi res difficiles adeo excellunt, ut uberrima atque incorrupta illius doctrina, cum revelatis veritatibus

famous pupil became his close friend, and in the end Albert came forward to defend him when in 1277 the bishop of Paris condemned as heretical some of Thomas' teachings.

32. **magister**: Thomas was appointed to teach in the University of Paris in 1252, and, as was the custom, earned his academic degrees while teaching, securing his doctorate in theology in 1257.

39. **Neapoli** ... This event took place two years before his death on December 6, 1273 and was witnessed by the sacristan. Thomas had just finished the tract on the Holy Eucharist for the third part of the *Summa Theologica*, but after this vision he never wrote again, saying to Brother Reginald, "The end of my labors is come. All that I have written appears to me as so much straw after the things that have been revealed to me".

mire consentiens, aptissima sit ad omnium temporum
errores pervincendos.

A summo Pontifice Urbano quarto Romam vocatus, eius iussu ecclesiasticum lucubravit Officium in Corporis Christi solemnitate celebrandum. Oblatos vero honores et Neapolitanum archiepiscopatum, etiam deferente Clemente quarto, recusavit. A praedicatione divini verbi non desistebat; quod

49. **aptissima sit**... Thomas' teaching was not always so highly regarded. In his own day it was opposed by another Doctor of the Church, St. Bonaventure (1221–1274), and many reputable theologians. After his death some of his doctrines were included in a list of theses condemned as unorthodox by Tempier, the bishop of Paris. For one thing, his Aristotelian approach (cf. 14.64n.) to Christian theology, being an innovation, was highly suspect and seemed too rationalistic. But in 1278 his teaching was embraced by the Dominicans as the official teaching of the order, and other religious groups later followed the same course.

51. **Romam vocatus.** Thomas was summoned to Rome by Urban IV (1261–1264) in 1261. He remained in Italy preaching and writing for seven years. During this time he completed the *Summa contra Gentiles* and began work on the *Summa Theologica*, his most famous work. In 1268 he returned to Paris and in 1272 was sent to the Dominican house of studies in Naples.

52. **lucubravit officium.** The Feast of Corpus Christi was established by Urban in 1264. Thomas' Office and Mass, the most beautiful in all the liturgy, contain the famous hymns *Lauda Sion, Sacris Solemniis, Verbum Supernum* and *Pange Lingua*. The last two contain the Benediction hymns *O Salutaris Hostia* and *Tantum Ergo*.

55. **Clemente quarto.** Clement IV (1264-1268) appointed him Archbishop of Naples in 1265 but Thomas begged to be excused.

cum faceret per octavam Paschae in basilica sancti
Petri, mulierem, quae eius fimbriam tetigerat, a flu-
xu sanguinis liberavit. Missus a beato Gregorio de-
60 cimo ad concilium Lugdunense, in monasterio
Fossae Novae in morbum incidit, ubi aegrotus
Cantica Canticorum explanavit. Ibidem obiit quin-
quagenarius anno salutis millesimo ducentesimo
septuagesimo quarto, Nonis Martii. Miraculis etiam
65 mortuus claruit; quibus probatis a Ioanne vigesimo
secundo in Sanctorum numerum relatus est anno
millesimo tercentesimo vigesimo tertio, translato
postea eius corpore Tolosam ex mandato beati
Urbani quinti. Cum sanctis angelicis spiritibus non
70 minus innocentia quam ingenio comparatus, Doctoris Angelici nomen iure est adeptus, eidem aucto-

58. **mulierem ... liberavit.** cf. *Acta Sanctorum*, p. 674.

59. **Missus a ... Gregorio.** Soon after his election, Gregory X (1271–1276) summoned a general council to concern itself primarily with reunion with the Greeks. Thomas' treatise *Contra Errores Graecorum* was used both at the Council of Lyons and later at the Council of Florence (1439). cf. 15.26n.

61. **in morbum incidit.** Thomas had been in failing health for some time, but was determined to make the journey to Lyons. But when near the Cistercian Abbey of Fossa Nuova near Terracina south of Rome, he became too ill to continue.

66. **in Sanctorum numerum.** John XXII (1316–1334) canonized him July 18, 1323.

67. **translato ... corpore.** The monks of Fossa Nuova had tried to keep his remains, but on orders of Urban V (1362–1370) the body was finally given to the Dominicans and laid to rest in the Dominican Church in Toulouse in 1369. It now reposes in the Church of St. Sernin in that city.

ritate sancti Pii quinti confirmatum. Leo autem decimus tertius, libentissime excipiens postulationes et vota omnium paene Sacrorum antistitum orbis catholici, ad tot praecipue philosophicorum systematum a veritate aberrantium luem propulsandam, ad incrementa scientiarum et communem humani generis utilitatem, eum ex sacrorum Rituum Congregationis consulto per apostolicas litteras caelestem patronum scholarum omnium catholicarum declaravit et instituit.

Oratio

Deus, qui Ecclesiam tuam beati Thomae Confessoris tui mira eruditione clarificas et sancta operatione fecundas, da nobis, quaesumus, et quae docuit intellectu conspicere et quae egit imitatione complere. Per Dominum nostrum.

---

72. **Pii quinti.** Pius V (1566–1573; cf.24) declared him a Doctor of the Church in 1567, almost three centuries after his death.

Leo XIII (1878–1903) declared him the patron of Catholic schools by a Brief dated August 4, 1880.

9. ST. GREGORY I THE GREAT

March 12   c. 540-604

Gregorius Magnus, Romanus, Gordiani senatoris filius, adulescens philosophiae operam dedit. Praetorio officio functus, patre mortuo sex monasteria in Sicilia aedificavit, Romae septimum sancti

1. **Magnus.** Few have been more deserving of the title, for Gregory's influence on the doctrine, organization and discipline of the Church was extraordinary. Gregory is also revered as a Doctor of the Church (so declared by Boniface VIII in 1295).

3. **Praetorio officio.** In 573 Gregory was appointed prefect of the city by Justin II (565–574). Rome was in ruins following the invasions of the Ostrogoths, when it had been conquered and reconquered four times in twenty years. The Ostrogoth Totila (cf. 13.31n.) had been defeated in 552, but in 568 the first of the Lombard invasions descended on Italy. As prefect, Gregory demonstrated the administrative wisdom and ability he would later put to the service of the Church as it began to fill more and more the void created by the absence of responsible civil government both in Rome and in Italy.

    patre mortuo. His father owned large estates in Sicily which Gregory inherited. Little is known about his mother Silvia, who is revered as a saint in the Martyrology (Nov. 3).

4. **Romae septimum.** It is agreed today that Gregory adopted the Rule of St. Benedict, which a later work of his, the *Dialogues*, served to make known throughout the West. Today the monastery is Camaldolese. (For the *Dialogues*, see also 13. 1n.)

Andreae nomine in suis aedibus prope basilicam sanctorum Ioannis et Pauli ad clivum Scauri, ubi Hilarione ac Maximiano magistris monachi vitam professus, postea abbas fuit. Mox diaconus cardinalis creatus, Constantinopolim a Pelagio Pontifice ad Tiberium Constantinum imperatorem legatus mittitur; apud quem memorabile etiam illud effecit, quod Eutychium patriarcham, qui scripserat contra veram ac tractabilem corporum resurrectionem, ita convicit ut eius librum imperator in ignem iniceret.

      6. **ad clivum Scauri**, on the western slope of the Coelian Hill.

      7. **Hilarione ... magistris.** Gregory studied under at least one abbot. Hilarion is the name (wrongly) given by John the Deacon, Gregory's ninth century biographer, but Gregory himself calls him Valentio (*Dial.* 1,4; 3,22). A second abbot, Maximianus, is also mentioned, whom Gregory succeeded. cf. *Acta Sanctorum*, March vol. 2, p. 122; 137.

      monachi vitam. St. Gregory referred to these early years as the happiest of his life, though the excessive fasting of this period was responsible for the gastritis that bothered him all his life. (cf. line 59).

      8. **Mox ...** In 578 Pope Pelagius II (579-590) ordained him one of the seven deacons responsible for the district churches of Rome. cf. 26.19n. (*Cardinalis* refers here to the fact that such clerics were attached to a *cardo* or cathedral church).

      10. **ad Tiberium** (Tiberius II 578-582). Gregory was sent in 579 to secure aid against the Lombards from the imperial court at Constantinople. His failure to do so convinced him that Italy in the future could be saved only by vigorous action on its own.

      14. **imperator ...** The Emperor had intervened in the bitter dispute, and after both had stated their views, ordered Eutychius' book burned.

ST. GREGORY THE GREAT SEEN BY PETER THE DEACON. Miniature from a twelfth century manuscript from Liège. **Bibliothèque Royale, Brussels. Courtesy, The Mansell Collection**

15 Quare Eutychius paulo post cum in morbum incidisset, instante morte pellem manus suae tenebat multis praesentibus dicens: "Confiteor quia omnes in hac carne resurgemus."

   Romam rediens, Pelagio pestilentia sublato
20 summo omnium consensu Pontifex eligitur. Quem honorem ne acciperet, quamdiu potuit, recusavit; nam alieno vestitu in spelunca delituit; ubi deprehensus indicio igneae columnae, ad sanctum Petrum

---

19. **Romam rediens** . . . Gregory returned in 585 to St. Andrew's, where as abbot he lectured on the Scriptures and revised the commentary on Job (the *Moralia*), which he had written in Constantinople at the request of St. Leander of Seville (cf. 16. 3n).

   pestilentia sublato. In 590 inundations of the Tiber were followed by a plague which killed the Pope and decimated the population.

20. **eligitur.** The election of the Popes at this time was in the hands of the clergy and people of Rome. (cf. 6.56n)

21. **ne acciperet**; construe with **recusavit**: 'he refused to accept'.

   quam diu potuit. Gregory appealed to the Emperor Maurice (582-602) not to confirm the election, but when six months later the Emperor sent his confirmation, Gregory allowed his consecration.

22. **nam alieno** . . . This story, with its variants, is pure invention; it appears first in an eighth century biography by a monk of Whitby. cf. *Acta Sanctorum*, March vol. 2, p. 144.

   ubi deprehensus . . . 'and having been apprehended there . . .'

23. **ad sanctum Petrum**, 'in St. Peter's basilica'.

consecratur. In pontificatu multa successoribus doctrinae ac sanctitatis exempla reliquit. Peregrinos
cotidie ad mensum adhibebat; in quibus et Angelum
et Dominum Angelorum peregrini facie accepit.
Pauperes et urbanos et externos, quorum numerum
descriptum habebat, benigne sustentabat. Catholicam fidem multis locis labefactatam restituit; nam
Donatistas in Africa, Arianos in Hispania repressit,
Agnoitas Alexandria eiecit. Pallium Syagrio Augus-

24. **doctrina**; especially the *Regula Pastoralis*, on the responsibilities of a bishop, a book which for centuries contributed to the formation of the clergy of the West.

28. **externos**; particularly those whom the Lombard invasions drove for refuge into Rome.

quorum numerum ..., 'whose number he kept written down...'

31. **Donatistas**. This sect, which arose following the persecution of Diocletian in 305 in Africa, claimed that the validity of the sacraments depended on the moral character of the minister. (cf. 15.34) Named after Donatus, a bishop of Carthage, the sect was condemned by various councils and Popes, but curiously survived into the seventh century.

Arianos in Hispania. For Arianism, see 24, 5n. King Reccared of the Visigoths (cf. 16.9, 14n.), the Arian conquerors of Catholic Spain, became a Catholic and convoked a council of Arian and Catholic bishops at Toledo in 589, at which Arianism was abjured and the nation declared Catholic. King Reccared began a correspondence with Gregory which foreshadowed the future close relations between Spain and Rome.

32. **Agnoitas.** As monophysites (cf. 17.21n.), the Agnoetae (ἀ γιγνώσκω -to know) specifically denied Christ's omniscience. The brief notices in these sentences, drawn from the fourteen books of Gregory's correspondence, are intended to give a general idea of his extensive activity as head of a far-flung growing Church.

todunensi episopo dare noluit nisi neophytos haereticos expelleret ex Gallia. Gothos haeresim Arianam
relinquere coegit. Missis in Britanniam doctis et
sanctis viris Augustino et aliis monachis, insulam ad
Iesu Christi fidem convertit, vere a Beda presbytero
Angliae vocatus Apostolus. Ioannis patriarchae Con-
stantinopolitani audaciam fregit, qui sibi universalis
Ecclesiae episcopi nomen arrogabat. Mauritium imperatorem, eos qui milites fuissent monachos fieri
prohibentem, a sententia deterruit.

Ecclesiam ornavit sanctissimis institutis et legibus. Apud sanctum Petrum coacta synodo, multa
constituit; in iis, ut in Missa *Kyrie eleison* novies
repeteretur; ut extra id tempus quod continetur

Pallium Syagrio. The pallium is the circular band of wool worn around the breast, neck and shoulders and only over the chasuble by the Pope and by metropolitans who receive it personally from the Pope as the sign of their pastoral authority. In 599 Gregory granted the pallium to Syagrius. There were several conditions, however. One of them was that Syagrius should see to it that neophytes were not admitted to Holy Orders too soon after their conversion. This is the condition the text has reference to, though it is wrong as it stands. (cf. *P.L.* 77, 937; 1008–1014; cf. *Acta Sanctorum,* March vol. 2, p. 160.)

36. **Augustino**; see 34; for Bede see 33.

39. **universalis**... Gregory protested the patriarch's assumption of the title Ecumenical Bishop in a synod in 588. A firm champion of the prerogatives of the see of Rome, Gregory referred to himself, subsequent to this controversy, by the title *Servant of the Servants of God,* a title which his successors continue to use.

40. **Mauritium**; cf. above, 21n. The decree was issued in 592 and Gregory eventually secured its mitigation.

Septuagesima et Pascha, *Alleluia* diceretur; ut adderetur in Canone *diesque nostros in tua pace disponas*. Litanias, Stationes et ecclesiasticum officium
50 auxit. Quatuor conciliis, Nicaeno, Constantinopolitano, Ephesino, Chalcedonensi, tamquam Evangeliis honorem haberi voluit. Episcopis Siciliae, qui ex antiqua ecclesiarum consuetudine Romam singulis trienniis conveniebant, quinto quoque anno semel
55 venire indulsit. Multos libros confecit; quos cum dictaret, testatus est Petrus diaconus se Spiritum Sanctum columbae specie in eius capite saepe vidisse. Admirabilia sunt quae dixit, fecit, scripsit, decrevit, praesertim infirma semper et aegra valetudine.
60 Qui denique multis editis miraculis, pontificatus an-

49. **Stationes.** *Statio* refers to the custom of designating one or another church in Rome as the place where the people, clergy and pope would gather each day in Lent to offer Mass. The station church for each Lenten Mass is listed in the Roman Missal, for the custom is still observed.

50. **auxit;** i.e., he re-established and re-organized the *statio,* etc., which the troubled times had interrupted. Tradition also assigns to Gregory the organizing of the liturgical chant of the Church, now called after him *Gregorian.*

54. **quoque,** ablative of *quisque.*

56. **Spiritum Sanctum...vidisse.** The story is told by John the Deacon (*Vita* 4, 14 in *Acta Sanctorum*, March vol. 2, p. 200.) Peter the Deacon, Gregory's close companion with whom he converses in the *Dialogues,* reported the vision to the people soon after Gregory's death, to save the pope's library which the people were about to destroy in revenge for a famine they felt was due to his extravagance. In most pictures of Gregory, a dove is depicted whispering into his ear, symbolizing this ancient belief that his every word and action was directly inspired by the Holy Spirit. cf. 31. 53n.

no decimo tertio, menso sexto, die decimo, quarto
Idus Martii, qui dies festus a Graecis etiam propter
insignem huius Pontificis sapientiam ac sanctitatem
praecipuo honore celebratur, ad caelestem beatitu-
dinem evocatus est. Cuius corpus sepultum est in
basilica sancti Petri.

Oratio

Deus, qui animae famuli tui Gregorii aeternae
beatitudinis praemia contulisti, concede propitius ut
qui peccatorum nostrorum pondere premimur, eius
apud te precibus sublevemur. Per Dominum
nostrum.

65. in basilica...The inscription on his tomb called him, significantly, *Consul Dei*.

10. ST. PATRICK

March 17   c. 385-c. 461

Patricius, Hiberniae dictus Apostolus, Calphurnio patre, matre Conchessa, sancti Martini Turonensis episcopi ut perhibent consanguinea, maiori in Britannia natus, puer in barbarorum saepius inci-

1. **Calphurnio.** His father was a decurion or a member of the town council and as such was a man of wealth and standing.

3. **maiori in Britannia,** i.e., in that part of the island which was a Roman Province. (Britannia minor was Brittany in NW France.) The location of his birthplace is generally accepted as on the Severn River in Wales. Roman control at this time was weak and the territory was exposed to frequent raids from the Irish and North Britains, which reached a peak c. 368.

4. **puer.** "In my youth when I was still no more than a beardless boy I was taken captive before I knew what to seek or what to desire or what to avoid..." So he states himself in his *Confessio*, a priceless document of unquestioned authenticity in which the saint again comes to life as a dedicated and ascetic apostle. cf. *Acta Sanctorum*, March vol. 2, pp. 530-534. He was sixteen when he was captured at his father's home and led to Ireland with many hundreds of others. Tradition says he became a slave to a petty king in the north-east county of Antrim.

in ... captivitatem. The object of the preposition is rarely postponed so long. For another unusual word order, see 1. 23, **Frequentissimi ... lavacro.** The student must acquire a facility in handling the stylistic arrangement of Latin words, which has no parallel in English.

saepius. There is great confusion among the various bidit captivitatem. Eo in statu pascendis gregibus praepositus, iam tum futurae sanctitatis specimen praebuit; fidei namque divinique timoris et amoris spiritu repletus, antelucano tempore per nives, gelu ac pluvias ad preces Deo fundendas impiger consurgebat; solitus centies interdiu centiesque noctu Deum orare. A servitute tertio exemptus et inter clericos relatus, in divinis lectionibus longo se tempore exercuit. Gallia, Italia insulisque Tyrrheni maris labore summo peragratis, divino tandem monitu ad Hibernorum salutem advocatur; et facta a beato Caelestino Papa Evangelii nuntiandi potestate con-

ographers as to the number of times Patrick was captured. A three-fold captivity is often found: he was first captured by the Scots when sixteen and brought to Ireland, but escaped in 379; after three months back home, he was again captured, this time by the Picts, from whom he soon escaped on board a ship bound for the Continent. There he and the crew were for a brief time taken captive, perhaps by the Vandals who were then ravaging Gaul.

7. **fidei namque** ... These are his own sentiments, as expressed in his *Confessio*.

13. **insulisque Tyrrheni** ... On these visits, which he later fondly recalls, Patrick came in contact not only with the many ascetics who lived on the islands, but also with the important monastery of Lérins ruled by St. Honoratus. Though facts and dates are extremely uncertain, he is said to have spent some eighteen years at Auxerre where he received his ecclesiastical training under St. Germain (c. 389-448) and was ordained (**inter clericos relatus** 1. 10). cf. *Acta Sanctorum*, p. 541.

16. **Caelestino.** Pope St. Celestine (422-432) had sent St. Palladius in 431 as the first bishop to the Irish. When Palladius died the following year, Patrick was commissioned to replace him. He was consecrated by St. Maximus of Tours.

ST. PATRICK PREACHING. Painting by G. Battista Tiepolo (1696-1770). **Municipal Museum, Padua. Courtesy, Alinari**

secratusque episcopus, in Hiberniam perrexit.

　　Eo in munere mirum quot vir apostolicus mala, quot aerumnas et labores, quot pertulerit adversarios. Verum Dei afflante benignitate, terra illa, idolorum antea cultrix, eum mox praedicante Patricio fructum dedit, ut Sanctorum insula deinde fuerit appellata. Frequentissimi ab eo populi sacro sunt regenerati lavacro; episcopi clericique plurimi or-

---

　　18. **mirum**, sc. *est.*—**quot** ... **mala**.... In his *Confessio* Patrick mentions frequently the dangers and insults that had to be endured both by himself and his people: "It is too long a story to relate the events of my work one by one or in parts. Briefly I shall mention how the most loving God often delivered me from slavery and from the twelve perils in which my life was endangered..." (*Conf.* 15)

　　19. **quot ... adversarios**. Tradition especially cites the Druids, though in many instances they welcomed the faith and helped in its spread.

　　21. **eum ... fructum ... ut**. Eum here means 'such', 'such great', and introduces the ut result clause.

　　22. **fuerit appellata**, instead of *sit* **appellata**. In forming the perfect passive forms the past tenses of *sum* are occasionally found; e.g. *perpessus fuit*, 11.23; *restitutus fuit*, 11.37; *fuisse illustratam*, 11.44

　　23. **Frequentissimi**, 'in large numbers'. cf. above 3n.

　　24. **lavacro**. The word, used since Tertullian (c. 160-c. 240), expresses the idea of purification in Baptism. cf. *Tit.* 3,5

　　episcopi. It is important to note how determined Patrick was to establish a native clergy and hierarchy to carry on his work. Second in importance to the hierarchy was his establishment of monasteries, and particularly with respect to nuns (whom he calls *virgines*, cf. 1.22), he was amazed at the numbers who desired to consecrate their lives to God.

25 dinati; virgines ac viduae ad continentiae leges institutae. Armachanam sedem Romani Pontificis auctoritate totius insulae principem metropolim constituit, Sanctorumque reliquiis ab Urbe relatis decoravit. Supernis visionibus, prophetiae dono,
30 ingentibusque signis et prodigiis a Deo exornatus adeo refulsit, ut longe lateque celebrior Patricii se fama diffuderit.

Praeter cotidianam ecclesiarum sollicitudinem, invictum ab oratione spiritum numquam relaxabat.
35 Aiunt enim integrum cotidie Psalterium una cum canticis et hymnis ducentisque orationibus consuevisse recitare, tercenties per dies singulos flexis genibus Deum adorare, ac in qualibet Hora diei ca-

26. **Romani Pontificis,** Leo I; see 17.

27. **metropolim constituit,** in 444. Tradition records a personal visit to Rome, from which Patrick brought back relics of Sts. Peter and Paul and the martyrs Stephen and Lawrence (Jocelin, ch. 17; see below 35n.) The visit may have occurred at this time when he was establishing a metropolitan see.

29. **Supernis visionibus.** Patrick relates many visions that came to him in sleep. Popular legend developed them into the visit of an angel named Victor. Most fully described by Patrick is a vision he had when back home in Britain, in which he was given a letter entitled *The Voice of the Irish*. As he read he thought he heard the voices of people he had known crying out, "Come back to us, holy youth, and walk among us once more." (*Conf.* 10)

35. **Aiunt enim....** The authority here is the *Vita* (ch. 18) by Jocelin, a monk of Furness Abbey in England, who wrote after 1180. The extravagant description of Patrick's spiritual practices as recorded by Jocelin make the above account seem restrained. cf. *Acta Sanctorum*, March vol. 2, p. 574.

nonica centies se crucis signo munire. Noctem tria in
spatia distribuens, primum in centum Psalmis per-
currendis et bis centies genuflectendo, alterum in
reliquis quinquaginta Psalmis, algidis aquis immersus, ac corde, oculis manibusque ad caelum erectus,
absolvendis insumebat; tertium vero super nudum
lapidem stratus tenui dabat quieti. Humilitatis eximius cultor, apostolico more a manuum suarum labore non abstinuit. Assiduis tandem curis pro Ecclesia consumptus, verbo et opere clarus, in extrema
senectute divinis mysteriis refectus, obdormivit in
Domino sepultusque est apud Dunum in Ultonia
a christiana salute saeculo quinto.

Oratio

Deus, qui ad praedicandam gentibus gloriam
tuam beatum Patricium Confessorem atque Pontificem mittere dignatus es, eius meritis et intercessione concede ut quae nobis agenda praecipis, te
miserante adimplere possimus. Per Dominum
nostrum.

48. **extrema senectute**. Some legends had him live to be 120.

50. **sepultus est**. The early lives (by Muirchu and Tirechan before the seventh century) say that on Patrick's orders his body was buried secretly. Many believe that his death and burial took place at Saul where he built his first church. (cf. *Acta Sanctorum*, p. 528)

51. **saeculo quinto**. The generally accepted date is 461, though 493 has also found support.

11. ST. CYRIL OF JERUSALEM

March 18 c. 315-386

Cyrillus Hierosolymitanus a teneris annis divinarum Scripturarum studio summopere deditus, adeo in earum scientia profecit ut orthodoxae fidei strenuus assertor evaserit. Monasticis institutis im-
5 butus, perpetuae continentiae omnique severiori vivendi rationi se addictum voluit. Postquam a sancto Maximo, Hierosolymae episcopo, presbyter ordinatus fuit, munus verbi divini fidelibus praedicandi et catechumenos edocendi summa cum laude implevit, at-
10 que illas vere mirandas conscripsit catecheses, quibus totam ecclesiasticam doctrinam dilucide et copiose complexus, singula religionis dogmata contra fidei hostes solide propugnavit. Ita vero in his enucleate et distincte disseruit, ut non solum iam exortas haere-
15 ses sed futuras etiam quasi praesagiens everterit;

1. **Hierosolymitanus.** Cyril was brought up and educated in Jerusalem, but whether he was born there is uncertain.

7. **ordinatus fuit,** in 345.

10. **catecheses.** Cyril's twenty-four catechese (κατηχησις —religious instruction) represent the oldest extant methodical explanation of the Creed. Nineteen of them were given during the Lent of 347 or 348 to candidates preparing for Baptism at Easter; the remaining five, on Baptism, Confirmation and the Eucharist, were given during Easter week.

quemadmodum praestitit asserendo corporis et sanguinis Christi realem praesentiam in mirabili Eucharistiae sacramento. Vita autem functo sancto Maximo, a provinciae episcopis in illius locum suffectus est.

In episcopatu iniurias multas et calamitates, non secus ac beatus Athanasius, cui coaevus erat, ab Arianorum factionibus fidei causa perpessus fuit. Hi

16. **quemadmodum**, 'as for example.'
17. **realem praesentiam.** "Since he himself has declared and said of the Bread, 'This is My Body', who shall dare to doubt any more? And when he asserts and says, 'This is My Blood,' who shall even hesitate and say it is not His Blood?" Cyril speaks as one no longer hindered by the 'Discipline of the Secret,' the practice of the ancient church whereby knowledge of some of the mysteries of the faith, as the Trinity and Eucharist, were kept secret from non-Christians and catechumens early in their instruction, to prevent ridicule and misunderstanding.
19. **in illius locum** . . . , c. 350. There is some obscurity about the circumstances surrounding Cyril's succession. The different accounts in Jerome (*Chron. ad Ann.* 352) and Socrates (*H.E.* 2, 38) are to be attributed to calumnies spread by Cyril's enemies (cf. 1.21) and too easily believed.
23. **Arianorum factionibus.** For Arianism, see 24. The heresy was condemned by the Council of Nicaea in 325, and the term *homoousios* (*consubstantialis* in Latin), adopted to express the doctrine that the Son is of the very same essence as the Father. Subsequently, under the leadership of Eusebius of Nicomedia, an Arian party took shape which refused to accept the Nicene formula. Eventually three 'parties' emerged among the hierarchy: some accepted the Nicene formula *homoousios;* others denied the orthodox doctrine out-right; while a middle group claimed to be orthodox, but refused to use the term *homoousios,* suggesting the vague term *homoiousios,* of similar or like substance. Cyril for a

ST. CYRIL OF JERUSALEM. Engraving by Sansoni from **Sancti Cyrilli Opera, Venice 1763.**

enim aegre ferentes Cyrillum vehementer haeresibus obsistere, ipsum calumniis aggrediuntur, et in conciliabulo depositum e sua sede deturbant. Quorum furori ut se subtraheret, Tarsum Ciliciae aufugit, et quoad vixit Constantius, exsilii rigorem pertulit. Post illius mortem, Iuliano Apostata ad

time was of this group. The Arian party received the support of the Emperor Constantius (337-361), and orthodox bishops soon found themselves exiled from their sees. The bitter heresy threatened to cleave Christianity asunder.

26. **conciliabulo.** The term is used to indicate a synod of heretical bishops. In 357 the Arian Acacius of Caesarea quarrelled with Cyril, according to some on the matter of the precedence of their respective sees, but doctrinal differences were no doubt the cause of the attack on Cyril. Acacius summoned a small council of bishops of his own party and had Cyril deposed.

27. **Tarsum ... aufugit.** Cyril was driven from Jerusalem (deturbant) and took refuge with the semi-Arian Silvanus of Tarsus, having appealed his sentence to a higher court. In 359 his appeal was approved by a council held at Seleucia and Cyril was reinstated in Jerusalem. But the following year his deposition was again decreed, this time by Constantinople. At the same time Arian bishops were appointed to the Eastern capital and elsewhere.

29. **Post illius mortem.** Constantius' death in 361 marked the beginning of the slow return to orthodoxy.

Iuliano. Julian (361-363), called the Apostate, determined to stamp out Christianity. Paganism was once again made the official religion of the Empire, and was enhanced with a liturgy and hierarchy of its own, in mimicry of Christianity. In the hope of sowing greater confusion in the Church, Julian recalled all the bishops exiled by Constantius, but the plan backfired as the return to orthodoxy was speeded by the many councils held at this time and by former *homoiousions* like Cyril defending the Nicene formula. Julian was killed in 363 while at

30 imperium evecto, Hierosolymam redire potuit, ubi
ardenti zelo gregi suo ab erroribus et a vitiis revocando operam navavit. Sed iterum Valente imperatore exsulare coactus est, donec reddita Ecclesiae
pace per Theodosium Magnum et Arianorum cru-
35 delitate audaciaque repressa, ab eodem imperatore
tamquam fortissimus Christi athleta honoribus susceptus, suae sedi restitutus fuit. Quam strenue et
sancte sublimis officii sui munia impleverit, luculenter apparet ex florenti tunc temporis Hierosolymi-
40 tanae ecclesiae statu, quem sanctus Basilius loca
sancta veneraturus ibi aliquamdiu commoratus describit.

 Venerandi huius praesulis sanctitatem caelesti-

---

war with Persia, and his successor Jovian (363-364) made Christianity again the religion of the Empire.

 32. **Valente.** Valens (364-378), co-ruler with Valentinian I (364-375) in the East and like Constantius a determined Arian, ordered the general banishment of all bishops who had returned from exile under Julian, both Catholic and Arian alike. Cyril's third banishment lasted nearly twelve years.

 34. **Theodosium.** Theodosius the Great (379-395), the last emperor to rule a united Roman Empire, promulgated the Nicene faith as a law of the Empire. Cyril was restored to his see in 378.

 36. **athleta**, the favorite term used of those who suffer much for the faith. cf. 2 *Tim.* 2,5.

 40. **Basilius.** Despite Basil's impressions of the Holy City, his friend Gregory of Nyssa, who had been sent on request to assist Cyril, found the city orthodox, but disturbed by factions and corrupt in morals. Basil the Great (329-379) led the resistance to Arianism after Athanasius' death. (cf. 24; 27.4n.)

 41. **veneraturus**, 'to venerate'; the future participle often expresses purpose.

bus signis a Deo fuisse illustratam, memoriae
traditum accepimus. Inter haec recensetur praeclara
crucis, solis radiis fulgentioris, apparitio, quae
episcopatus eius initia decoravit. Huiusmodi prodigii
ethnici et christiani testes oculares fuerunt cum ipso
Cyrillo, qui gratiis primum in ecclesia Deo redditis,
illud per epistulam Constantio imperatori narravit.
Nec minus admiratione dignum, quod Iudaeis,
templum a Tito eversum restaurare ex impio imperatoris Iuliani iussu conantibus, evenit. Vehementi
enim terraemotu oborto et ingentibus flammarum
globis e terra erumpentibus, omnia opera ignis con-
sumpsit, ita ut Iudaei et Iulianus deterriti ab incepto
destiterint; prout scilicet indubitanter futurum Cyrillus praedixerat. Qui demum paulo ante obitum

---

50. **per epistulam.** The letter has been preserved. It was in the first year of Cyril's episcopate, on Pentecost at 9:00 A.M., that the cross appeared "just over Golgotha, reaching as far as the holy Mount of Olives." It lasted several hours and was seen by the whole city. The phenomenon was described also by St. Jerome (*Chron. ad ann.* 357) and Socrates (*H.E.* 2, 28).

53. **Iuliani iussu.** Julian the Apostate determined to rebuild the temple which had been destroyed by the Roman general and later Emperor Titus (79-81) in 70 A.D. Titus' sack of the city had fulfilled the prophecy of Christ (*Mt.* 24,2), which Julian intended now to prove wrong. The extraordinary phenomena are recorded not only by the Church historians Socrates (*H.E.* 3,20) and Theodoret (*H.E.* 3,15) but also by the contemporary pagan historian Ammianus Marcellinus (23, 1,2).

57. **futurum,** sc. *esse,* as often; 'as Cyril had confidently predicted *would happen.*'

concilio oecumenico Constantinopolitano interfuit,
in quo Macedonii haeresis et iterum Ariana condemnata est. Ac Hierusalem inde reversus, fere septuagenarius tricesimo quinto sui episcopatus anno sancto fine quievit. Eius Officium ac Missam Leo decimus tertius Pontifex maximus ab universa Ecclesia celebrari mandavit.

Oratio

Da nobis, quaesumus, omnipotens Deus, beato Cyrillo Pontifice intercedente, te solum verum Deum et quem misisti Iesum Christum ita cognoscere, ut inter oves quae vocem eius audiunt, perpetuo connumerari mereamur. Per eumdem Dominum nostrum.

---

59. **concilio** ... The Second Ecumenical Council met in 381 and condemned Macedonius, the Arian bishop of Constantinople, who had denied the Divinity of the Holy Spirit, and reaffirmed the Nicene Creed. cf. 27.19n.

64. **Leo XIII.** On July 28, 1882, Leo also declared Cyril a Doctor of the Church.

12. ST. JOSEPH

March 19

 Quis et qualis homo fuerit beatus Ioseph conice ex appellatione, qua licet dispensatoria meruit honorari a Deo, ut pater Dei dictus et creditus sit. Conice et ex proprio vocabulo, quod *augmentum* non
5 dubitas interpretari. Simul et memento magni illius quondam Patriarchae venditi in Aegypto, et scito

  About St. Joseph very little is known. In the Gospels he figures solely in the events of Christ's birth and infancy, and as he never appears with Mary during the public life of Christ, it is probable that he died prior to it. The apocryphal gospels, it is true, provide elaborate information about him, but none of it is reliable. Joseph's Mass and Office were extended to the universal Church by Gregory XV in 1621, and Pius IX proclaimed him Patron of the Universal Church in 1870.

  This selection is a homily by St. Bernard of Clairvaux (1090-1153). (*Hom.* 2 in *Lk.* 1,26,27.) The foremost promoter of the Cistercian reform in France, Bernard was renowned throughout Europe for his wisdom and sanctity, and was called upon by Eugenius III to preach the Second Crusade. He is a Doctor of the Church.

  2. **qua licet dispensatoria**, 'by which, although as a steward, he deserved to be honored'.

   a **Deo**; so *P.L.* 183, 69, for breviary *adeo*.

  4. **augmentum**; in Hebrew: "May God add."

THE MARRIAGE OF JOSEPH AND MARY. Fresco by Giotto (1266-1337). Scrovegni Chapel, Padua.
Courtesy, Alinari

ipsius istum non solum vocabulum fuisse sortitum, sed castimoniam adeptum, innocentiam assecutum et gratiam.

10 Siquidem ille Ioseph, fraterna ex invidia venditus et ductus in Aegyptum, Christi venditionem praefiguravit; iste Ioseph, Herodianam invidiam fugiens, Christum in Aegyptum portavit. Ille domino suo fidem servans, dominae noluit commisceri; iste
15 Dominam suam Domini sui matrem, virginem agnoscens, et ipse continens fideliter custodivit. Illi data est intellegentia mysteriis somniorum; isti datum est conscium fieri atque participem caelestium sacramentorum.

20 Ille frumenta servavit non sibi sed omni populo; iste Panem vivum e caelo servandum accepit tam sibi quam toti mundo. Non est dubium quin bonus

---

7. **ipsius istum.** For a similar juxtaposition, cf. 1.12 **Dominam suam Domini sui.** ipsius refers to Joseph the Patriarch; **istum** to St. Joseph.

8. **adeptum,** from *adipiscor; fuisse* is to be understood with **adeptum** and **assecutum.**

   10. ille . . . iste, 'one Joseph' . . . 'the other Joseph.'
       venditus; cf. *Gen.* 37.
   13. Christum . . . portavit; cf. *Mt.* 2, 13-15.
   14. **noluit commisceri;** cf. *Gen.* 39.
   15. virginem agnoscens . . . **custodivit;** cf. *Mt.* 1, 18-25.
   17. **somniorum;** cf *Gen.* 40,41.
   19. **sacramentorum,** 'secrets'. cf. *Mt.* 1, 20. *Sacramentum* (μυστηριον) has a long history. cf. Harper's Latin Dictionary and theology texts on the Sacraments in General. cf. particularly *Dan.* 2, 18-47; *Col.* 1, 26-27; *Eph.* 3, 3-12.
   20. **frumenta;** cf. *Gen.* 41,42.
   21. **Panem vivum;** cf. *Jn.* 6,51.

et fidelis homo fuerit iste Ioseph, cui Mater desponsata est Salvatoris. Fidelis, inquam, servus et prudens, quem constituit Dominus suae Matris solacium, suae carnis nutricium, solum denique in terris magni consilii coadiutorem fidelissimum.

Oratio

Sanctissimae Genetricis tuae Sponsi, quaesumus, Domine, meritis adiuvemur, ut quod possibilitas nostra non obtinet, eius nobis intercessione donetur: Qui vivis et regnas.

---

24. **Fidelis servus**; cf. *Mt*. 25,21.

13. ST. BENEDICT

March 21   c. 480-c. 547

    Benedictus Nursiae nobili genere ortus, Romae liberalibus disciplinis eruditus, ut totum se Iesu Christo daret, ad eum locum, qui Sublacus dicitur, in altissimam speluncam penetravit; in qua sic per
5 triennium delituit, ut unus id sciret Romanus mona-

    The main sources for the life of St. Benedict are his own Rule, which conveys much of his spirit and character, and Book Two of the *Dialogues* of Gregory the Great. (cf. 9.4n.) Gregory states that four of Benedict's own disciples (two of whom succeeded him as abbots of Monte Cassino) are the source of his information about the saint. Written in 593, fifty years after Benedict's death, the *Dialogues* relate the life and miracles of Italian saints, and present a vivid picture of religious life in Italy during the chaotic sixth century, the century that ushered in the Dark Ages. Much of the miraculous that characterizes the work is due to the avid interest of the people in the supernatural, since they saw in such phenomena a sign that God had not completely abandoned the world.

    2. **eruditus**. Scandalized by the dissolute life led by his school associates, Benedict determined to leave Rome, being about twenty at the time. His first vocation was as a solitary.

    3. **Sublacus**, fifty miles east of Rome. Sublacus (the modern Subiaco) received its name from the artifical lake formed by a dam built by the emperor Claudius (41-54) across the Anio River. It was destroyed by floods in 1305.

    5. **Romanus**. Benedict met Romanus while on his journey to Subiaco. Having counselled Benedict, Romanus undertook to

chus, quo ad vitae necessitatem ministro utebatur.
Dum igitur ei quodam die ardentes ad libidinem
faces a diabolo subicerentur, se in vepribus tamdiu
volutavit, dum lacerato corpore voluptatis sensus
10 dolore opprimeretur. Sed iam erumpente ex illis
latebris fama eius sanctitatis, quidam monachi se
illi instituendos tradiderunt. Quorum vivendi licentia cum eius obiurgationes ferre non posset, venenum
in potione ei dare constituunt. Verum poculum ei
15 praebentibus, crucis signo vas confregit, ac relicto
monasterio in solitudinem se recepit.

provide him with food which he used to let down into Benedict's cave by a long rope.

10. **erumpente.** Some shepherds discovered him and soon after word about him started to circulate.

11. **quidam monachi.** When the abbot of a near-by monastery died, the monks entreated Benedict to come and govern them. At first Benedict refused because he knew the laxity of their monastic observance (**vivendi licentia**) was not to his liking. He finally agreed, however, but the monks soon found that they could not accept his strict rule. The incident is indicative of the amorphous condition of western monasticism prior to Benedict.

15. **vas confregit.** "When the cup was offered, according to the custom, to the abbot to bless, Benedict made the sign of the Cross and immediately the cup, that was held afar off, broke in pieces, as though the sign of the Cross had been a stone thrown against it." (*Dial.* 2, 3)

praebentibus, sc. *eis,* and abl. absol.

relicto monasterio. Of his abandonment of these monks, Gregory makes the following not unobscure comment: "You will quickly see that Benedict forsook not so many in one place who were unwilling to be taught, as he did in many other places raise up from the death of the soul many more who were willing to be taught." (ibid.)

Sed cum multi ad eum cotidie discipuli convenirent, duodecim monasteria aedificavit, eaque sanctissimis legibus communivit. Postea Cassinum migravit, ubi simulacrum Apollinis, qui adhuc ibi colebatur, comminuit, aram evertit et lucos succendit; ibique sancti Martini sacellum et sancti Ioannis aediculam exstruxit, oppidanos autem et incolas christianis praeceptis imbuit. Quare augebatur in dies magis divina gratia Benedictus, ut etiam prophetico spiritu

18. **duodecim.** Each monastery was given a small community of twelve monks. Later at Monte Cassino Benedict kept all his monks in the one monastery. At this time many parents began to entrust their children to Benedict for their education. (cf. 8.9n.)

19. **legibus.** There was still no written rule; the monks were taught the religious life only by following the example of Benedict. His famous Rule, with its mature wisdom, was written after 530 and at Monte Cassino. cf. 27.6n.

Cassinum migravit, c. 429. It is not known how long he stayed at Subiaco, but his departure was sudden, brought on by trouble stirred up by an envious priest.

22. **Martini,** i.e., St. Martin of Tours (c. 316-397), who established near Poitiers the first monastery in France, and was one of Benedict's precursors in the history of Western monasticism. To Benedict, however, is reserved the title of its Founder and Patriarch.

22. **Ioannis,** i.e., St. John the Baptist. It was here that Benedict was buried.

25. **prophetico spiritu.** Among other things, Benedict prophesied that Monte Cassino would be destroyed. This prophecy came true in 581 when the monastery was sacked by the Lombards. Rebuilt in the eighth century, it was again destroyed in 883 by the Saracens. In 1944 the monastery, built up over six centuries after an earthquake in 1349, was destroyed by Allied bombers during the invasion of Italy.

THE DEATH OF ST. BENEDICT. Fresco by Spinello Aretino (c. 1346-1410). S. Miniato al Monte, Florence.
Courtesy, Alinari

ventura praediceret. Quod ubi accepit Totila Gothorum rex, exploraturus an res ita esset, spatharium suum regio ornatu et comitatu praemittit, qui se regem simularet. Quem ut ille vidit, "Depone," inquit, "fili, depone quod geris; nam tuum non est." Totilae vero praedixit adventum eius in Urbem, maris transmissionem et post novem annos mortem.

Qui aliquot mensibus antequam e vita migraret, praemonuit discipulos quo die esset moriturus; ac sepulchrum, in quo suum corpus condi vellet, sex diebus antequam eo inferretur, aperiri iussit; sextoque die deferri voluit in ecclesiam, ubi sumpta Eucharistia, sublatis in caelum oculis orans, inter manus discipulorum efflavit animam. Quam duo monachi euntem in caelum viderunt, pallio ornatam pretiosissimo, circum eam fulgentibus lampadibus; et clarissima et gravissima specie virum, stantem

26. **Quod ubi accepit**, 'And when he *heard* this'.

27. **exploraturus**; the future participle often expresses purpose. cf. **veneraturus**, 11.40.

28. **qui ... simularet**; a relative clause of purpose.

31. **Totilae ... praedixit**, in 543, the only certain date in his life, and the year some maintain he died. The prophecy was fulfilled: Totila captured and sacked Rome in 545, again in 549; later he crossed to Sicily and plundered the island; he was killed in 552 by the forces of the Emperor Justinian (527 - 565). (cf. 9.3n.)

39. **duo monachi**. According to the *Dialogues*, two monks, one of whom was in his cell, the other far distant, both had the same vision. In the same way Benedict is said to have seen the soul of his sister St. Scholastica ascending to heaven.

supra caput ipsius, dicentem audierunt: "Haec est via, qua dilectus Domini Benedictus in caelum ascendit."
45

Oratio

Intercessio nos, quaesumus, Domine, beati Benedicti Abbatis commendet, ut quod nostris meritis non valemus, eius patrocinio assequamur. Per Dominum nostrum.

14. ST. JOHN DAMASCENE

March 27   c. 609-c. 749

    Ioannes, a patrio loco Damascenus dictus, nobili genere natus, humanis divinisque litteris a Cosma monacho Constantinopoli fuit excultus. Cumque ea tempestate imperator Leo Isauricus nefario bello
5 sacrarum imaginum cultum insectaretur, Ioannes hortatu Gregorii tertii Romani Pontificis et sermone et scriptis sanctitatem illius cultus sedulo propugna-

    2. **Cosma**, a Sicilian monk captured by the Arabs and ransomed by John's father. He is said to have taught John grammar, logic, arithmetic, geometry and theology, though John was not at the time contemplating the priesthood.
    3. **Constantinopoli.** He was educated not at Constantinople but at home.
    4. **Leo** III the Isaurian (717-740) published an edict in 726 forbidding the use of sacred images. Because of the devout and widespread use of such images, the edict caused riots in the Empire and even revolution in Greece, but Leo triumphed over all opposition and ordered the Patriarch of Constantinople to countersign the edict. When he refused, Leo appointed another patriarch, who signed and drew many other bishops into heresy with him.
    6. **Gregorii.** Gregory III (731-741) excommunicated in 731 all who destroyed images or forbade their veneration. In reply, Leo sent a fleet to Italy to seize the Pope, and when it perished in the Adriatic, he occupied the papal estates in Sicily and southern Italy.

vit. Quo facto tantam Leonis adversum se invidiam
concitavit, ut hic confictis litteris ipsum tamquam
10 proditorem accusarit apud Damasci calipham, qui
Ioanne consiliario et administro utebatur. Credulus

    10. **accusarit** = *accusaverit*.
    apud Damasci calipham. Damascus in 611 became the residence of the caliphs or 'successors' to Mohammed. Mohammed (570-632) claimed to have received revelations from God and to be his last and greatest prophet, and founded c. 622 the Islamic religion, which accepted some Biblical teachings but held that the Koran, containing Mohammed's revelation, superseded the Bible. In 633 his followers began a 'Holy War' to further the spread of Islamism. With a united Arab world behind them, they conquered Damascus (635), Jerusalem (637) and Alexandria (642). With Syria, Palestine and Egypt subjugated, they pushed their new empire further west. By 681 all of North Africa had fallen and in 711 Visigothic Spain (cf. 16.9n.) The Graeco-Roman Christian culture in these territories was engulfed and submerged, but a new culture soon flowered, especially in Spain, which stimulated the renaissance of science and philosophy in the twelfth and thirteenth centuries. (cf. 8.31; 16.58n)
    11. **administro.** John succeeded his father as chief revenue officer for the caliph. (His grandfather had negotiated the surrender of Damascus in 635.) As a subject of the Arab caliph, John was out of reach of the authority of the Byzantine emperors and in a position to fight Iconoclasm unmolested. According to the story (which is now regarded as apocryphal, as is the caliph's punishment and the cure), Leo resolved to destroy John by stratagem and sent a forged letter purporting to have been written by John in which he informed the emperor that Damascus was poorly defended and offered his help if Leo attacked it. (*Acta Sanctorum*, May vol. 2, p. 114)

5. *Latin Book*

fraudi princeps Ioanni, nequidquam calumniam eiuranti, praecidi dexteram iussit. Verum innocentiae vindex adfuit clienti suo sanctissima Virgo, cuius
15 opem precibus enixe imploraverat, eiusque beneficio trunca manus restituta ita bracchio coaluit ac si divisa numquam fuisset. Quo maxime miraculo permotus, Ioannes quod pridem animo conceperat, exsequi statuit. Itaque aegre a calipha impetrato secessu,
20 suas omnes facultates in egenos distribuit et servos libertate donavit. Tum sacra Palaestinae loca peregrinus lustravit, ac demum una cum Cosma institutore suo in lauram sancti Sabbae prope Hierosolymam concessit, ibique presbyter initiatus est.

13. **eiuranti,** dative modifying **Ioanni,** a dative of possession with **dexteram:** 'ordered that John's right hand be cut off, though he swore in vain that the story was a calumny...'. The Gospel of St. John's Mass is the story of the miraculous cure of the man with the withered hand, *Lk.* 6,6-11.

17. **Quo maxime miraculo....** There are grounds for believing, however, that John's early works against Iconoclasm (the first appeared in 726) were written *after* he had left the caliph's service and was a monk at Mar Saba.

18. **quod,** 'that which', 'what'; the clause is object of **exsequi.**

22. **Cosma institutore.** According to the biography of John, written in the tenth century by the Patriarch of Jerusalem and the only source for details of his life, this Cosmas was not his teacher, but his adopted *brother,* who had been taught with John by Cosmas, the ransomed monk. cf. *Acta Sanctorum,* p. 113; 115.

23. **lauram.** This Greek word was used to designate monasteries in Palestine of the semi-eremitical type. Sabas, a Cappadocian, founded Mar Saba in 483.

ST. JOHN DAMASCENE (left) AND COSMAS.
Miniature from the Menology of Basil II (tenth century).
Vatican Library

In religiosae vitae palaestra praeclariora virtutum exempla monachis praebuit, demissionis potissimum et oboedientiae. Abiectissima quaeque coenobii munia, veluti sibi propria, deposcebat ac sedulo obibat. Contextas a se sportulas venditare Damasci iussus, in ea nimirum civitate, ubi olim summis honoribus perfunctus fuerat, irrisiones ac ludibria vulgi avide captabat. Oboedientiam adeo coluit, ut non modo ad quemlibet praesidum nutum praesto esset, sed ne causam quidem eorum quae praecipiebantur, quamvis ardua essent et insolita, quaerendam sibi umquam putarit. Inter has virtutum exercitationes, catholicum dogma de sanctarum imaginum cultu impense tueri numquam destitit. Quare ut ante Leonis Isaurici, ita postmodum Constantini Copronymi adversum se odia vexationesque provocavit; eo vel magis quod libere arrogantiam

27. **Abiectissima quaeque**, 'all the most menial tasks'.

32. **ut non modo ... putarit**, 'so that not only was he ready for any and every nod of his superiors, but never did he think that he should ask even the reason for the things which were commanded...' **putarit** = *putaverit*.

39. **Constantini**. Constantine V Copronymus (740-775) continued his father's policy of later years, which was to further the cause of Iconoclasm without persecution. But in 752 hostilities were renewed. A new edict was countersigned by over three hundred bishops, whose purged ranks had been summoned to council at Hieria. A violent persecution was carried on until the emperor's death, particularly against the monks, who, unlike the bishops, refused to yield and whose influence was greatly resented.

41. **eo vel magis quod**, 'even all the more because...'

imperatorum retunderet, qui fidei negotia pertractare deque his sententiam arbitratu suo ferre audebant.

45 Mirum sane est quam multa tum ad fidem tutandam tum ad pietatem fovendam et soluta et astricta numeris oratione Ioannes elucubraverit; dignus sane qui ab altera Nicaena synodo amplissimis laudibus celebraretur, et ob aureum orationis
50 flumen *Chrysorrhoas* appellaretur. Neque solum contra Iconomachos orthodoxam fidem defendit; sed

42. **fidei negotia.** The line between Church and State had never been drawn or observed by the emperors, particularly the Byzantine ones. Their interference in Church affairs was ultimately an attempt at Caesaro-papism, i.e., to be both Caesar and Pope at once.

46. **et soluta ... oratione,** 'both in free-flowing speech and in speech confined to meter'; i.e., both prose and poetry. St. John was regarded as one of the two greatest poets of the Eastern Church, some of whose hymns were made part of the liturgy.

48. **altera Nicaena synodo.** In 787 the seventh Ecumenical Council was convoked by Adrian I (772-795) at the proposal of the Empress Irene, regent for her son after the death of her husband Leo IV (775-780). At this council, the second held at Nicaea, the pseudo-council of Hieria (above n. 39) was condemned and the Catholic doctrine on veneration of images set forth. (The Council of Trent (1545-1563) later reiterated the same teaching to the iconoclasts among the Protestant reformers of the sixteenth century.)

50. **Chrysorrhoas,** i.e., 'one who pours forth gold'; χρυσος, gold; ῥέω, to flow.

51. **Iconomachos,** 'fighters against images;' εἰκων, image; μαχομαι, to fight; also Iconoclasts; κλαω, to break.

omnes ferme haereticos, praesertim Acephalos, Monothelitas, Theopaschitas, strenue impugnavit. Ecclesiae iura potestatemque egregie vindicavit.
55 Primatum Principis Apostolorum disertissimis verbis asseruit, ipsumque ecclesiarum columen, infractam petram, orbis terrarum magistrum et moderatorem saepius nominat. Universa autem eius scripta non modo eruditione et doctrina praestant, sed etiam
60 quemdam ingenuae pietatis sensum praeferunt, praecipue cum Genetricis Dei laudes praedicat, quam singulari cultu et amore prosequebatur. Illud vero maxime in laudem Ioannis cedit, quod primus universam theologiam recto ordine comprehenderit

52. **Acephalos**, i.e., the Headless (ἀ κεφαλοι, heads), a Monophysite sect, so named perhaps because originally they had withdrawn from the party of the Patriarch of Constantinople in 482 when he tried to form an ambiguous creed acceptable to orthodox and monophysite alike. cf. 17.21n.

Monothelitas. Monothelites held to one will (θελημα) in Christ.

53. **Theopaschitas.** This sect held that the human nature of Christ was absorbed into the divine and that the sufferings and death of Christ were to be attributed to the divine nature (θεος, God; πασχω, to suffer.) St. John also wrote against the Manichaeans, the Mohammedans, and the Nestorians.

62. **Illud ... quod,** 'This most of all belongs to John's praises, the fact that ...'

64. **universam theologiam**: in the work *On The Orthodox Faith*, the third part of his *Fountain of Wisdom*, the most famous of his dogmatic works, regarded in the East as highly as the *Summa Theologica* of St. Thomas Aquinas in the West. A twelfth century Latin translation of this work was used by both Peter Lombard and Thomas Aquinas. For this reason, and be-

65 et sancti Thomae viam complanaverit ad sacram
doctrinam tam praeclara methodo tractandam. Tandem vir sanctissimus meritis plenus devexaque iam
aetate, in pace Christi quievit anno circiter septingentesimo quinquagesimo quarto. Eius Officium et
70 Missam Leo decimus tertius Pontifex maximus addito Doctoris titulo universae Ecclesiae concessit.

Oratio

Omnipotens sempiterne Deus, qui ad cultum
sacrarum imaginum asserendum, beatum Ioannem
caelesti doctrina et admirabili spiritus fortitudine
75 imbuisti, concede nobis eius intercessione et exemplo, ut, quorum colimus imagines, virtutes imitamur
et patrocinia sentiamus. Per Dominum nostrum.

---

cause he made extensive use of Aristotelian philosophy. John has been called the forerunner of scholasticism.

68. **septingentesimo.** . . . John's death must be placed no later than 754 when an Iconoclastic Synod anathematized his memory. 749 is the probable date.

71. **Doctoris.** . . . The last of the Greek Fathers of the Church was named a Doctor in 1890.

15. ST. JOHN OF CAPISTRANO

March 28   1386-1456

Ioannes, Capistrani in Pelignis ortus et Perusium studiorum causa missus, in christianis et liberalibus disciplinis adeo profecit, ut ob egregiam iuris scientiam aliquot civitatibus a Neapolis rege Ladis-
5 lao praefectus fuerit. Dum autem earum rempublicam sanctissime gerens perturbatis rebus tranquilli-

> 1. **in Pelignis**, 'in the country of the Peligni', an ancient people of central Italy. St. John's father was not Italian, but of French or German ancestry.
> **Perusium.** Perugia was an important town in both ancient Etruria and medieval Tuscany. Long loyal to the Holy See, it revolted in 1375, became subject again in 1403, but subsequently fell into the power of King Ladislaus of Naples, who held it until 1416. Its university was founded in 1320.
> 4. **a Neapolis rege**... The Kingdom of Naples (or, together with Sicily, the Kingdom of the Two Sicilies) included all of Italy south of the Papal States. Established by the Normans in 1091, it became part of the Holy Roman Empire in the thirteenth century. It was conquered by Charles of Anjou in 1266, who was expelled in 1282 and replaced by the Spanish House of Aragon. The mainland, however, remained Angevin until 1435 when it reunited with Sicily under Spanish rule. Ladislaus I inherited the throne in 1386. To restore the kingdom to its former prominent position in Italy, he invaded the Papal States in 1408, even entered Rome in 1410. St. John was appointed governor of Perugia in 1412.

tatem revocare studet, capitur ipse et in vincula conicitur. Quibus mirabiliter ereptus, Francisci Assisiensis regulam inter Fratres Minores profitetur.
10 Ad divinarum litterarum studium progressus, praeceptorem nactus est sanctum Bernardinum Senensem, cuius et virtutis exempla, in cultu potissimum sanctissimi nominis Iesu ac Deiparae propagando, egregie est imitatus. Aquilanum episcopatum re-
15 cusavit, et severiore disciplina atque scriptis, quae plurima edidit ad mores reformandos, maxime enituit.

Praedicationi verbi Dei sedulo incumbens, Italiam fere universam lustravit; quo in munere et

7. **capitur ipse**. The city revolted in 1416 and John was thrown into prison. While there he made his decision to abandon the world and enter the Franciscans.

8. **Francisci**. Curiously St. Francis (1182-1226) had once been a prisoner himself in Perugia, after a battle between that city and Assisi, and had subsequently left the world for an austere life of poverty and penance. The first of the rules he wrote for his small band of followers was verbally approved by Innocent III in 1210. Honorius III in 1223 approved a more detailed rule for his fast growing order.

11. **Bernardinum**. St. Bernardine of Siena (1380-1444) was ordained a Franciscan in 1404 and twelve years later began the eloquent preaching journeys through Italy which bore tremendous fruit and won for him the title of Apostle of Italy. Popular devotion to the Holy Name of Jesus owes its origin to him.

18. **Praedicationi ... incumbens.** St. John accompanied Bernardine on his missions and in 1420 as a deacon was permitted to preach.

virtute sermonis et miraculorum frequentia innumeras prope animas in viam salutis reduxit. Eum Martinus quintus ad exstinguendam Fraticellorum sectam inquisitorem instituit. A Nicolao quinto contra Iudaeos et Saracenos generalis inquisitor in Italia constitutus, plurimos ad Christi fidem convertit. In Oriente multa optime constituit, et in concilio

20. **innumeras prope animas.** John met with an extraordinary response, yet the biographies of him, written by three of his companions, often exaggerate when they speak of 100,000 or 150,000 people attending a single sermon.

22. **Martinus quintus** (1417-1431) was elected at the Council of Constance (1414-1418) to end the Great Western Schism.

Fraticelli (Italian for Little Brothers), an heretical sect which separated from the Franciscans in the fourteenth century because of disputes over poverty. Originally a group of extreme Spirituals, the sect believed that the Church had deserted the faith since the time of John XXII (1323), that they alone constituted the true Church and retained the Sacraments and priesthood. (The two branches of the Franciscan Order, the Observants or Spirituals and the Conventuals, formally date from the Council of Constance, but the division had appeared immediately after the death of St. Francis two hundred years before. St. Bernardine had been the vicar-general of the Observants (1438-1442).)

23. **Nicolao quinto.** A patron of literature, Nicolaus V (1447-1455) founded the Vatican Library, performed the last imperial coronation in Rome, that of Frederick III (1440-1493) in 1452.

26. **concilio Florentino.** The seventeenth Ecumenical Council met 1438-1445 to heal the schism between East and West. Like its predecessor at the second Council of Lyons (1274; cf. 8. 59n.), the agreement at Florence failed to achieve a lasting union. Of the Eastern Rites now in union with Rome, all but one have returned since the sixteenth century.

ST. JOHN OF CAPISTRANO. Painting by Bartholomeo Vivarini (c. 1425-c. 1499). **Louvre Museum, Paris. Courtesy, Giraudon**

Florentino, ubi veluti sol quidam fulsit, Armenos
Ecclesiae catholicae restituit. Idem Pontifex, postu-
lante Friderico tertio imperatore, illum apostolicae
30 Sedis nuntium in Germaniam legavit, ut haereticos
ad catholicam fidem et principum animas ad concor-
diam revocaret. In Germania aliisque provinciis Dei
gloriam sexennali ministerio mirifice auxit, Hussitis,
Adamitis, Thaboritis, Hebraeisque innumeris doc-
35 trinae veritate ac miraculorum luce ad Ecclesiae
sinum traductis.

27. **Armenos.** St. John had done much to have the Armenians, whose patriarchs at one time or another had been in communion with Rome, included with the Greeks at the council,
though between the early and the final sessions he had been
away as apostolic commissary in Jerusalem.

33. **Hussitis.** The Hussites were an heretical sect in Bohemia,
named after John Huss (1369-1415), a priest whose teachings
had been condemned by Constance in 1414. Their distinctive
teaching was the necessity of receiving Holy Communion under
both species.

34. **Adamitis.** By no means the first sect professing to have
recovered Adam's original innocence, this sect was an over-
ardent off-shoot of the Hussites, which was annihilated by the
Hussite Ziska in 1421.

Thaboritis. The Taborites were the left-wing of the
Hussites, an extreme anti-clerical group who claimed *inter alia*
that sacraments administered by a sinful priest were invalid.
(cf. 9. 31n.)

35. **miraculorum.** St. John's companions recorded all the
miracles that occurred wherever he went. John attributed them
to the relics of St. Bernardine with which he blessed the sick.
John's mission, which included trips to Bavaria, Saxony, Austria,
Bohemia and Poland, began in 1451 and ended when he was
ordered to preach a crusade against the Ottoman Turks, who in

Cum Callistus tertius, ipso potissimum deprecante, cruce signatos mittere decrevisset, Ioannes per Pannoniam aliasque provincias volitavit, qua
40 verbo, qua litteris principum animos ita ad bellum accendit, ut brevi millia Christianorum septuaginta conscripta sint. Eius consilio et virtute potissimum Taurunensis victoria relata est, centum ac viginti Turcarum millibus partim caesis, partim fugatis.
45 Cuius victoriae cum Romam nuntius venisset octavo Idus Augusti, idem Callistus eius diei memoriae solemnia Transfigurationis Christi Domini perpetuo consecravit. Lethali morbo aegrotum et Villacum delatum viri principes plures visitarunt; quos ipse
50 ad tuendam religionem hortatus, animam Deo sancte

1453 had captured Constantinople and whose empire now extended through the Balkans to the Danube and was threatening European Christendom.

38. **cruce signatos**, 'those signed with the cross'; i.e., crusaders, who received a cross from the pope or his legate and wore a cross as a badge on their outer garment. Callistus III (1455-1458) organized this crusade against the Turks.

39. **qua verbo, qua litteris**, 'where by word and by letter'. Actually his efforts met with little response and in 1456 the situation was desperate. Mustering most of the forces in Hungary, John led the troops himself to Belgrade and urged on the left wing during the battle.

43. **Taurunensis**. Taurunum was a strong fortress opposite Belgrade.

relata est, 'was won', 'secured', on July 21, 1456. In 1521, however, the Turks succeeded in capturing the city.

45. **octavo Idus Augusti**, August 6.

48. **Lethali morbo**. Infection from unburied bodies killed first the great general Hunyady and then St. John.

reddidit, anno salutis millesimo quadringentesimo quinquagesimo sexto. Eius gloriam post mortem Deus multis miraculis confirmavit; quibus rite probatis, Alexander octavus anno millesimo sexcentesimo
55 nonagesimo Ioannem in Sanctorum numerum retulit, eiusque Officium ac Missam Leo decimus tertius altero ab eius canonizatione saeculo ad universam extendit ecclesiam.

Oratio

Deus, qui per beatum Ioannem fideles tuos in
60 virtute sanctissimi nominis Iesu de crucis inimicis triumphare fecisti, praesta, quaesumus, ut spiritualium hostium eius intercessione superatis insidiis, coronam iustitiae a Te accipere mereamur. Per Dominum nostrum.

---

54. **Alexander octavus** in his own pontificate (1689-1691) came to the aid of his native Venice against the Turks.

60. **de ... triumphare**, 'to triumph *over* the enemies of the cross'.

16. ST. ISIDORE OF SEVILLE

April 4   c. 560-636

Isidorus, natione Hispanus, Doctor egregius, ex nova Carthagine Severiano patre, provinciae duce, natus, a sanctis episcopis Leandro Hispalensi et Fulgentio Carthaginiensi fratribus suis pie et liber-
5 aliter educatus, Latinis, Graecis et Hebraicis litteris, divinisque et humanis legibus instructus, omni scientiarum atque christianarum virtutum genere praestantissimus evasit. Adhuc adulescens haeresim Arianam, quae gentem Gothorum, Hispaniae latissi-

    2. **nova Carthagine**. Named after the mother city in N. Africa, New Carthage was founded c. 225 B.C. as the start of a new Punic Empire in Spain, but in 210 B.C. it was captured by the Romans who made the entire country a Roman province and established a capital at Toledo.
    3. **Leandro.** Orphaned when very young, Isidore's education was supervised by his older brother Leander at the cathedral school of Seville, the first of its kind in Spain where the liberal arts, divided into *trivium* (grammar, rhetoric and dialectic) and the *quadrivium* (arithmetic, geometry, music, astronomy), were taught.
    9. **gentem Gothorum.** Spain had been conquered 409-411 by the Vandals, who moved on into Africa in 429. In 456 the Visigoths moved from Gaul into Spain and secured control by 477. As pious and fanatical Arians, they persecuted the native Catholic population and hierarchy. For their conversion to Catholicism, much credit must be given to St. Leander, who

me dominantem, iampridem invaserat, tanta constantia palam oppugnavit, ut parum abfuerit quin ab haereticis necaretur. Leandro vita functo, ad Hispalensem cathedram invitus quidem sed urgente in primis Reccaredo rege magnoque etiam cleri populique consensu assumitur; eiusque electionem sanctus Gregorius Magnus, nedum auctoritate apostolica confirmasse, sed et electum transmisso de more pallio decorasse, quin etiam suum et apostolicae Sedis in universa Hispania vicarium constituisse perhibetur.

In episcopatu quantum fuerit constans, humilis, patiens, misericors, in christiana et ecclesiastica disciplina instauranda sollicitus, eaque verbo et scriptis

directed the Council of Toledo of 589 when the Visigoths under Reccared declared themselves Catholic. see 9.19n., 31n.

11. **ut parum abfuerit...**, 'that he was not very far from being killed by the heretics'.

12. **vita functo**, in 599.

14. **Reccaredo.** In 586 Reccared succeeded his father Leovigild as king of the Visigoths. Having converted to Catholicism himself, he set about the conversion of his people. cf. 9.31n. An older brother, Hermenegild, who had become a Catholic, but had been slain in 585 for his faith by his father, is revered as a martyr and a saint. (April 13)

15. **eiusque electionem ... perhibetur**, 'Gregory, to say nothing of having confirmed the election, is reported to have honored the elected bishop by sending him the pallium as customary, and moreover to have appointed him his own vicar and that of the Apostolic See in Spain.'

18. **pallio.** cf. 9.32n.

21. **quantum fuerit constans...**, 'how firm he was...'; indirect questions depending on **enarrare**, 1.25.

ST. ISIDORE OF SEVILLE AND BRAULION. A miniature from the **Codex Monacensis**. **Bavarian State Library, Munich.**

stabilienda indefessus, atque omni demum virtutum
25 ornamento insignitus, nullius lingua enarrare sufficeret. Monastici quoque instituti per Hispaniam promotor et amplificator eximius, plura construxit monasteria, collegia itidem aedificavit, ubi studiis sacris et lectionibus vacans, plurimos discipulos, qui
30 ad eum confluebant, erudivit, quos inter sancti Ildefonsus Toletanus et Braulio Caesaraugustanus episcopi emicuerunt. Coacto Hispali concilio, Acephalorum haeresim, Hispaniae iam minitantem, acri et eloquenti disputatione fregit atque contrivit. Tan-
35 tam apud omnes sanctitatis et doctrinae famam adeptus est, ut elapso vix ab eius obitu sextodecimo anno, universa Toletana synodo duorum supra quinquaginta episcoporum plaudente ipsoque etiam

26. **Monastici ... amplificator.** His work *Regula Monachorum* laid down rules for the monastic life and was generally followed throughout Spain.

28. **collegia ... aedificavit.** The ancient institutions and classical learning of the Romans was fast disintegrating before the Gothic barbarians. Realizing that education and religion were his main resources for blending the various racial elements in Spain into a new nation, Isidore set himself to the task of promoting Christian learning. In his own cathedral school Latin and Greek were prescribed, medicine and law were encouraged. Later at the Fourth Council of Toledo (55n.) he promulgated a decree which required all bishops to establish a cathedral school in their diocese along the pattern of his own in Seville.

30. **quos inter;** anastrophe.

32. **Hispali concilio,** in 619.—**Acephalorum,** cf. 14.52n.

36. **elapso ... anno,** 'when the sixteenth year after his death had hardly gone by'; i.e., in 653, when the Eighth National Council met at Toledo.

sancto Ildefonso suffragante, Doctor egregius, ca-
40 tholicae Ecclesiae novissimum decus, in saeculorum
fine doctissimus, et cum reverentia nominandus ap-
pellari meruerit; eumque sanctus Braulio non modo
Gregorio Magno comparaverit sed et erudiendae
Hispaniae loco Iacobi Apostoli caelitus datum esse
45 censuerit.
 Scripsit Isidorus libros etymologiarum et de ecclesiasticis officiis aliosque quamplurimos christianae et ecclesiasticae disciplinae adeo utiles, ut

40. **in saeculorum fine,** a difficult phrase; perhaps: 'in these last centuries'. This accolade was reiterated at the fifteenth council in 688.

43. **erudiendae Hispaniae,** dative of the gerundive to express purpose.

44. **Iacobi,** James the Greater, brother of St. John the Evangelist. Tradition asserts that James preached the Gospel in Spain, later returned to Jerusalem where he was martyred in 44. (*Acts.* 12, 1-2) His body was miraculously brought to Compostela which became a national shrine and the scene of pilgrimages through the Middle Ages.

46. **etymologiarum.** Written shortly before his death, the *Etymologiae* represents his most important and best known work. Taking its name from the subject matter of just one of the twenty books, the work was a scholarly compilation of all the learning possessed in his time and became a standard textbook through the Middle Ages.

de ecclesiasticis officiis. In this work Isidore discusses divine worship, the old Spanish (Mozarabic) liturgy, the Eucharist, the hierarchy and the various states in life.

47. **aliosque.** His *History of the Goths* is regarded as the chief authority on Gothic history in the West.

sanctus Leo Papa quartus ad episcopos Britanniae
scribere non dubitaverit, sicut Hieronymi et Augustini, ita Isidori dicta retinenda esse, ubi contigerit
inusitatum negotium, quod per canones minime
definiri possit. Plures etiam ex eiusdem scriptis
sententiae inter canonicas Ecclesiae leges relatae
conspiciuntur. Praefuit concilio Toletano quarto,
omnium Hispaniae celeberrimo. Denique cum ab
Hispania Arianam haeresim eliminasset, morte sua
et regni vastatione a Saracenorum armis publice
praenuntiata, postquam quadraginta circiter annos
suam rexisset Ecclesiam, Hispali migravit in caelum
anno sexcentesimo tricesimo sexto. Eius corpus inter
Leandrum fratrem et Florentinam sororem, ut ipse

49. **Leo Papa.** In his letter Leo (847-855) discusses, among other things, the norms which the bishops should follow in making judgments. He prescribes particularly the decrees of Church Councils, which he calls "... Sanctorum Patrum (statuta), quae apud nos *canones* praetitulantur." Jerome, Augustine, and Isidore are the only Fathers cited by name. cf. *P.L.* 115, 667.

55. **Toletano quarto.** The Fourth National Council was held in 633. These national councils were not solely concerned with church affairs, but also formulated civil legislation, and were a fundamental institution of the Visigothic State. Modern historians regard them as exercising an important influence on the origins of representative government.

58. **Saracenorum.** In 711 the Saracens or Arab Moslems overthrew the Visigothic monarchy and overran Spain in three years without serious opposition. They remained for eight hundred years, and though after the eleventh century their control was confined to the Kingdom of Granada in the south, the culture that developed had a far-reaching influence. cf. 14.10n.

mandaverat, primo conditum, Ferdinandus primus
Castellae et Legionis rex, ab Eneto Saraceno Hispali
65 dominante magno pretio redemptum, Legionem
transtulit; et in eius honorem templum aedificatum
est, ubi miraculis clarus magna populi devotione
colitur.

Oratio

Deus, qui populo tuo aeternae salutis beatum
70 Isidorum ministrum tribuisti, praesta, quaesumus, ut
quem Doctorem vitae habuimus in terris, intercessorem habere mereamur in caelis. Per Dominum
nostrum.

63. **Ferdinandus**, King of Castile, married in 1029 the sister of Bermudo III, King of Leon. When Bermudo was killed in battle, the united crowns of Castile and Leon became Ferdinand's. The relics of St. Isidore were brought from Seville to Leon and buried in the ancient church of St. John the Baptist, which had been rebuilt and dedicated to Isidore, December 21, 1063. Isidore was declared a Doctor of the Church in 1722 by Innocent XIII (1721-1724.)

17. ST. LEO I THE GREAT

April 11   c. 390-461

    Leo: primus, Etruscus, eo tempore praefuit Ecclesiae cum rex Hunnorum Attila, cognomento Flagellum Dei, in Italiam invadens, Aquileiam triennii obsidione captam diripuit et incendit. Unde cum
5 Romam ardenti furore raperetur iamque copias, ubi Mincius in Padum influit, traicere pararet, occurrit

    1. **Etruscus**. The place and date of Leo's birth are uncertain. His family was Tuscan, but he may have been born in Rome. He is first met as a deacon under Celestine I. (cf. 4.27n.) He was elected Pope in 440, and became one of the three whom posterity has called Great. For another, see Gregory, 9.
    2. **Attila**. In 433 Attila became king of the Huns, an Asian people who had forced the Visigoths in the previous century to move into the Empire. Having invaded the Eastern Empire in 441, they moved across Germany into France, where they were finally stopped in 451 by the combined forces of the Romans and Visigoths. In the next year the Huns descended again on Italy, but Attila died the same year and his empire collapsed.
    3. **Aquileiam**. Built by Rome in 180 as a fortress against the Illyrians on the northern frontier, Aquileia was soon a flourishing commercial city. After its destruction by the Huns, the people fled south to the lagoons and islands that eventually became the city of Venice.
    5. **ubi**, 'at the place where'; at Peschiera near Verona.
    6. **occurrit ei Leo**. Leo had been asked to go on this famous embassy by the Emperor Valentinian III (425-455) and

ei Leo, malorum Italiae impendentium misericordia permotus; cuius divina eloquentia persuasum est Attilae ut regrederetur. Qui interrogatus a suis quid esset quod praeter consuetudinem tam humiliter Romani Pontificis imperata faceret, respondit se astantem quemdam alium, illo loquente, sacerdotali habitu veritum esse, sibi stricto gladio minitantem mortem nisi Leoni obtemperaret. Quare in Pannoniam reversus est.

Leo autem Romae singulari omnium laetitia exceptus, paulo post invadenti Urbem Genserico eadem eloquentiae vi et sanctitatis opinione persuasit ut ab incendio, ignominiis ac caedibus abstineret. Sed cum Ecclesiam a multis haeresibus oppugnari maximeque a Nestorianis et Eutychianis exagitari

was accompanied by one of the consuls and some of the Senators of Rome. cf. *Acta Sanctorum*, April vol. 2, p. 18. The incident demonstrates the growing influence and authority of the papacy as well as the confidence the people had in turning to it for help.

8. **persuasum est Attilae,** impersonal construction: 'Attila was persuaded.'

11. **respondit** . . . The legends about Attila which fill medieval hagiography demonstrate the impact made on the times by both Attila and Leo's encounter with him.

14. **Pannonia.** The Roman province included present day Hungary and Jugoslavia.

17. **paulo post.** Three years later, in 455, the Vandals under Genseric invaded Italy from Africa (which they had occupied after leaving Spain; cf. 16.9n.). Leo was not as successful with Genseric, for the city was in fact captured and pillaged, though the inhabitants were spared and the city not fired.

21. **Nestorianis**; cf. 4.23sqq.

Eutychianis. The Eutychians were the followers of

videret, ad eam purgandam et in fide catholica confirmandam concilium Chalcedonense indixit, ubi sexcentis triginta coactis episcopis, Eutyches et Dioscorus et iterum Nestorius condemnati sunt; eiusdemque concilii decreta sua auctoritate confirmavit.

His actis sanctus Pontifex se ad reficiendas et aedificandas ecclesias convertit. Cuius suasu Demetria, pia femina, sancti Stephani ecclesiam construxit in suo fundo via Latina tertio ab Urbe mil-

Eutyches, abbot of a monastery near Constantinople, who was supported by Dioscurus, the successor of St. Cyril (cf. 5) as Patriarch of Alexandria. Eutyches was a monophysite who held to a 'fusion' of the divine and human natures in Christ.

exagitari. The new crisis came seventeen years after the Council of Ephesus (cf. 4. 35n.) in 448, when Flavian, the Patriarch of Constantinople, was forced to depose and excommunicate Eutyches for his refusal to retract his heretical teachings. A council held at Ephesus in 449, presided over by Dioscurus, acquitted Eutyches and condemned Flavian. Pope Leo responded by declaring the council invalid, and agreed to call a new one, which finally met in 451 at Chalcedon.

23. **Chalcedonense.** This most important of the first four General Councils set forth with superb clarity the Church's teaching on Christ and the Trinity, and established the terminology the Church continues to use today. The Council acclaimed the famous *Dogmatic Epistle* sent by Leo to Flavian in which the Pope set forth the faith of the Church with regard to the Person of Christ, and gave witness to its acceptance of the primacy by declaring, "Thus through Leo has Peter spoken."

29. **Stephani.** The ruins of this long-forgotten basilica were found in 1858, along with a dedicatory inscription.

30. **via Latina** followed a more inland route than the Via Appia which it joined at Beneventum.

ST. LEO STOPPING ATTILA. Fresco by Raphael (1483-1520). Raphael Apartments, Vatican Palace. Courtesy, Alinari

6. Latin Book

liario; ipse via Appia sub nomine sancti Cornelii alteram condidit. Multas praeterea et sacras aedes et sacra earum vasa restituit. In tribus basilicis, Petri, Pauli et Constantiniana, cameras exstruxit;
35 aedificavit monasterium vicinum basilicae sancti Petri; sepulchris Apostolorum custodes adhibuit, quos cubicularios appellavit. Statuit ut in actione mysterii diceretur: *Sanctum sacrificium, immaculatam hostiam.* Sanxit ne monacha benedictum capitis

31. **Cornelii**; Pope St. Cornelius, martyred in 253 and buried in the catacombs of St. Callistus on the Via Appia. (cf. 4. 18n.)

34. **Pauli.** The basilica of St. Paul's Outside the Walls, was begun under Valentinian II (375-392) in 386 over the tomb of the Apostle.

Constantiniana, i.e., the Lateran Basilica, begun by Constantine and dedicated to the Holy Savior; rededicated to St. John the Baptist in 898. The adjoining palace was the residence of the Popes until the Avignon Captivity in 1307. (cf. 23.39n.)

37. **cubicularios**, 'custodians' of the shrines.

in actione mysterii, 'in the celebration of the mystery'; i.e., of the Mass. The words are found at the end of the second prayer after the consecration.

39. **Sanxit ne monacha.** ... The text no doubt refers to the fifteenth canon of the Council of Chalcedon which states: "Diaconissam mulierem non posse ordinari ante annum quadragesimum et cum diligenti probatione." The use and place in the Church of deaconesses varied greatly over the centuries. In the West they were accepted with great reluctance, and although they had some ecclesiastical standing in the fourth and fifth centuries, the Church as a whole rejected the conferring on them of the Sacrament of Orders and accounted them as lay

40 velamen reciperet nisi quadraginta annorum virginitatem probasset. His et aliis praeclare gestis, cum multa sancte et luculenter scripsisset, quarto Idus Novembris obdormivit in Domino. Sedit in pontificatu annos viginti unum, mensem unum, dies
45 tredecim.

Oratio

Gregem tuum, Pastor aeterne, placatus intende et per beatum Leonem Summum Pontificem perpetua protectione custodi, quem totius Ecclesiae praestitisti esse pastorem. Per Dominum nostrum.

persons. In the beginning only a widow could become a deaconess. The strict age of sixty was later relaxed in some places to forty.

42. **multa... scripsisset.** Extant are ninety-six of his sermons and one hundred forty-three letters.

quarto Idus Novembris; November 10. His feast on April 11 is in commemoration of one of the translations of his remains. Leo was buried in St. Peter's Basilica. Benedict XIV (1740-1758) declared him a Doctor of the Church in 1754.

18. ST. JUSTIN MARTYR

April 14   †165

    Iustinus, Prisci filius, ex Graeco genere Flaviae Neapolis in Syria Palaestina natus, adulescentiam in litterarum omnium studiis transegit. Vir factus adeo philosophiae amore correptus est, ut ad veritatem
5 assequendam quotquot aderant philosophorum sectis nomen dederit, eorumque praecepta scrutatus sit. Cum in his fallacem tantum sapientiam erroremque

    1. **Flaviae Neapolis...natus.** Flavia Neapolis, modern Nablus, was built in 72 by the Emperor Vespasian (69-79) near the ruins of the ancient Sichem in Samaria. Justin was born a pagan of Greek parents. The main source for details of his life is his *Dialogue with Trypho*, a work written to convince the Jews that Christ was the Messiah.
    2. **in Syria Palaestina.** The Roman province of Palestine (Judaea) was under the general supervision of the Emperor's *legatus* in Syria.
    5. **quotquot...sectis,** 'to as many sects of philosophers as existed.' In the *Dialogue,* Justin tells how he went to the Stoics, to the Peripatetics, to the Pythagoreans, and finally to the Platonists, who satisfied him for a time. (cf. *Dial.* 2; *P.G.* 6, 475) Justin's account may not be so much strict autobiography, as an arrangement allowing him to set forth the major pagan philosophies and show their weak points. His own works, however, reveal an eclecticism in which Stoic and Platonic elements predominate.
    7. **fallacem tantum sapientiam,** 'deceptive wisdom only'.

reperisset, superna illustratione per senem quemdam ignotum aspectuque venerabilem edoctus, verae
10 christianae fidei philosophiam amplexus est. Hinc sacrae Scripturae libros diu noctuque prae manibus habens, ita ex eorum meditatione divinus ignis in anima eius exarsit, ut ea qua pollebat eruditionis vi, eminentem Iesu Christi scientiam adeptus, plurima
15 conscripserit volumina ad christianam fidem exponendam magisque propagandam.

Inter praeclarissima Iustini opera binae emi-

8. **per senem quemdam.** cf. *Dial.* 3. Justin probably met the stranger in Ephesus, though nothing is known for certain about Justin's movements, except that he travelled extensively, spent some time in Ephesus, knew Alexandria, and visited Rome twice.

10. **amplexus est**; c. 130. The date can be fixed approximately by the time when the *Dialogue* is described as having taken place. The place is not certain, but was probably Ephesus.

Hinc, 'From that time on'.

11. **Scripturae libros:** particularly the Psalms and the Prophets, especially Isaias, to judge from the quotations in his works. cf. 36n.

14. **plurima ... volumina.** Eusebius (*H.E.* 4, 18) mentions nine or ten of Justin's works, but apart from a few fragments, only three authentic works are extant, the *Dialogue* and the two *Apologies*.

17. **binae ... apologiae.** The first *Apology* was written c. 155 in the reign of Antoninus Pius (138-161), the second soon after as an appendix to the first. Justin sought first to defend the Christians against the false charges of atheism and immorality for which they were being condemned. Secondly, he set forth the teachings of Christianity, particularly the moral teachings, which had from the beginning made a profound impression upon him. He described the exemplary moral lives of

nent fidei christianae apologiae. Quas cum coram
senatu et imperatoribus Antonino Pio eiusque filiis
20 Marco Antonino Vero et Lucio Aurelio Commodo,
Christi asseclas saevissime divexantibus, porrexisset,
eamdemque fidem disputando strenue propugnasset,
obtinuit ut a Christianorum caede publico principum
edicto temperatum fuerit. Verum Iustino haud par-
25 citum est. Nam Crescentis Cynici, cuius vitam et
mores nefarios redarguerat, insidiis accusatus, a
satellitibus comprehensus est. Adductus autem ad

the Christians, and emphasized their charity, continence and
fortitude in the face of martyrdom. In this Justin is the first
significant Christian apologist, and exerted a strong influence
on some of the later Greek Apologists, especially Tatian and
Athenagoras later in the second century.

19. **eiusque filiis** . . . i.e., the Emperor's adopted sons. At
the insistence of the Emperor Hadrian (117-138), Antoninus
Pius had adopted his wife's nephew M. Aurelius Verus (the
future Emperor (161-180) Marcus Aurelius Antoninus), and
Lucius Commodus, the son and namesake of the man Hadrian
had first chosen to be his own successor and at whose prema-
ture death he had adopted Antoninus. Lucius Commodus was
co-regent with Marcus Aurelius until his death in 169.

24. **temperatum fuerit**; impersonal construction. So also:
parcitum est; cf. 17.8n.

25. **Crescentis Cynici.** Justin and the Cynic philosopher
Crescens had debated publicly in Rome (cf. *Apol.* 2,3), in the
course of which Justin had accused him of ignorance and wil-
ful misrepresentation. Despite the assertion of Tatian (*Oratio
adv. Graecos* 19) whom Eusebius (*H.E.* 4, 16) quotes, it remains
uncertain that the intrigues of Crescens brought about Justin's
death.

ST. JUSTIN MARTYR. A mural in the Church of St. Vito, Rome. Courtesy, Alinari

Romae praesidem nomine Rusticum, cum hic ab eo quaesivisset quaenam essent Christianorum praecepta, hanc bonam confessionem coram multis testibus confessus est: Rectum dogma, quod nos christiani homines cum pietate servamus, hoc est: ut Deum unum existimemus, factorem atque creatorem omnium quae videntur quaeque corporeis oculis non cernuntur; et Dominum Iesum Christum Dei Filium confiteamur, olim a prophetis praenuntiatum, qui et humani generis iudex venturus est.

Quoniam Iustinus in prima sua apologia ad repellendas ethnicorum calumnias palam exposuerat quomodo Christiani convenirent ad sacra celebranda et quaenam fuerint sacri huius conventus mysteria,

---

28. **Rusticum.** Q. Junius Rusticus was prefect of Rome 163-167. The Acts of the trial and martyrdom of Justin and his six companions, based on an official court record, are accepted as authentic, though their date and author are unknown. (cf. *P.G.* 6, 1567.) The *Acta* thus rank with the Acts of Perpetua (cf. 7), Polycarp (d. 155) and Ignatius (his *Epistle to the Romans*; cf. 1) as among the few authentic Acts that have been preserved. The *Chronicon Paschale* fixes his martyrdom as happening in 165.

30. **hanc confessionem.** cf. *Acta Martyrii* 1.

33. **existimemus,** 'that we believe in'; Gr. ἡγέομαι = νομίζω, to believe in.

36. **a prophetis.** In more than a third of the *Apology* and almost all of the *Dialogue*, Justin draws his arguments for Christianity from the fulfillment of the Old Testament prophecies by Christ and the Church.

41. **quaenam ... mysteria ...** *Apol.* 1, 61-67 describes in fine detail the rite of Baptism, the Eucharist and the Sunday observance, and clearly sets forth also the doctrine of the Real

exquisivit ab eo praeses in quonam loco conveniret
ipse et ceteri huius Urbis Christifideles. Iustinus autem reticens conventuum loca, ne sancta et fratres
45   proderet canibus, domicilium tantum suum indicavit,
ubi manere et discipulos excolere solebat penes cele-
brem titulum Pastoris in aedibus Pudentis. Demum
praeses optionem ei dedit vel ut diis sacrificaret vel
per totum corpus flagellis caedi perferret. Cum invic-
50   tus fidei vindex assereret se in votis semper habuisse
cruciatus perpeti propter Dominum Iesum Christum,
a quo magnam in caelis mercedem consequi exspec-
tabat, praeses in eum capitalem sententiam pronun-
tiavit. Itaque mirabilis p h i l o s o p h u s Deum

Presence. In this Justin is the chief witness of the faith and worship of the Church in the second century.
    45. **domicilium... suum.** Justin said he lived near (*prope*)
a certain Martin near (*ad*) the Timiotine baths. cf. *Acta* 2.
    46. **discipulos excolere.** Some of his pupils, Tatian among
them, later became well known as Christian teachers and writers.
    47. **titulum Pastoris;** i.e., *a chapel*, in memory of St Pastor,
the brother of St. Pius I (142-157). Today it is enshrined as a
side chapel in the church of St. Pudentiana, believed to be the
most ancient church in Rome, where St. Peter himself taught and
lived. The old mosaic floor of the chapel is said to have belonged
to the house of Pudens, which has been excavated beneath the
church. Pudens is mentioned by St. Paul (2 *Tim.* 4, 21), and
tradition asserts he was a senator and his family among Paul's
first converts in Rome.
    53. **capitalem sententiam.** The martyrs were beheaded,
though a curious but absurd addition to some copies of the *Acta*
states that Justin died by hemlock, à la Socrates.
    54. **philosophus.** Even after his conversion to Christianity,
Justin continued to wear the philosopher's mantle (cf. *Dial.* 1),

collaudans, post verbera fuso pro Christo sanguine glorioso martyrio coronatus est. Quidam vero fideles clam illius sustulerunt corpus et in loco idoneo condiderunt. Leo decimus tertius Pontifex maximus eiusdem Officium et Missam ab universa Ecclesia celebrari praecepit.

Oratio

Deus, qui per stultitiam crucis eminentem Iesu Christi scientiam beatum Iustinum Martyrem mirabiliter docuisti, eius nobis intercessione concede ut errorum circumventione depulsa fidei firmitatem consequamur. Per eumdem Dominum nostrum.

and it was through philosophy and as a layman that he propagated the Christian faith. He was also the first to attempt to bridge Christianity and pagan philosophy. Posterity however revers him as Justin *Martyr,* because he sealed his witness by the shedding of his blood.

61. **stultitiam crucis.** cf. 1 *Cor.* 1, 23-25.

62. **scientiam . . . Iustinum;** double accusative with *doceo.*

64. **errorum circumventione,** 'the cunning deceitfulness of error.' cf. *Eph.* 4, 14.

19. ST. ANSELM

April 21 1033-1109

Anselmus Augustae Praetoriae in finibus Italiae Gundulpho et Ermemberga nobilibus et catholicis parentibus natus, a teneris annis assiduo litterarum studio atque perfectioris vitae desiderio, non obscu-
5 rum futurae sanctitatis et doctrinae specimen dedit. Et licet iuvenili ardore aliquando ad saeculi illecebras traheretur, brevi tamen in pristinam viam revocatus, patria et bonis omnibus derelictis, ad monasterium Beccense ordinis sancti Benedicti se

1. **Augustae Praetoriae.** Augusta Praetoria, modern Aosta, at the juncture of the St. Bernard Passes in the Alps, was established by the Emperor Augustus (27 B.C.–14 A.D.) in 24 B.C. There are remains of the ancient amphitheatre and triumphal arch.

3. **parentibus.** Anselm's father was a Lombard; his mother belonged to an old Burgundian family.

4. **perfectioris vitae desiderio.** At fifteen Anselm sought in vain for admission to a monastery. So his biographer Eadmer, who was a monk of Canterbury, and a friend and secretary to Anselm. His biography is a chief source for the saint's life. (cf. P.L. 158, 49.)

6. **ad saeculi illecebras.** . . . For a time his great love for his mother restrained him, but her death ended even that check on his worldliness, which he greatly repented later in life.

8. **patria . . . derelictis.** Because of his father's sternness and harshness, Anselm decided to leave home. He wandered for three years through Burgundy and France, eventually came to Avranches in Normandy where he settled for a time.

ad . . . Beccense. The monastery had been founded about

10 contulit; ubi emissa regulari professione sub Her-
luino abbate observantissimo et Lanfranco viro
doctissimo, tanto animi fervore et iugi studio in litteris et virtutibus assequendis profecit, ut mirum in
modum tamquam sanctitatis et doctrinae exemplar
15 ab omnibus haberetur.

Abstinentiae et continentiae tantae fuit, ut

> thirty years before by Herluin, a Norman knight, who was con-
> secrated its abbot in 1037. The abbey took its name from the
> second location selected by Herluin on the banks of the Bec
> (Danish for brook). In its golden age under Lanfranc and An-
> selm, Bec exerted a far-reaching influence, trained many of
> the future hierarchy, including Pope Alexander II (1061-1073),
> and helped the spread of theological learning. The monastery
> continued in existence until the French Revolution. Its ruins may
> be viewed today in the village of Le Bec-Hellouin.
>
> 10. **regulari professione**, religious profession as required by
> monastic rule. After spending some time studying under Lan-
> franc, Anselm decided in 1060 to enter the monastery.
>
> 11. **Lanfranco.** Born and educated as a lawyer at Pavia in
> Italy, Lanfranc (1005-1089) as a young man left Pavia and
> made his way to France where he became well known as a
> teacher in Avranches in Normandy. In 1042 he joined the new
> abbey at Bec and opened a school which soon was drawing
> scholars from many parts of Europe. As counsellor to William,
> Duke of Normandy, Lanfranc is believed to have helped in the
> planning of William's invasion of England. After the defeat of
> King Harold at the famous battle of Hastings in 1066, Lanfranc
> was appointed, at William the Conqueror's insistence, to the
> see of Canterbury in 1070. (cf. 34.26n.) While remaining as
> William's chief counsellor, he did much to further the church
> in England by bringing it into closer contact with the learning
> and practice of the Continent.

ST. ANSELM AND TWO MONKS. Miniature from a twelfth century manuscript of his **Monologium**.
Municipal Library, Rouen

assiduitate ieiunii omnis paene ciborum sensus in
eo videretur exstinctus. Diurno enim tempore in
exercitiis monasticis docendo et respondendo variis
20 de religione quaesitis emenso, quod reliquum erat
noctis somno subtrahebat, ut divinis meditationibus,
quas perenni lacrimarum imbre fovebat, mentem
recrearet. Electus in priorem monasterii invidos
fratres ita caritate, humilitate et prudentia lenivit,
25 ut quos aemulos acceperat, sibi et Deo amicos,
maximo cum regularis observantiae emolumento,

17. **omnis ... exstinctus.** The statement is based on Eadmer's life, ch. 11: *Quid namque de illius ieiunio dicerem cum ab initio prioratus sui tanta corpus suum inedia maceraverit, ut... omnis illecebra gulae penitus in eo postmodum exstincta sit... Comedebat tamen ut alii homines sed omnino parce.*

23. **Electus in priorem.** In 1062 when Lanfranc was appointed abbot of St. Stephen's in Caen, newly founded by William, Anselm was elected to succeed him as Prior of Bec.

invidos fratres ... lenivit. As a young man and only three years a monk, his election was resented by some who felt they had better claim to the office. At this time Anselm demonstrated the kindness and sympathy that won him countless friends all his life.

26. **maximo ... emolumento,** 'along with very great advantage to the observance of the rule'. During this period Anselm wrote some of his theological and philosophical works, which greatly influenced the course of medieval thought and won for him the title of Doctor of the Church from Clement XI (1700-1721) in 1720. Anselm is regarded as one of the fathers of scholastic theology, though his influence was obscured by men like Peter Lombard (c. 1110-1164) and Thomas Aquinas whose works were better suited as textbooks. Of particular note is his ontological argument for the existence of God, which may be summarized: God exists in reality, since God is that than which nothing

redderet. Mortuo abbate et in eius locum licet invitus suffectus, tanta doctrinae et sanctitatis fama ubique refulsit, ut non modo regibus et episcopis venerationi esset, sed sancto Gregorio septimo etiam acceptus, qui tunc magnis persecutionibus agitatus, litteras amoris plenas ad eum dedit, quibus se et Ecclesiam catholicam eius orationibus commendabat.

Defuncto Lanfranco archiepiscopo Cantuariensi, eius olim praeceptore, Anselmus urgente Willelmo Angliae rege et instantibus clero ac populo, ipso tamen repugnante, ad eiusdem ecclesiae regi-

---

greater can be thought of, and to exist in reality is greater than to exist in the mind. (cf. *Proslogium de Dei Existentia*, ch. 3; P.L. 158,223.) Though rejected by some, the argument has been accepted by many notable thinkers, e.g., Descartes, Hegel, over the centuries.

27. **Mortuo abbate.** Herluin died in 1078. As abbot of Bec Anselm was at once brought into contact with England where the abbey had several possessions. In his first year he visited Canterbury where he was welcomed by Lanfranc.

29. **regibus;** among them, William the Conqueror, who asked for Anselm on his death-bed.

30. **Gregorio septimo;** cf. 31.

36. **Willelmo.** William Rufus (1087-1100), a younger son of William the Conqueror. It was perhaps on Lanfranc's advice that he left England to his second son Rufus, and left Normandy to his elder son Robert.

38. **ad ... vocatus,** in 1093. William Rufus had kept the see vacant after Lanfranc's death for four years, in order to enjoy its revenues. On his death-bed from a serious illness, William repented, and yielded to entreaties to appoint the reluctant monk to the see. But his subsequent recovery belied the genuineness of

men vocatus, statim, ut corruptos populi mores re-
formaret, verbo et exemplo prius, dein scriptis et
conciliis celebratis, pristinam pietatem et ecclesiasticam disciplinam reduxit. Sed cum mox idem Willelmus rex vi et minis Ecclesiae iura usurpare tentasset,
ipse sacerdotali constantia restitit; bonorumque di-
reptionem et exsilium passus, Romam ad Urbanum
secundum se contulit, a quo honorifice exceptus et
summis laudibus ornatus est, cum in Barensi concilio Spiritum Sanctum etiam a Filio procedentem,

his repentance, and Anselm soon found himself embroiled with the king over the question of investitures.

44. **bonorumque ... passus.** After constant and fruitless quarrels with Rufus, Anselm sought leave to refer the matter to Rome in person. Permission, first denied, was later granted, though the king swore that he would not allow Anselm back into England. In his absence, the king converted the possessions of Canterbury to his own use. During his exile, Anselm completed his work *Cur Deus Homo,* an influential work on the theology of the Incarnation and Atonement.

45. **Urbanum secundum.** The early years of Urban II (1088-1099) were troubled by the anti-pope Guibert, and the controversy had repercussions in England for Anselm. Urban was responsible for the organizing of the First Crusade (1096-1099) which successfully captured Jerusalem from the Turks.

47. **in Barensi concilio ...** This council was summoned in 1098 to attempt a reconciliation with the Greeks on the *Filioque* controversy. The Greeks held that the Holy Spirit proceeded only from the Father, while the Western Church taught that the Holy Spirit proceeded from both the Father and the Son.

48. **Spiritum ... procedentem,** i.e., the doctrine that the Holy Spirit proceeds from the Son as well. Anselm's arguments were later enlarged into a treatise. (cf. *P.L.* 158, 285-326.)

contra Graecorum errorem, innumeris Scripturarum
50 et sanctorum Patrum testimoniis propugnasset. E
vivis Willelmo sublato, ab Henrico rege, eius fratre,
in Angliam revocatus, obdormivit in Domino, famam non solum miraculorum et sanctitatis (praecipue ob insignem devotionem erga Domini nostri
55 passionem et beatam Virginem eius Matrem) assecutus, sed etiam doctrinae, quam ad defensionem
christianae religionis, animarum profectum et nor-
mam omnium theologorum, qui sacras litteras scholastica methodo tradiderunt, caelitus hausisse ex eius
60 libris omnibus apparet.

    51. **Willelmo sublato.** He was killed in a hunting accident in 1100. The controversy over investitures was renewed with King Henry (1100-1135), since Anselm had, among other things, refused to consecrate bishops invested by the king. Finally a council in 1107 determined that the king would renounce the right of investing bishops and abbots, while prelates would do homage to the king for the temporal fiefs that were assigned by the king to the bishoprics. The pact was a victory for Anselm.
    52. **obdormivit,** in 1109.
        famam ... assecutus, 'having attained a reputation not only for miracles and sanctity ... , but also for learning'.
    56. **quam ... apparet,** 'which it is apparent from all his books he drew by divine inspiration, for the defense of the Christian religion ... ' **quam** is the object of **hausisse,** whose subject is *eum* understood.
    58. **scholastica methodo;** the characteristic method of investigation and exposition in both philosophy and theology, as developed by the Schoolmen of Western Europe from the ninth to the fifteenth century.

Oratio

Deus, qui populo tuo aeternae salutis beatum Anselmum ministrum tribuisti, praesta, quaesumus, ut quem Doctorem vitae habuimus in terris, intercessorem habere mereamur in caelis. Per Dominum nostrum.

20. ST. MARK

April 25   First Century

Marcus, discipulus et interpres Petri iuxta quod Petrum referentem audierat, rogatus Romae a fratribus, breve scripsit Evangelium. Quod cum Petrus audisset, probavit et Ecclesiae legendum sua auc-
5 toritate dedit, sicut Clemens in sexto Ὑποτυπώσεων libro scribit et Papias Hierapolitanus episco-

---

The text is taken from St. Jerome's *De Viris Illustribus*, ch. 8. (cf. 1) Jerome's account is based on Eusebius, *H.E.* 2,15.

1. **Marcus.** The author of the second Gospel is to be identified with the Mark and John Mark mentioned in the *Acts of the Apostles* (4,36; 12,12;25; 15,39) and Pauline Epistles (*Col.* 4,10; *Philem.* 24; 2 *Tim.* 4,11). John was his Jewish name and Marcus his adopted Roman surname. His mother was prominent in the Christian community and it was to her house that St. Peter went after his release from prison (*Acts* 12,12).

interpres Petri. Far more prominent in the New Testament is Mark's association with St. Paul. His association with St. Peter is reported by the early Fathers.

3. **scripsit Evangelium.** Tradition in general states that the Gospel was written at Rome, though a few authorities say Alexandria. Its date of composition was 53-63.

5. **Clemens**; i.e., Clement of Alexandria (c. 150-c.215), in his Ὑποτυπώσεις or *Outlines*, eight books of commentary on the Bible.

6. **Papias**, second century friend of St. Polycarp, known through fragments in Irenaeus and Eusebius.

pus. Meminit huius Marci et Petrus in Epistula prima, sub nomine Babylonis figuraliter Romam significans: "Salutat vos Ecclesia quae in Babylone est
¹⁰ coelecta, et Marcus filius meus." Assumpto itaque Evangelio quod ipse confecerat, perrexit in Aegyptum, et primus Alexandriae Christum annuntians, constituit Ecclesiam tanta doctrina et vitae continentia, ut omnes sectatores Christi ad exemplum sui
¹⁵ cogeret.

Denique Philo, disertissimus Iudaeorum, videns Alexandriae primam ecclesiam adhuc iudaizantem, quasi in laudem gentis suae librum super eorum conversatione scripsit. Et quomodo Lucas

    7. **in Epistula prima**; 1 *Pet.* 5,13. The epistle was written some time before 64 to Christian communities in Asia Minor, to whom St. Mark must have been known.

    10. **coelecta**, i.e., chosen, called by God, as the Asia Minor churches had been.

    12. **primus ... annuntians**, 'being the first to announce... '

        Alexandriae ... constituit Ecclesiam. This ancient tradition is testified to by Eusebius (*H.E.* 2, 16;24), but is rendered uncertain by the strange silence of two prominent Alexandrians, Origen (185-254) and Cyril (cf. 4). While the date is uncertain, the decade 50-60, when the New Testament is silent about him, is the most likely time during which Mark established the Alexandrian church.

    16. **Philo** (c.25 B.C.-40 A.D.) was a prominent Alexandrian Jew, noted for his allegorical commentaries on the Jewish law and influential philosophical system which owed much to the Greek philosophers.

    17. **iudaizantem**. The church was still characterized by many Jewish practices. The break between Church and Synagogue was slow and painful. cf. *Acts* 15.

    19. **Lucas narrat ...** cf. *Acts* 2, 44sqq; 4.32.

ST. MARK. Mosaic (sixth century) in the **Basilica of St. Vitale**, Ravenna. Courtesy, Alinari.

20 narrat Hierosolymae credentes omnia habuisse communia, sic et ille, quod Alexandriae sub Marco fieri doctore cernebat, memoriae tradidit. Mortuus est autem octavo Neronis anno et sepultus Alexandriae, succedente sibi Aniano.

Oratio

25 Deus, qui beatum Marcum Evangelistam tuum evangelicae praedicationis gratia sublimasti, tribue, quaesumus, eius nos semper et eruditione proficere et oratione defendi. Per Dominum nostrum.

22. **Mortuus ... anno**; i.e., in 62/63, but the fact of his death at this time is quite uncertain, since Jerome's statement is based on Eusebuis (*H.E.* 2,24), who says only that that was the year Anianus succeeded to the see. Since Mark is mentioned in 2 *Tim.*, which was written 66/67, he may well have *resigned* the see to Anianus and joined Peter and Paul in Rome. There is also an account of Mark's martyrdom in Alexandria at this time, but its date is no earlier than the fourth century. cf. *Acta Sanctorum*, April vol. 3, p. 350-351.

23. **sepultus Alexandriae**. Mark's body was transferred in the ninth century to Venice, the city with which he is today most commonly associated. cf. *Acta Sanctorum*, p. 354-358, for an account of the transfer. The genuineness of the relics in Venice depend of course on the genuineness of the Alexandrian tradition.

24. **Aniano**. The unreliable Acts of Mark's martyrdom relate that Anianus had been a shoemaker whose hand had been injured by an awl and healed by Mark when he first came to the city. *Acta Sanctorum*, p. 350.

21. ST. PETER CANISIUS

April 27   1521-1597

Petrus Canisius Noviomagi in Gelria eo ipso anno natus est, quo Lutherus in Germania aperta rebellione ab Ecclesia descivit, et Ignatius de Loy-

1. **Noviomagi in Gelria.** Nijmegen was in the county of Gelre of the Holy Roman Empire. In 1579 Gelre joined the other Protestant counties of the Netherlands in the revolt from Spain. Canisius' father was nine times burgomaster of the town.

2. **Lutherus** (1483-1546) had proclaimed his ninety-five theses dealing with many points of Catholic doctrine and practice, particularly indulgences, on October 13, 1517. When some of them were denounced as heretical, Luther was summoned to Rome, but did not go. A fruitless meeting with the papal legate Cajetan in 1518 was followed by a defiant appeal to a general council. Public debates with John Eck at Leipsig in 1519 furthered the development of his heretical teachings, which were condemned by papal decree June 15, 1520. On January 3, 1521 Luther was finally excommunicated by Leo X (1513-1521) and on May 25 placed under the ban of the Empire by the Diet of Worms.

3. **Ignatius.** As a Spanish officer defending the citadel of Pamplona in 1521 against the French, Ignatius (1491-1556) was injured in the legs by a cannon ball. His long hospitalization proved the turning point in his life. After recovering he retired to Montserrat and Manresa and his religious experiences there were later made the foundation of his *Spiritual Exercises*. A constitution drawn up for his band of followers known as the Society of Jesus was approved in 1541.

ola in Hispania terrestri militia abdicata ad praeli-
anda praelia Domini se convertit; Deo nimirum
portendente quos ille posthac adversarios, quem
sacrae militiae ducem esset habiturus. Coloniae
Agrippinae, quo studiorum causa concesserat, perpetuo castitatis voto se Deo obstrinxit et paulo post
Societati Iesu nomen dedit. Sacerdotio auctus, catholicam fidem contra novatorum insidias legationibus, sermonibus, scriptis libris statim defendendam
suscepit. Ob praeclaram sapientiam et exploratum
rerum usum a Cardinali Augustano et a pontificiis
legatis magnopere expetitus, semel atque iterum
concilio Tridentino interfuit; cuius etiam decreta ex

6. **quos adversarios...**, 'what adversaries, what leader he was going to have...'

7. **Coloniae Agrippinae.** The Roman settlement was named for the mother of Nero; it is today Cologne. When only nineteen Canisius received a master of arts degree from the University. In 1543 he made the Spiritual Exercises of St. Ignatius under Bl. Peter Faber, one of Ignatius' closest followers, and entered the new Society. He was ordained three years later in 1546.

11. **fidem ... defendendam suscepit**, 'undertook the defense of the faith'.

novatorum, 'the reformers', the leaders in the Protestant revolt.

13. **exploratum rerum usum**, 'his known experience'.

14. **Cardinali ...** Canisius was theologian to Cardinal Truchsess of Augsburg. He had gained his reputation by his 1546 edition of the works of Cyril of Alexandria and Leo the Great. For his knowledge of the Fathers, cf. 35.

16. **concilio Tridentino.** The nineteenth Ecumenical Council opened in 1545 under Paul III (1534-1549) and closed under Pius IV (1559-1565) in 1563. Called to define the doctrine

ST. PETER CANISIUS BEFORE EMPEROR
FERDINAND I AND CARDINAL OTTONE.
Painting by Cesare Fracassini (1838-1868). **Vatican Gallery of Modern Art**

auctoritate Pii quarti Pontificis maximi rite per
Germaniam promulganda et in morem inducenda
curavit. A Paulo quarto ad conventum Petricoviensem ire iussus, aliisque a Gregorio decimo tertio
legationibus obeundis adhibitus, alacri semper et
numquam fracto difficultatibus animo, gravissima
religionis negotia tractavit, ac vel inter praesentia
vitae discrimina ad felicem exitum perduxit.

    Superno caritatis igne, quem in Basilica Vati-

of the Church against the teaching of the Protestants and to institute a renewal within the Church by removing abuses, Trent passed decrees on Sacred Scripture, original sin, justification, the Sacraments, veneration of saints. Canisius spoke twice at the early sessions. He was called to Trent again in 1562 as papal theologian.

19. **curavit.** Actually this was Canisius' life-long work, as he travelled extensively in Central Europe preaching, conducting missions, and establishing schools. But Pius IV in 1561 entrusted him with the specific mission of delivering the decrees of Trent to Germany and urging the Catholic princes at the next diet to defend the faith.

Petricoviensem. While attending the first General Congregation of the Jesuits in Rome, Canisius was sent to Poland in 1558 to the imperial diet held at Piotrków. Here he also aided the work of renewal and checked the alarming progress of the Revolt.

20. **Gregorio** ... Gregory (1572-1585) was a zealous promoter of the Tridentine reforms. Among his achievements was the reform of the calendar which was adopted by the Catholic countries in 1578 and later by the Protestant countries.

25. **Basilica Vaticana,** i.e., St. Peter's, built near the ancient Vatican Hill.

cana e penetralibus Cordis Iesu olim copiose hauserat, inflammatus, et divinae gloriae amplificandae unice intentus, dici vix potest quot per annos amplius quadraginta labores susceperit aerumnasque
30 pertulerit, ut complures Germaniae civitates ac provincias vel ab haereseos contagione defenderet vel haeresi infectas catholicae fidei restitueret. In Ratisbonensi et in Augustano conventu imperii proceres ad iura Ecclesiae tuenda et mores populorum
35 emendandos excitavit; in Vormatiensi insolescentes impietatis magistros ad silentium adegit. A sancto Ignatio Germaniae superioris provinciae praefectus,

26. **Cordis Iesu.** Peter was one of the precursors of modern devotion to the Sacred Heart.

28. **amplius quadraginta:** *quam* is usually omitted after *amplius* before numbers; 'for more than forty years'. cf. 33. 45n.

32. **infectas**, agreeing with **provincias**; 'or restored those tainted with heresy to the Catholic faith.

33. **Ratisbonensi.** The imperial diet met in Ratisbon in the winter 56/57, and at Augsburg in 1555, when the terms of the Peace of Augsburg between the Lutherans and the Catholics were drawn up, dividing the Empire and establishing the devisive principle, *cuius regio, eius religio* (the ruler determines the region's religion).

35. **Vormatiensi.** The diet met at Worms in 1556/57 and Canisius took part in the religious discussions between Catholic and Protestant theologians. Prominent among the latter was Melanchthon, who in 1530 had drawn up the Augsburg Confession, which was accepted as the new Lutheran creed.

37. **Germaniae superioris.** The new province of Upper Germany included Swabia, Bavaria, Bohemia, Hungary, and Austria. Peter was superior 1556-1569.

domos et collegia multis locis condidit. Collegium
Germanicum, Romae constitutum, omni ope pro-
vehere atque amplificare studuit; in academiis
sacrarum humanarumque disciplinarum studia,
miserandum in modum collapsa, instauravit; contra
Centuriatores Magdeburgenses duo volumina egregie conscripsit; et summam doctrinae christianae,
theologorum iudicio et publico trium saeculorum
usu ubique probatissimam, aliaque complura ad
populorum institutionem valde accommodata in
vulgus edidit. Quam ob rem haereticorum malleus
et alter Germaniae apostolus appellatus, plane dig-

38. **condidit**, at Ingolstadt, Prague, Munich, Innsbruck, Dillingen and elsewhere.

Collegium Germanicum. The second oldest college in Rome was initiated by Ignatius c. 1552 and founded by Gregory XIII.

43. **Centuriatores**; a group of Protestant historians, who wrote an anti-Catholic history of the Church, century by century, hence the name. Their work was published at Basel 1559-1574 and was financially supported by the kings and princes devoted to the Protestant cause.

duo volumina. Entrusted by St. Pius V (cf. 26) with the task of refuting the Centuriators, Canisius published one work in 1571 refuting the principal errors of Protestantism, and another in 1577 on the Blessed Virgin, which has been called a classic defence of Catholic teaching on Mary. cf. 35.

44. **summam**... Canisius' most important work was his Catechism which was published in 1555. Recognized even by Protestant historians and theologians as a master-piece, the Catechism appeared in more than two hundred editions in fifteen languages during his own lifetime.

47. **in vulgus edidit**, 'published'.

49. **alter Germaniae apostolus**. That much of Germany was

50 nus habitus est qui ad tutandam in Germania religionem divinitus electus putaretur.

Inter haec, precatione crebra et assidua rerum supernarum commentatione, lacrimis saepe perfusus ei animo interdum a sensibus abducto, Deo se
55 coniungere solitus erat. A viris principibus vel sanctitate clarissimis et a quatuor summis Pontificibus magno in honore habitus, adeo de se demisse sentiebat, ut se omnium minimum et diceret et haberet. Vindobonensem episcopatum semel, iterum
60 ac tertio recusavit. Moderatoribus suis obsequentissimus, paratus erat ad ipsorum nutum omnia relinquere aut aggredi, etiam cum valetudinis et vitae periculo. Voluntaria sui ipsius coercitione castitatem perpetuo saepsit. Demum Friburgi Hel-
65 vetiorum, ubi plurimum pro Dei gloria et salute

saved to the Catholic faith was due to the work of the Jesuits, and in this Canisius was the leader. For this he is ranked with the English Benedictine St. Boniface (cf. 33.30n.) as the second Apostle of Germany.

50. **qui ... putaretur:** a relative cause of purpose: 'he has been regarded as worthy to be thought divinely chosen ...'

59. **Vindobonensem.** Because of his successful work in restoring the faith in Vienna, the Emperor and the Pope were both anxious to have Canisius accept the vacant see. In 1557 he consented to administering the see for one year only.

60. **obsequentissimus.** So did Ignatius himself find Canisius, at the time when he had spent several months with the Jesuit founder after having been summoned by him from Trent in 1547.

64. **Friburgi** ... Canisius' stay in Fribourg began in 1580, when he laid the foundation-stone of the new Jesuit college (which developed into the present University). The authorities there successfully opposed all subsequent transfers.

animarum ultimis vitae suae annis desudaverat, migravit ad Deum die vigesima prima Decembris anno millesimo quingentesimo nonagesimo septimo, aetatis suae septimo supra septuagesimum. Hunc vero strenuum catholicae veritatis propugnatorem Pius Papa nonus Caelitum beatorum honoribus adauxit; novis autem fulgentem signis Pius undecimus Pontifex maximus anno iubilaei Sanctorum numero accensuit simulque Doctorem universalis Ecclesiae declaravit.

Oratio

Deus, qui ad tuendam catholicam fidem beatum Petrum Confessorem tuum virtute et doctrina roborasti, concede propitius ut eius exemplis et monitis errantes ad salutem resipiscant, et fideles in veritatis confessione perseverent. Per Dominum nostrum.

---

71. **Pius Papa nonus** (1846-1878) approved four of the miracles submitted and beatified Canisius November 20, 1869.
74. **anno iubilaei**, 1925. cf. 5.81n.

22. ST. PAUL OF THE CROSS

April 28   **1694-1775**

 Paulus a Cruce Uvadae in Liguria natus, sed e Castellatio prope Alexandriam Statiellorum nobili genere oriundus, qua futurus esset sanctitate clarus innotuit miro splendore qui noctu implevit parientis
5 matris cubiculum, et insigni augustae caeli Reginae beneficio, quae puerum in flumen delapsum a certo naufragio illaesum eripuit. A primo rationis usu Iesu Christi crucifixi amore flagrans, eius contemplationi prolixius vacare coepit, et carnem innocen-

---

  1. **a Cruce**, 'of the Cross', his name in religion. (cf. 30.34) He was born Paul Francis Danei.
   Liguria, the coastal province in Italy between France and Tuscany.
   sed ... oriundus, 'but descended from the Statielli family of Castellazzo near Alessandria'. The family had to move when war broke out between Louis XIV and Piedmont in 1693. cf. 26.1n.
  3. **qua ... claritate ... innotuit**, 'for what (great) sanctity Paul would be renowned, became known...'
  4. **miro splendore**. Beginning with Ven. Vincent Strambi, Paul's early biographers narrate many extraordinary events which surrounded his birth. The light referred to here is said to have shone so brightly that it obscured the lamps and dazzled those who were present. Again, when still children, Paul and his younger brother one day fell into the Tanaro. A 'beautiful lady' helped them out of the water and then disappeared. (cf. 31.4n.)

10 tissimam vigiliis, flagellis, ieiuniis, potu in sexta
feria ex aceto cum felle mixto ac dura quavis
castigatione conterere. Martyrii desiderio incensus,
exercitui se adiunxit, qui Venetiis ad bellum Turcis
inferendum comparabatur. Cognita vero inter oran-
15 dum Dei voluntate, arma ultro reddidit, praestan-
tiori militiae operam daturus, quae Ecclesiae
praesidio esse aeternamque hominum salutem pro-
curare totis viribus niteretur. Reversus in patriam,
honestissimis nuptiis sibique delata patrui heredi-
20 tate recusatis, artiorem inire crucis semitam ac

   11. **ex aceto**...cf. *Jn.* 19,29; *Ps.* 68,22.
   12. **conterere**, complimentary to **coepit**, line 9.
   13. **qui Venetiis**... By 1571 the Turkish Empire had reached the limit of its extension, for in that year the famous battle of Lepanto destroyed the Turkish naval power in the Mediterranean. See 26.34n. A century later, the unsuccessful siege of Vienna in 1683 marked the Empire's last assault on the West. In 1714 when the Sultan Ahmed III (1703-1730) broke the 1699 Treaty of Karlowitz, Paul joined the army being prepared under the auspices, spiritual and financial, of Clement XI (1700-1721), to whom great credit in the subsequent victory in Rumania in 1716 was attributed. (cf. 15.35n.)
   16. **daturus**, 'to give'; the future active participle expressing purpose.
      quae...niteretur, (a military service) 'which would strive to...'
      Ecclesiae praesidio, a double dative; cf. 6.14n.
   18. **patriam**, i.e., Castellazzo, his father's home, to which the family was able to return after peace was restored in 1709.
   19. **patrui hereditate.** From this inheritance from a priest-uncle, Paul kept only the breviary.

ST. PAUL OF THE CROSS. Anonymous modern portrait. **Paulist Curia, Rome**

rudi tunica a suo episcopo indui voluit. Tum eius iussu ob eminentem vitae sanctimoniam et rerum divinarum scientiam, nondum clericus, Dominicum agrum maximo cum animarum fructu divini verbi
25 praedicatione excoluit.

Romam profectus, theologicis disciplinis rite imbutus, a summo Pontifice Benedicto decimo tertio ex oboedientia sacerdotio auctus est. Facta sibi ab eodem potestate aggregandi socios, in soli-
30 tudinem recessit Argentarii montis, quo eum beata Virgo iampridem invitaverat, veste illi simul ostensa atri coloris, passionis Filii sui insignibus decorata, ibique fundamenta iecit novae congregationis. Quae

21. **rudi tunica**... After his military discharge, Paul spent several years in intense prayer, and in 1720 received three visions, which he described in the introduction to the Rule written later the same year, of a black habit with a badge on the breast bearing the name of Jesus in white letters surmounted by a white cross. On the third occasion, our Lady appeared to him attired in the habit and told him he was to found a congregation devoted to the memory of her Son's passion. cf. line 36.

24. **agrum ... excoluit**. While still a layman, Paul assisted the local clergy in teaching catechism and giving missions, but only for a short time, as he knew he would have to go to Rome to seek papal approval for his Rule and Congregation, in accordance with the advice given him by Bishop di Gattinara of Alessandria.

27. **Benedicto**... Benedict XIII (1724-1730) gave vocal approval to his plans for a congregation in 1725. Then on June 7, 1727 he and his younger brother John Baptist, his constant companion and life-long cooperator in his work, were ordained to the priesthood.

brevi, plurimis ab eo toleratis laboribus, praeclaris
35 aucta viris, cum Dei benedictione valde succrevit,
a Sede apostolica non semel confirmata, una cum
regulis quas orando ipse a Deo acceperat, et quarto
addito voto, pergratam Dominicae passionis memo-
riam promovendi. Sacras virgines quoque instituit,
40 quae excessum caritatis divini Sponsi sedulo meditarentur. Haec inter, animarum inexhausta aviditate
ab Evangelii praedicatione numquam deficiens,
homines paene innumeros, etiam perditissimos aut
in haeresim lapsos, in salutis tramitem adduxit.
45 Praesertim Christi enarranda passione mirifica eius
orationis vis erat, qua una cum astantibus in fletum
effusus, quaelibet obdurata corda ad paenitentiam
scindebat.

 Tandem, asperrimi vitae generis ad longam us-
50 que senectutem tenacissimus, anno millesimo septingentesimo septuagesimo quinto, cum praeclara

  36. **non semel confirmata**. Benedict XIV (1740-1758) approved in 1741 a mitigated Rule. Final canonical approval was given to the Passionist Congregation by Clement XIV (1769-1774) in 1769 and reaffirmed by Pius VI (1775-1799) in 1775.

  37. **quarto ... voto**, in addition to the three traditional vows of poverty, chastity, and obedience. cf. 27.6n.

  39. **virgines ... instituit**. The first house was opened at Corneto, the ancient Tarquinia, 100 miles north of Rome, in 1771, though Paul was not well enough to attend. He further never saw his Nuns in their religious habit.

  40. **quae ... meditarentur**; relative clause of purpose, 'who should meditate...'

  49. **generis ... tenacissimus**, 'most tenacious of the harshest manner of life'.

monita, veluti sui spiritus transmissa hereditate, alumnis tradidisset, Ecclesiae sacramentis ac caelesti visione recreatus, Romae qua praedixerat die migravit in caelum. Eum Pius nonus Pontifex maximus in Beatorum, novisque deinde fulgentem signis in Sanctorum numerum retulit.

52. **monita ... tradidisset.** In this connection it is worth noting that Paul from his earliest days was deeply interested in the conversion of England. Seventy years after his death, in 1845, the Passionist Dominic Barberi, beatified by Paul VI (1963-   ) in 1963, received into the Church John Henry, later Cardinal, Newman and other prominent members of the Oxford movement.

veluti ... hereditate, 'as if handing on the heredity of his own spirit'.

53. **caelesti visione.** Rosa Calabresi, a young woman whom Paul directed in 1775, testified for his cause that in his last year the saint had frequent ecstasies, lasting from fifteen to thirty minutes, during which he beheld a vision of Our Lady and the Child Jesus. During his last months, he received favors which were as extraordinary as the visions of his youth. On Good Friday, for example, in 1768, Mary appeared to him in the attitude of the Pietá.

54. **qua praedixerat die** ... The antecedent **die** is incorporated into the relative clause; 'on the day which he had predicted'. cf. 32. 44n.

55. **in Beatorum,** sc. *numerum retuit,* line 47. Pius IX (1846-1878) beatified Paul October 1, 1852, and canonized him June 29, 1867. His body is buried in the Basilica of Sts. John and Paul in Rome, which was built in memory of two other brothers, officers in the household of the daughter of Constantine, who were martyred under Julian the Apostate.

Oratio

60 Domine Iesu Christe, qui ad mysterium crucis praedicandum sanctum Paulum singulari caritate donasti, et per eum novam in Ecclesia familiam florescere voluisti, ipsius nobis intercessione concede ut passionem tuam iugiter recolentes in terris, eiusdem fructum consequi mereamur in caelis: Qui vivis.

23. ST. CATHERINE OF SIENA

April 30   1347-1380

Catharina, virgo Senensis, piis orta parentibus, beati Dominici habitum, quem Sorores de Paenitentia gestant, impetravit. Summa eius fuit abstinentia et admirabilis vitae austeritas. Inventa est aliquando
5 a die Cinerum usque ad Ascensionem Domini ieiunium perduxisse, sola Eucharistiae communione contenta. Luctabatur quam frequentissime cum dae-

    1. **Senensis.** The city of Siena in central Tuscany, which dates back to the ancient Etruscans, was at this time a Republic and an important rival of Florence. Like so many others during this period, it was torn by rival factions and parties. In 1348, thirty thousand of the population died in the Black Death.
    piis parentibus. Catherine was the youngest of twenty-five children born to Giacomo di Benincasa, a prosperous wool-dyer, and Monna Lapa, whose spacious house is still preserved today much as it was in Catherine's time.
    2. **Dominici habitum.** When she was sixteen, Catherine was admitted to the Third Order of St. Dominic, the formation of which had been approved fifty years before by Honorius IV (1285-1287). The group in Siena was especially strong and the list of its members from 1311 on is extant. St. Catherine is today the patron of the Third Order.
    3. **Summa**; predicate, as is **admirabilis, fuit** being taken again with the second adjective.
    7. **quam frequentissime. Quam** is here used to strengthen the superlative, has the force of 'very'.

monibus, multisque illorum molestiis vexabatur;
aestuabat febribus nec aliorum morborum cruciatu
10 carebat. Magnum et sanctum erat Catharinae nomen, et undique ad eam aegroti et malignis vexati
spiritibus deducebantur. Languoribus et febribus in
Christi nomine imperabat, et daemones cogebat ab
obsessis abire corporibus.
15 Cum Pisis immoraretur, die Dominico refecta
cibo caelesti et in exstasim rapta, vidit Dominum crucifixum magno cum lumine advenientem, et ex eius
vulnerum cicatricibus quinque radios ad quinque
loca sui corporis descendentes. Ideoque mysterium
20 advertens, Dominum precata est ne cicatrices apparerent, et continuo radii colorem sanguineum
mutaverunt in splendidum, et in forma purae lucis
pervenerunt ad manus, pedes et cor eius; ac tantus
erat dolor quem sensibiliter patiebatur, ut nisi Deus

8. **molestiis vexabatur.** Catherine was indeed favored by heavenly visions, but she was also subjected to vivid sensual temptations, and periods of spiritual desolation when she felt utterly abandoned by God. She had her first vision at the age of six when she saw Christ, in glory with Sts. Peter, Paul, and John, extend his hand to bless her. For three years after becoming a Tertiary, Catherine remained in her own room, speaking to no one except her confessor, and practising the severest austerities. This period in her life closed on Shrove Tuesday, 1366, when Christ appeared to her and espoused her to himself by placing on her finger a ring which remained visible to herself alone. She was soon ordered to resume her activity in the world and labor for its sanctification.

11. **aegroti.** Catherine's activity was particularly noted and admired in tending those suffering from the most repulsive diseases, and during plagues.

25 minuisset, brevi se crederet morituram. Hanc itaque gratiam amantissimus Dominus nova gratia cumulavit, ut sentiret dolorem, illapsa vi vulnerum, et cruenta signa non apparerent. Quod ita contigisse Dei famula confessario suo Raymundo retulit. (Ut
30 oculis etiam repraesentaretur, radios in imaginibus beatae Catharinae, ad dicta quinque loca pertingentes, pia fidelium cura pictis coloribus expressit.)

Doctrina eius infusa, non acquisita fuit; sacrarum litterarum professoribus difficillimas de divini-

    28. **cruenta signa.** The Stigmata (Greek for 'marks', 'brands'), when visible, are external manifestations of the suffering which is the essential feature of the phenomenon, for the stigmatic shares in the intense pain and suffering of the crucified Christ and offers up the suffering for the expiation of sin. (The phenomenon is known to have existed in over three hundred individuals, all of whom were also ecstatics. The first was St. Francis of Assisi in the thirteenth century.) St. Catherine received the Stigmata on the Fourth Sunday of Lent in the Church of St. Christina in 1375. During her life-time the marks did not appear on her body, but they became clearly visible after her death. In our own day the Stigmata have appeared on Theresa Neumann of Germany (d. 1963) and Padre Pio, a Capuchin monk in Italy, though in both cases the Church has declined to verify the supernatural character of the wounds.

    Quod ita contigisse, 'that this had happened in this way'; indirect statement introduced by **retulit.**

    29. **Raymundo;** Blessed Raymond of Capua (d. 1399), later Master General of the Dominicans, whose biography of Catherine is the most important source for details of her life. cf. *Acta Sanctorum,* April vol. 3, p. 862-967.

    33. **Doctrina ... fuit.** It became clear from the theological discussions, held at Siena, Avignon and Genoa, that some of Catherine's knowledge was infused. This same conclusion is also

ST. CATHERINE OF SIENA RECEIVING THE
STIGMATA. Fresco by Bernardino Fungai (c. 1460-1516).
House of St. Catherine, Siena. Courtesy, Alinari

tate quaestiones proponentibus respondit. Nemo ad
eam accessit, qui non melior abierit. Multa exstinxit
odia et mortales sedavit inimicitias. Pro pace
Florentinorum, qui cum Ecclesia dissidebant et
interdicto ecclesiastico suppositi erant, Avenionem
ad Gregorium undecimum Pontificem maximum
profecta est; cui etiam votum eius de petenda Urbe,
soli Deo notum, sese divinitus cognovisse monstravit,
deliberavitque Pontifex ea etiam suadente ad Sedem

reached from her famous mystical treatise, the *Dialogues*, which her confessor said was dictated under the inspiration of the Holy Spirit.

38. **Florentinorum**. Florence had rebelled against the Holy See and its French legates, because of their mismanagement of the Papal States. Within a short space of time, eighty cities had joined Florence. Catherine had been sent in 1375 to secure the neutrality of Pisa (cf. line 15), but her mission for Florence in 1376 to the Pope was fruitless, except for the profound impression she personally made on Gregory. In 1378 he sent her to Florence to make a new attempt to secure peace, but he died before this was achieved.

39. **interdicto**. An interdict is an ecclesiastical censure which, unlike excommunication, does not exclude from Church membership, but does deprive the faithful of certain spiritual goods, such as some liturgical services, some of the sacraments, and Christian burial, though the sacraments may be given to the dying. The interdict may be personal, or territorial as in this case.

Avenionem. This French city was made the residence of the Popes in 1309 by Clement V (1305-1314), the former Archbishop of Bordeaux. Seven Popes resided here during what came to be termed the Avignon 'Captivity', until Gregory XI (1370-1378) returned under Catherine's prodding to Rome in 1376.

suam Romanam personaliter accedere; quod et
fecit. Eidem Gregorio et Urbano sexto eius successori acceptissima fuit, adeo ut legationibus eorum fungeretur. Denique post innumera virtutum insignia, dono prophetiae et pluribus clara miraculis, anno aetatis suae tertio circiter et tricesimo migravit ad Sponsum; quam Pius secundus Pontifex maximus sanctarum Virginum numero ascripsit.

45. **Urbano sexto.** Urban's election in 1378 was challenged as invalid by certain Cardinals who elected a Frenchman as Clement VII (1378-1394; Avignon). Clement received the support of the French clergy and King Charles V. The Christian world was soon divided into two camps, in support of either the Rome or the Avignon claimant to the Papacy. The confusion was increased by the fact that each side could number saints of the Church among its supporters. The schism, later known as the Great Western Schism, was finally healed by the election of Martin V in 1417. cf. 15.22n.

46. **acceptissima...** Urban VI summoned Catherine to Rome in 1378 where she remained until her death, endeavoring to win supporters for Urban's claims to the Papacy and urging him to modify his harshness and tactlessness which was widening the rift. Many of her four hundred extant letters, which today form a priceless historical collection, were written at this time. Addressed to kings and princes, popes and bishops, individuals in the world and in religion, these letters are remarkable for their fine Italian style, their content, and the insights they give into the personality of this saint who has been called 'the greatest woman in Christendom.'

49. **migravit...** Catherine died of a stroke after three months of intense agony during which she had the sensation that the Bark of Peter was crushing her by its weight.

50. **ad Sponsum.** cf. 8n. for an account of her mystical experience known as the Spiritual Espousals.

Pius secundus (1458-1464) canonized her in 1461.

Oratio

Da, quaesumus, omnipotens Deus, ut qui beatae Catharinae Virginis tuae natalitia colimus, et annua solemnitate laetemur et tantae virtutis proficiamus exemplo. Per Dominum nostrum.

24. ST. ATHANASIUS

May 2   c. 295-373

Athanasius Alexandrinus, catholicae religionis propugnator acerrimus, ab Alexandro episcopo Alexandrino diaconus factus est, in cuius locum successit; quem etiam antea secutus fuerat ad Ni-

    1. **Alexandrinus.** It is most probable that Athanasius was born at Alexandria, though the date is uncertain. Authorities generally favor 295. About his parents practically nothing is known. He was given an excellent education, to judge from the learning evident in his writings, in which he quotes the classics, Homer, Pindar, Euripides, Plato, as well as the Scriptures and patristic commentaries.
    2. **Alexandro.** Bishop Alexander was bishop of Alexandria 313-328. Some of his letters and sermons are extant (cf. *P.G.* 18, 547), as well as two of his pastoral letters concerning the condemnation of Arius (cf. Theodoret, *H.E.* 1,3; *P.G.* 82,887; Socrates, *H.E.* 1,6; *P.G.* 67,42). Alexander ordained Athanasius a deacon in 318 and made him his secretary and adviser. At this time Athanasius wrote the *Oratio contra Gentes* (*P.G.* 25, 3-96), on the worship of the true God, and the *De Incarnatione Verbi* (*P.G.* 25, 96-198) The work on the Incarnation does not discuss the deeper questions of the nature of Christ's relationship to His Father and other Christological problems which occupied his later life, when almost unaided he defended the Catholic faith against heretical bishops and emperors.
    4. **Nicaenum:** cf. 11.23n. for the Council and an account of the theology involved in the Arian controversy.

5 caenum concilium, ubi cum Arii impietatem repressisset, tantum odium Arianorum suscepit, ut ex eo tempore ei insidias moliri numquam destiterint. Nam coacto ad Tyrum concilio magna ex parte Arianorum episcoporum, subornarunt mulierculam quae accu-

    5. **Arii.** Arius (c. 256-336), a parish priest in Alexandria much admired for his asceticism, had accused Bishop Alexander in 318 of holding the heresy that the Father became man in Christ and died for men (Sabellianism; Patripassianism). At the same time he himself was teaching that the Son of God was not eternal, had come into being, was subordinate to the Father by whom He was created. (The significance of this heretical teaching can scarcely be minimized, for it assailed Christian theology and belief at its very foundations by denying the basic truths of the Trinity and Incarnation.) Arius' teachings spread remarkably quickly as they were embodied in hymns set to popular tunes. In 321 a synod of one hundred bishops of Egypt and Libya condemned and deposed him. After having moved to Palestine and then Bithynia, Arius found support in Bishop Eusebius of Nicomedia (an old school-mate), who in 330 endeavored to have him reinstated through his great influence with Constantine. Athanasius' adamant refusal to reinstate the heretic brought on him the life-long animosity of the Arian party.

    8. **coacto ... concilio.** The Council of Tyre, summoned in 335 by Constantine himself, was presided over by an Arian and packed with Arian bishops. Athanasius had been compelled by the Emperor to attend and answer charges brought against him by the Eusebians. (Even before this, he had been obliged to answer before the Emperor to charges brought by Egyptian schismatics in collusion with Eusebius.) For the accusation described here, cf. Ruffinus, *H.E.* 1, 17 (*P.L.* 21,489); Theodoret, *H.E.* 1,28, (*P.G.* 82,986); Sozomen, *H.E.* 2,25 (*P.G.* 67,1003); *Acta Sanctorum*, May vol. 1, p. 200.

    9. **quae accusaret**; relative clause of purpose: 'to accuse'.

ST. ATHANASIUS. Mosaic (twelfth century) in the **Basilica of St. Mark,** Venice

10 saret Athanasium quod hospitio acceptus sibi stuprum per vim intulisset. Introductus igitur est Athanasius, et una cum eo Timotheus presbyter, qui simulans se esse Athanasium, "Egone", inquit, "mulier, apud te sum deversatus? ego te violavi?"
15 Cui illa petulanter: "Tu mihi vim attulisti." Idque iureiurando affirmans, iudicum fidem obtestabatur ut tantum flagitium vindicarent. Qua cognita fraude reiecta est mulieris impudentia.

Arsenium quoque episcopum ab Athanasio in-
20 terfectum Ariani pervulgarunt. Quem dum occulte detinent, manum mortui deferunt in iudicium, ad usum magicae artis Arsenio amputatam criminantes. At Arsenius noctu aufugiens, cum se in conspectu totius concilii statuisset, Athanasii inimicorum im-
25 pudentissimum scelus aperuit; quod illi nihilominus magicis artibus Athanasii tribuentes, vitae eius insidiari non desistebant. Quam ob rem in exsilium actus, in Gallia apud Treviros exsulavit. Gravibus

10. **sibi**, 'on her'; indirect reflexive.

19. **interfectum**, sc. *esse*: indirect statement after **pervulgarunt**.

22. **amputatam**, sc. *esse*: 'making the accusation that the hand had been cut off from Arsenius'; **Arsenio** is a dative of separation; cf. 3.23n.

27. **in exsilium actus**. After the Council of Tyre condemned and deposed Athanasius, Constantine exiled him to Trier. The exile ended two years later with the death of Constantine in 337. Athanasius' return to Alexandria was celebrated with great rejoicing. The Arians had now suffered a series of setbacks in Athanasius' restoration, Constantine's death, and the death of Arius himself in 336.

deinceps ac diuturnis sub Constantio imperatore,
30 Arianorum fautore, tempestatibus iactatus et incredibiles calamitates perpessus, magnam orbis terrae partem peragravit; ac saepe e sua ecclesia eiectus, saepe etiam in eamdem et Iulii Romani Pontificis auctoritate et Constantis imperatoris, Constantii
35 fratris, patrocinio, decretis quoque concilii Sardicensis ac Hierosolymitani, restitutus est, Arianis interea illi semper infestis. Quorum pertinacem iram et summum vitae discrimen fugiens, in sicca cister-

29. **Constantio.** On the death of Constantine, the Empire was divided between his sons, Constans in the West and Consantius in the East. Eusebius (who died in 339) soon succeeded in winning over the new Eastern Emperor to the Arian party. Athanasius was again exiled, and an Arian bishop installed in his place. Athanasius appealed directly to Pope St. Julius I (337-352) who summoned a synod which vindicated him. This vindication was reaffirmed in 343 by the Council of Sardica, which had been summoned as a representative council of East and West to settle the Arian controversy. But the council failed in its purpose when the Eastern bishops withdrew in defiance. Athanasius did not actually recover his see until 346, after Constantius, out of political expediency, yielded to his Catholic brother Constans, and after the Arian usurper had died.

38. **vitae discrimen fugiens** ... The murder of Constans in 350 removed all hesitancy from Constantius, now sole ruler of the entire Empire. He at once moved against his avowed adversary in a series of councils (Arles, 353; Milan, 355; Constantinople, 360) which deposed Athanasius after he had been in possession of his see for ten years. Athanasius barely escaped with his life from the soldiers who burst into church to arrest him. (Of the Council of Constantinople of 360 and its Arian creed signed by nearly all the bishops of the world,

8. *Latin Book*

na quinque annis se abdidit, eius rei tantum conscio
quodam Athanasii amico qui eum clam sustentabat.

Constantio mortuo, cum Iulianus Apostata, qui
ei in imperio successit, exsules episcopos ad suas ecclesias redire permisisset, Athanasius Alexandriam
reversus, summo honore exceptus est. Sed non multo
post iisdem Arianis impellentibus a Iuliano exagitatus, rursus discedere cogitur. Cumque ab eius satellitibus ad necem conquireretur, qua fugiebat navicula
conversa in contrariam fluminis partem, iis qui se
insequebantur ex industria occurrit, et quaerentibus
quantum inde abesset Athanasius, respondit eum non
longe abesse. Itaque illos, contrarium tenentes cursum, effugit, atque Alexandriam rediens ibidem
usque ad Iuliani obitum occultus permansit. Paulo

St. Jerome said, "The whole world groaned and marvelled to find itself Arian.") Athanasius' third exile lasted six years, which were spent in the deserts of Upper Egypt, where he lived the life of the monks and hermits, hiding at times in cisterns, and protected by the hermits. During this period many of his important writings were composed, especially the *Apologia contra Arianos* (*P.G.* 25, 247-410).

43. **Alexandriam reversus.** Constantius died in 361 and Athanasius returned early in 362.

44. **non multo post**. A few months after his restoration, Julian the Apostate (cf. 11.29n.) ordered his expulsion on the grounds that he had never been included in the original edict which permitted all exiled bishops to return to their sees.

47. **navicula ... conversa**; abl. absol., 'after the boat by which he was fleeing had been turned in the opposite direction on the river.' cf. 22.54n.

53. **ad Iuliani obitum.** Julian was killed in 363. Athanasius was reinstated by Jovian his successor. cf. 11.29n

post, Alexandriae alia exorta tempestate, quatuor
55 menses in paterno sepulchro delituit. Ac denique ex
tot tantisque periculis divinitus ereptus, Alexandriae
mortuus est in suo lectulo sub Valente; cuius vita
et mors magnis nobilitata est miraculis. Multa pie
et ad illustrandam catholicam fidem praeclare scrip-
60 sit, sexque et quadraginta annos in summa temporum
varietate Alexandrinam ecclesiam sanctissime gu-
bernavit.

Oratio

Exaudi, quaesumus, Domine, preces nostras
quas in beati Athanasii Confessoris tui atque Pontifi-
65 cis solemnitate deferimus, et qui tibi digne meruit
famulari, eius intercedentibus meritis ab omnibus
nos absolve peccatis. Per Dominum nostrum.

54. **alia exorta tempestate.** Jovian died in 364 and Valens (cf. 11.32n.) exiled Athanasius for the fifth time, together with all the bishops restored by Jovian. Athanasius withdrew quietly to prevent any disorders and remained in seclusion outside the city, spending four months in the family vault. (cf. Socrates, H.E. 4, 13) Valens, however, fearing the consequences of public disturbances, soon ordered the bishop's reinstatement. This last period of his life was spent in continuing his defence of the Nicene decrees on the Incarnation. The struggle with Arianism still continued after his death, but its force was spent and orthodoxy soon triumphed under orthodox bishops and emperors. Cardinal Newman called Athanasius the "principal instrument after the apostles by which the sacred truths of Christianity have been conveyed and secured to the world". Pius V (cf. 24) declared him a Doctor of the Church in 1568.

25. ST. MONICA

May 4   332-387

    Monica, sancti Augustini dupliciter mater, quia eum et mundo et caelo peperit, marito mortuo, quem senectute confectum Iesu Christo conciliavit, castam et operibus misericordiae exercitam viduitatem age-
5 bat. In assiduis vero ad Deum orationibus pro filio, qui in Manichaeorum sectam inciderat, lacrimas ef-

    1. **Monica** was born in 332 at Tagaste in North Africa, about sixty miles from Carthage.
    2. **eum ... peperit**. Augustine (354-430) was the eldest son; two other children are also known, a brother Navigius and a sister Perpetua.
    marito. Monica's husband Patricius, a magistrate of Tagaste, made her life very unhappy by his violent temper and dissolute habits, but she had the consolation of seeing him a Christian a short time before his death in 371 (cf. *Conf.* 9,9; Augustine makes only a passing reference to his father's death: *ibid*, 3, 7.)
    6. **Manichaeorum sectam**. The heresy was started by a Persian named Mani in the third century, and spread to the West and particularly N. Africa about fifty years before Augustine's birth. The system was based on a dual principle of creation, one good and from God, the other evil and from the evil spirit. Man's soul is from God and so is good, but his body is from Satan and is bad. Like many of his contemporaries, Augustine was attracted by the sect's claim to be a religion of pure reason, to have an answer for every question, and an explanation of all the mysteries of Christianity. Augustine was a member of the

fundebat; quem etiam Mediolanum secuta est, ubi ipsum frequenter hortabatur ut ad episcopum Ambrosium se conferret. Quod cum ille fecisset, eius 10 et publicis contionibus et privatis colloquiis catholicae fidei veritatem edoctus, ab eodem baptizatus est.

Mox in Africam redeuntes, cum ad Ostia Tibe-

sect for nine years, later wrote at least a dozen treatises in refutation of it.

  lacrimas effundebat. A bishop to whom Monica had gone for advice about her son consoled her with the famous words: "It is not possible that the child of those tears should perish." (*Conf.* 3, 21)

  7. **etiam Mediolanum.** In 384 Monica followed her son to Rome and then to Milan where he had gone to fill a position as a teacher of rhetoric.

  8. **Ambrosium.** Ambrose (340-397) had been consular governor of the territory of Liguria and Aemilia. In 374, when in charge of supervising an orderly election of a bishop to Milan, he found himself acclaimed by the people for the office, though he was only a catechumen at the time. Baptized, ordained and consecrated, Ambrose devoted himself to the study of the Scriptures and the Fathers, became one of the most important figures in the political and ecclesiastical affairs of his time, and by his writings exercised a great influence on the Middle Ages, for which he is revered as a Father and Doctor of the Church. Ambrose's personal magnetism and eloquent sermons in explanation of Christian doctrine eventually brought Augustine into the Church.

  11. **baptizatus.** Monica had been unable to have her children baptized, though Patricius had once given his consent when Augustine was seriously ill, but withdrew it when he recovered. When Augustine was thirty-three, after a long period of searching, he was baptized by Ambrose, Easter week, 387.

  12. **redeuntes.** They were returning home to Africa, the same year as Augustine's baptism.

THE DEATH OF ST. MONICA. Painting by Benozzo
Gozzoli (1420-1497). Church of St. Augustine,
San Gimignano, Italy. Courtesy, Alinari

rina constitissent, incidit in febrim. Quo in morbo cum eam quodam die anima defecisset, ut se collegit, "Ubi," inquit, "eram?" Et astantes intuens, "Ponite hic matrem vestram. Tantum vos rogo, ut ad altare Domini memineritis mei." Nono autem die beata mulier animam Deo reddidit. Eius corpus ibi in ecclesia sanctae Aureae sepultum est. Quod postea Martino quinto summo Pontifice Romam translatum, in ecclesia sancti Augustini honorifice conditum est.

Subdit vero Augustinus de matris morte disserens: Neque enim decere arbitrabamur funus illud questibus lacrimosis gemitibusque celebrare, quia illa nec misere nec omnino moriebatur. Hoc docu-

14. **eam ... anima defecisset**, 'when her breath had failed her'; 'when she had fainted away'.
16. **vestram**. Monica was addressing Augustine and his brother Navigius.
19. **in ecclesia ... sepultum est**. This burial took place only in the sixth century. Until then her body seems to have been almost forgotten.
   sanctae Aureae; virgin and martyr of the third century, whose feast is observed, according to the Roman Martyrology, on August 24. cf. *Acta Sanctorum*, August vol. 4, pp. 755-761.
20. **Romam translatam**. The relics were removed from Ostia to the Church of St. Trypho belonging to the Augustinians in 1430. In 1480 they were brought to the new church of St. Augustine. (cf. *Acta Sanctorum*, May vol. 1., pp. 493-496.)
22. **Subdit ...** The abridged quotation given here is taken from Book Nine of St. Augustine's *Confessions*, which contains the most moving passages in his work and is the principal source for her mother's life.
23. **Neque enim decere arbitrabamur**, 'For we did not think that it was fitting...'

mentis morum eius et fide non ficta rationibusque certis tenebamus. Atque inde paulatim reducebam in pristinum sensum ancillam tuam, conversationemque eius piam in te et sanctam, in nos blandam atque
30 morigeram, qua subito destitutus sum; et libuit flere de illa et pro illa. Et si quis peccatum invenerit, felvisse me matrem meam exigua parte horae, matrem oculis meis mortuam, quae me multos annos fleverat, ut oculis tuis viverem, non irrideat; sed
35 potius, si est grandi caritate, pro peccatis meis fleat ipse ad te, Patrem omnium fratrum Christi tui.

Oratio

Deus, maerentium consolator et in te sperantius salus, qui beatae Monicae pias lacrimas in conversione filii sui Augustini misericorditer suscepisti,
40 da nobis utriusque interventu peccata nostra deplorare et gratiae tuae indulgentiam invenire. Per Dominum nostrum.

    26. **fide non ficta;** cf. 1 *Tim.* 1:5.
    27. **reducebam ... tuam,** 'I recalled to my mind my former memory of thy handmaid'; lit., 'I brought back to my former mind thy handmaid'.
    32. **parte;** ablative of duration of time, instead of the classical accusative.
    34. **tuis;** i.e., God's, to whom Augustine addresses all his thoughts. cf. lines 29,36.
        non=*ne;* a late Latin use in prohibitions.
    36. **Christi tui;** cf. 28. 4n.

26. ST. PIUS V

May 5   1504-1572

    Pius in oppido Insubriae, quod Boschum vocant, natus, sed e Bononia oriundus ex nobili Ghisleriorum familia, cum quatuordecim esset annorum, ordinem Praedicatorum ingressus est. Erat
5 in eo admirabilis patientia, profunda humilitas, summa vitae austeritas, continuum orationis studium, et regularis observantiae ac divini honoris ardentissimus zelus. Philosophiae vero ac theologiae incumbens, adeo in iis excelluit, ut illas docendi munus
10 magna cum laude per multos annos exercuerit. Sacras contiones pluribus in locis cum ingenti audi-

    1. **Insubriae;** the country around Milan, modern Piedmont. At the time of Pius' birth, the ruling House of Savoy was at war with France for supremacy of northern Italy, which Savoy won in the Peace Treaty of 1559. cf. 22. 1n.
    3. **Ghisleriorum familia.** Pius was born Anthony Ghisleri. His family, though of the nobility, was poor. Thanks to the generosity of a neighbor, he was educated by the Dominicans, whom he joined when he was fourteen taking the name Michael. Later in life as Supreme Pontiff he was ever mindful of his humble origins.
    7. **divini honoris,** 'the glory of God'.
    9. **docendi munus.... exercuerit.** Ordained in Genoa in 1528, Ghisleri taught theology for sixteen years at the House of Studies in Pavia near Milan. During this period of his life, he was also Master of Novices and prior of several houses.

torum fructu habuit. Inquisitoris officium inviolabili animi fortitudine diu sustinuit, multasque civitates non sine vitae discrimine ab haeresi tunc grassante
15 immunes servavit.

A Paulo quarto, cui ob eximias virtutes carissimus erat, ad Nepesinum et Sutrinum episcopatum promotus, et post biennium inter Romanae Ecclesiae presbyteros cardinales ascriptus fuit. Tum ad ecclesiam Montis Regalis in Subalpinis a Pio quarto trans-
20

12. **Inquisitoris officium.** Ghisleri was appointed in 1544 as head of the inquisition for the diocese of Pavia, later for other dioceses. His activities were greatly resented, so that he was even physically mistreated, and have been criticized by some historians.

16. **Paulo quarto.** Paul IV (1555-1559), when Cardinal Caraffa, had been impressed when Ghisleri defended at Rome an order he had given for the confiscation of heretical books. In 1551 he appointed him Inquisitor General for all Italy. He was consecrated a bishop in 1556 and in 1557 created Cardinal and Inquisitor General for all Christendom.

18. **promotus:** sc. fuit, understood from line 19.

19. **presbyteros cardinales,** 'cardinal-priests'. Sixtus V (1585-1590) fixed the College of Cardinals at seventy, six cardinal-bishops, fifty cardinal-priests, and fourteen cardinal-deacons. (John XXIII (1958-1963) was the first officially to raise the number.) The three-fold division of the college is a vestige of the early (fifth century) government of Rome, when cardinal-bishops were in charge of the dioceses close to the city, cardinal-priests were in charge of the city's principal churches, and cardinal-deacons were responsible for the seven districts into which the city was divided for the care of the poor. cf. 9.8n.

20. **Pio quarto.** Pius IV (1559-1565; cf. 21.16n.) transferred Ghisleri to Mondovi in 1559, the year that saw the end to the war between France and Savoy. (cf. above 1n.) Because

ST. PIUS V. Monument in the Basilica of
St. Mary Major, Rome. Courtesy, Alinari

latus, cum plures in eam abusus irrepsisse cognovisset, totam dioecesim lustravit; rebusque compositis Romam reversus, gravissimis expediendis negotiis applicatus, quod iustum erat apostolica libertate et
25 constantia decernebat. Mortuo autem Pio praeter omnium exspectationem electus Pontifex, nihil in vitae ratione excepto exteriori habitu immutavit. Fuit in eo religionis propagandae perpetuum studium, in ecclesiastica disciplina restituenda indefes-
30 sus labor, in exstirpandis erroribus assidua vigilantia, in sublevandis egentium necessitatibus indeficiens beneficentia, in Sedis apostolicae iuribus vindicandis robur invictum.

Selimum Turcarum tyrannum multis elatum
35 victoriis, ingenti comparata classe ad Echinades in-

of the long conflict, conditions in the territory were in dire need of renewal.

24. **quod iustum erat ... decernebat**, 'with apostolic freedom and firmness, he decided what was just'. Pius IV called him to Rome frequently to consult on important matters.

26. **electus Pontifex**. His unexpected election, due in great part to the influence of his friend St. Charles Borromeo of Milan, was a victory for the reform party in the Church. Pius retained the simple habits that had characterized his life as a monk and a bishop, and was active in carrying out the reforms recommended by the recently ended Council of Trent. (cf. 21.16n.)

27. **excepto... habitu**. The white cassock now worn by the Pope is said to derive from Pius' white Dominican habit.

34. **Selimum Turcarum**. After Selim III (1566-1574) attacked the Venetian colony of Cyprus in 1570, Pius endeavored to prevail upon Maximilian II of the Holy Roman Empire, Philip II of Spain and Charles IX of France to form a league against the Turks whose power was becoming a serious threat.

sulas non tam armis quam fusis ad Deum precibus
devicit; quam victoriam ea ipsa hora qua obtenta
fuit Deo revelante cognovit suisque familiaribus indicavit. Dum vero novam in ipsos Turcas expeditio-
40 nem moliretur, in gravem morbum incidit, et
acerbissimis doloribus patientissime toleratis, ad extrema deveniens, cum sacramenta de more suscepis-
set, animam Deo placidissime reddidit anno milles-
mo quingentesimo septuagesimo secundo aetatis
45 suae sexagesimo octavo, cum sedisset annos sex,
menses tres, dies viginti quatuor. Corpus eius in

A Holy League was finally formed, which included only Spain, the Republic of Venice and the Holy See. A fleet was placed under the command of Philip's brother, Don Juan of Austria, with orders from the Pope that all soldiers of evil life be left behind. The brilliant victory in the Gulf of Lepanto on October 7, 1571 marked the end of the Western expansion of the Turkish Empire. Cf. 15.35,54; 22.13.

36. **fusis ad Deum precibus**, 'by prayers poured forth to God'. Since the very first year of his Pontificate, Pius had urged Christendom to do penance and to pray for a victory over the Turks. When the fleet had finally sailed, itself the result of the saintly pontiff's labors, Pius ordered public prayers for victory.

38. **Deo revelante cognovit**. Pius was confering with some of his cardinals when suddenly he looked out of the window, and after staring at the sky for some time, said, "Now is not the time for business. Go and thank God, for our fleet has met the Turk and has been victorious this very hour." cf. *Acta Sanctorum*, May vol. 1, p. 691. To commemorate the victory, the invocation *Help of Christians* was added to the Litany and the present Feast of the Holy Rosary established on October 7.

basilica sanctae Mariae ad Praesepe summa fidelium veneratione colitur, multis a Deo eius intercessione patratis miraculis. Quibus rite probatis a Clemente
50 undecimo Pontifice maximo Sanctorum numero ascriptus est.

Oratio

Deus, qui ad conterendos Ecclesiae tuae hostes et ad divinum cultum reparandum, beatum Pium Pontificem maximum eligere dignatus es, fac nos
55 ipsius defendi praesidiis et ita tuis inhaerere obsequiis, ut omnium hostium superatis insidiis, perpetua pace laetemur. Per Dominum nostrum.

47. **sanctae Mariae ad Praesepe**, 'St. Mary at the Crib', i.e., St. Mary Major, so named because of the Basilica's famous relic believed to be a portion of the Crib. The tomb of St. Pius V is in the Blessed Sacrament chapel.

49. **Clemente undecimo.** Clement XI (1700-1721) canonized him in 1712.

27. ST. GREGORY OF NAZIANZUS

May 9   c. 328-389

Gregorius, nobilis Cappadox, ex singulari divinarum litterarum scientia Theologi cognomen consecutus, Nazianzi in Cappadocia natus, Athenis in omni disciplinarum genere una cum sancto Basilio erudi-
5 tus, ad studia sacrarum litterarum se convertit. In quibus se in coenobio per aliquot annos exercuerunt,

    1. **Cappadox.** Gregory was born at Arianzus in Cappadocia but is named for the place with which he was closely associated most of his life. Both his parents, his brother and sister are revered as saints. He was sent to the famous school at Caesarea in Cappadocia, studied subsequenty at Caesarea in Palestine, Alexandria, and Athens, where he attended the famous schools of rhetoric.
    2. **Theologi.** Gregory won the title of Theologian for his discourses on the Trinity. see line 14n.
    4. **Basilio**; Basil the Great (329-379); cf. 11.40n. A very great friendship existed between the two men despite the great difference in their temperaments. Another school companion was the future Emperor Julian the Apostate, whose character Gregory said he knew and distrusted even then.
    6. **in coenobio.** cf. 6.24n. Gregory stayed with Basil for a time at his retreat in the province of Pontus, compiled with him a collection of the works of Origen (185-253), and helped him in the formulation of his famous rule. St. Basil, who was the first to draw up the three vows of poverty, chastity and obedience, is credited with organizing in the East the cenobitic form of religious life, and influenced St. Benedict who was acquainted with his writings.

illarum sententiam non ex proprio ingenio sed ex maiorum ratione et auctoritate interpretantes. Qui cum doctrina et vitae sanctitate florerent, vocati ad munus praedicandae evangelicae veritatis, plurimos Iesu Christo filios pepererunt.

Gregorius igitur aliquando domum reversus, primum Sasimorum episcopus creatus est, deinde Nazianzenam ecclesiam administravit. Tum Con-

7. **non ex proprio ingenio**. Contrast their approach to Scripture with one of the fundamental tenets of Protestantism. cf. 33.15n.

12. **aliquando domum reversus**. c. 361 Gregory returned home and was with great unwillingness ordained by his aged father. The experience caused him to flee in panic back to Basil's retreat, but within a few weeks he returned and wrote a magnificent treatise on the priesthood which was later used by St. John Chrysostom (c.347-407) and Gregory the Great in his *Regula Pastoralis* (cf. 9.24n.). During the next ten years Gregory administered his father's see and gained a wide reputation for the eloquence of his sermons.

13. **Sasimorum episcopus**. As the new (370) Bishop of Caesarea and metropolitan of Cappadocia, Basil consecrated his friend bishop of a new see in the town of Sasima. But Gregory soon found the place not at all to his liking and within a few weeks he resigned. He returned to Nazianzus where he was coadjutor to his father till his death in 374. Refusing then to become the bishop of the diocese, he retired to a monastery and spent the next three years in solitude and study, the surroundings most congenial to his disposition.

14. **Constantinopolim**. Following the death of Valens (cf. 11.32n.) in 378, the Catholic remnant of Constantinople, which for thirty years had been in the hands of Arian bishops, appealed to Gregory to become their bishop. In 379 Gregory took up residence in the city and commenced another task from which

ST. GREGORY OF NAZIANZUS. Miniature from a tenth century manuscript of his Homilies.
Bibliothèque Nationale, Paris

stantinopolim ad eam regendam ecclesiam arcessitus, cum civitatem, haeresum purgatam erroribus, ad catholicam fidem reduxisset, quod ei summum omnium amorem conciliare debebat, multorum paravit invidiam. Itaque cum inter episcopos magna propterea esset facta seditio, sponte cedens episcopatu, illud prophetae dictum usurpavit: "Si propter me commota est ista tempestas, deicite me in mare, ut vos iactari desinatis." Quare Nazianzum reversus, cum illi ecclesiae Eulalium praeficiendum curasset, totum se ad contemplationem et scriptionem divinarum rerum contulit.

he would soon seek to be released. At this time he delivered the discourses on the Trinity, which are noted for their precise terminology and later won for him the title of Theologian. Most of his extant discourses date from this two-year stay in Constantinople. As the Catholic candidate for the see, Gregory received the support of the Emperor Theodosius the Great (379-395; cf. 11.34n.), who demanded that bishops subscribe to the Nicene Creed and restored all churches in the capital to orthodox pastors.

17. **quod ... invidiam**, 'what should have won for him the greatest love of all, secured the ill-will of many'.

19. **inter episcopos**; i.e., the more than one hundred fifty bishops attending the second Ecumenical Council of Constantinople in 381. cf. 11.59n. Controversy soon swarmed around Gregory's head, and being in ill-health and inadequate to the task before him, he resigned his see and returned to the quieter life of Nazianzus.

21. **prophetae**; Jonas 1, 12.

24. **Eulalium**. Toward the end of 383 Gregory requested the new metropolitan to appoint his cousin Eulalius to the see of Nazianzus. Gregory then withdrew in retirement, probably to his birth-place, where he lived til his death six years later.

Scripsit autem multa et soluta oratione et versibus, mirabili pietate et eloquentia; quibus doctorum hominum sanctorumque iudicio id assecutus est, ut nihil in illis nisi ex verae pietatis et catholicae religionis regula reperiatur, ac nemo quidquam iure vocare possit in dubium. Consubstantialitatis Filii fuit acerrimus propugnator. Ut autem vitae laude nemo ei praepositus est, sic et orationis gravitate omnes facile superavit. In iis scribendi ac legendi studiis ruri vitam monachi exercens, imperatore Theodosio ad caelestem vitam senio confectus migravit.

27. **soluta oratione** . . . cf. 14.46. Gregory's poems, some deserving of high praise, were written in this last period of his life. One of them is two thousand lines of valuable autobiography. (cf. *P.G.* 37, 969-1452; the life in the *Acta Sanctorum*, May vol. 2. p. 378 sqq. is by Cardinal Baronius, 32.16n.) Gregory also kept up his letter writing, and was the first to collect and publish his own letters. He is most renowned as one of the greatest orators the Church has possessed and has been called the Christian Demosthenes.

30. **ut nihil** . . . **reperiatur**, 'that there may be found in them nothing except what is in conformity with (=*ex*) the rule of . . ."

32. **Consubstantialitatis**; cf. 11.23n.

33. **Ut** . . . , **sic et** . . . , 'Just as . . . , so also . . .'

34. **orationis gravitate**, 'in the seriousness of his prayer'.

37. **ad caelestem vitam** . . . **migravit**. Gregory's remains were first transferred to Constantinople, then at a later date to Rome, where they repose today in St. Peter's. He was declared a Doctor of the Church in the tenth century. In 1081 the Patriarch of Constantinople instituted a feast in honor of the three great Doctors of the Oriental Church, Sts. Gregory, Basil and John Chrysostom.

Oratio

Deus, qui populo tuo aeternae salutis beatum
40 Gregorium ministrum tribuisti, praesta, quaesumus, ut quem Doctorem vitae habuimus in terris, intercessorem habere mereamur in caelis. Per Dominum nostrum.

28. STS. PHILIP AND JAMES

May 11   First Century

Philippus, Bethsaidae natus, unus erat ex duodecim Apostolis qui primum a Christo Domino vocati sunt; a quo Nathanael, cum accepisset venisse Messiam in lege promissum, ad Dominum deductus
5 est. Quam vero Christus eum familiariter adhiberet,

1. **Bethsaidae**, a Hellenized town on the east bank of the Jordan near where it flows into the Sea of Galilee. Peter and Andrew were from the same town.

2. **vocati sunt.** See *Jn.* 1,40-45. Philip appears fifth in the lists of Apostles (*Mt.* 10,2-4; *Mk.* 3,14-19; *Lk.* 6,13-16), after the two pairs of brothers: Peter and Andrew, James (the Greater) and John.

3. **Nathanael**, commonly identified with Bartholomew. cf. *Jn.* 1,45-51.

4. **Messiam**, the transliteration of a Hebrew word meaning the Anointed One. The promised Messiah would be anointed as King and Priest. (cf. *Ps.* 2,2; *Dan.* 9,26) *Christ* comes from the Greek χριστος, anointed one.

lege; i.e., the Law of Moses; cf. *Dt.* 18, 18. The term usually embraces the Pentateuch, the first five books of the Bible. Other divisions of the Old Testament are the Prophets and the Wisdom literature.

5. **Quam...declarat**, 'How familiarly Christ dealt with him, the following fact readily declares, that...'

illud facile declarat quod Gentiles, Salvatorem videre cupientes, ad Philippum accesserunt, et Dominus, cum in solitudine hominum multitudinem pascere vellet, sic Philippum affatus est: "Unde ememus panes ut manducent hi?" Is, accepto Spiritu Sancto, cum ei Scythia ad praedicandum Evangelium obtigisset, omnem fere illam gentem ad christianam fidem convertit. Postremo, cum Hierapolim Phrygiae venisset, pro Christi nomine cruci affixus lapidibusque obrutus est Kalendis Maii. Eius corpus ibidem a Christianis sepultum, postea Romam delatum, in

6. **Gentiles ... ad Philippum;** cf. *Jn.* 12,21-23. Philip probably knew some Greek (to judge from his name and town), and would therefore have been of help to any strangers.

8. **in solitudine,** the uncultivated plain south-east of Bethsaida. cf. *Mt.* 14,15 (*desertus*) and 15,33 (*in deserto*). The reference here is to *Jn.* 6,5-7.

10. **accepto Spiritu sancto,** i.e., after Pentecost, *Acts* 2,1-4.

11. **Scythia:** an early tradition. Eusebius (*H.E.* 3,1) says Scythia fell to Andrew.

13. **Hierapolim.** Bishop Polycrates of Ephesus in a letter to Pope St. Victor (189-199) refers to Philip, one of the twelve Apostles, who died in Hierapolis. (in Eusebius, *H.E.* 3,31; 5,24) There is, however, some uncertainty whether the Philip buried at Hierapolis was the Apostle or Philip the Deacon and Evangelist (*Acts* 6,5; 8; 21,8-9), whose burial in the same city is mentioned in the *Dialogue of Caius to Proclus.* (Eusebius 3,31) There is also an account of Philip's martyrdom in Hierapolis but it is legendary. (cf. line 14.)

16. **Romam delatum.** The body of the Philip buried in Hierapolis was moved first to Constantinople, then to Rome, where it now reposes, together with the body of St. James, in the Basilica of the Twelve Apostles, which was built in honor of the two Apostles by Pelagius I (555-560).

STS. PHILIP AND JAMES. Mosaic (twelfth century) in the **Basilica of St. Mark,** Venice

basilica duodecim Apostolorum una cum corpore beati Iacobi Apostoli conditum est.

Iacobus frater Domini, cognomento Iustus, ab
20 ineunte aetate vinum et siceram non bibit, carne abstinuit, numquam tonsus est, nec unguento nec balneo usus. Huic uni licebat ingredi in Sancta sanctorum; idem lineis vestibus utebatur. Cui etiam assiduitas orandi ita callum genibus obduxerat, ut
25 duritie cameli pellem imitaretur. Eum post Christi ascensionem Apostoli Hierosolymorum episcopum creaverunt; ad quem etiam Princeps Apostolorum misit qui nuntiaret se e carcere ab Angelo eductum fuisse. Cum autem in concilio Hierosolymis contro-
30 versia esset orta de lege et circumcisione, Iacobus,

19. **Iacobus frater Domini.** In addition to James the Greater, son of Zebedee and brother of St. John, the following bear the name in the New Testament: James, the son of Alpheus, the Apostle (*Mt.* 10,3; *Mk.* 3,18; *Lk.* 6,15); James, the brother of the Lord (*Mt.* 13,55; *Mk.* 6,3; *Gal.* 1,19); James, the bishop of Jerusalem (*Acts* 12,17; 15, 13; 21,18). That one and the same person is identified in these ways is, in the absence of full evidence, the most probable view.

20. **siceram non bibit.** *Sicera* is a Latinized Hebrew word for intoxicating drink. This description of James will be found in Eusebius (*H.E.* 2,23) who quotes Hegesippus, a second century Jewish convert. See also Jerome, *De Viris Illustribus* 2. Most of this biography is based on Eusebius and Jerome.

21. **balneo usus**, 'frequent the baths'.

23. **idem**, 'he likewise'.

28. **misit qui nuntiaret**; supply an antecedent for **qui**: 'sent a man to announce...' cf. *Acts* 12, 17.

29. **concilio Hierosolymis.** The account of the Council of Jerusalem in 49 will be found in *Acts* 15.

Petri sententiam secutus, ad fratres habuit contionem, in qua vocationem Gentium probavit fratribusque absentibus scribendum esse dixit, ne Gentibus iugum Mosaicae legis imponerent. De illo et loquitur
35 Apostolus ad Galatas: "Alium autem Apostolorum vidi neminem nisi Iacobum fratrem Domini."

Tanta autem erat Iacobi vitae sanctitas, ut fimbriam vestimenti eius certatim homines cuperent attingere. Nam is nonaginta sex annos natus, cum tri-
40 ginta annis illi Ecclesiae sanctissime praefuisset, Christum Dei Filium constantissime praedicans, lapidibus primum appetitur; mox in altissimum Templi locum adductus inde praecipitatus est. Qui confractis cruribus iacens semivivus, manus tendebat ad
45 caelum Deumque pro illorum salute deprecabatur his verbis: "Ignosce eis, Domine, quia nesciunt quid

33. **ne ... imponerent**, 'that they should not impose ...'

35. **Apostolus**, i.e., St. Paul in *Gal.* 1,19, the text which is the main argument for the view that James the brother of the Lord and James the Apostle are one and the same.

Alium ... neminem, 'other of the Apostles (besides Peter; cf. *Gal.* 1,18) I saw no one ...'; 'no one else of the Apostles have I seen....'

36. **fratrem Domini**. The New Testament mentions a group of persons especially close to Christ, who are called the Brethren or the Brothers of the Lord, but their relationship to Christ was no closer than that of cousins. James is one of the four whose names are given.

38. **certatim ... cuperent attingere**, 'men vied with one another in their desire to touch ...'

41. **Christum Dei Filium**, 'Christ *as* the Son of God'.

faciunt." Qua in oratione graviter eius capite fullonis fuste percusso, animam Deo reddidit septimo Neronis anno, et iuxta Templum, ubi praecipitatus fuerat, 50 sepultus est. Unam scripsit epistulam, quae de septem catholicis est.

Oratio

Deus, qui nos annua Apostolorum tuorum Philippi et Iacobi solemnitate laetificas, praesta, quaesumus, ut quorum gaudemus meritis, instruamur exemplis. Per Dominum nostrum.

47. **fullonis fusto**, 'with the club of a fuller'. Eusebius, *H.E.* 2,23: "And one of the fullers among them took the club with which he used to beat out clothes and brought it down on the head of the Just...' (See a Dictionary of Antiquities for an account of the prominent trade of a fuller.)

48. **septimo Neronis anno**. Nero ruled 54-68, and James' death is usually dated c. 62.

50. **epistulam**... The Epistle of James was written at uncertain date to all Christian converts from Judaism. Its authenticity and inspiration were disputed in the early centuries, but by the fourth it was almost universally accepted.

de septem Catholicis, 'one of the seven Catholic Epistles'. The single epistles of James and Jude, the two of Peter and the three of John have been from the earliest times grouped together and called the *Catholic* Epistles. The term is usually taken to refer to the fact that they were written for a general audience and not a specific church.

29. ST. ROBERT BELLARMINE

May 13 1542-1621

Robertus Politianus e patricia Bellarminorum gente, matrem pientissimam habuit Cynthiam Cervini, Marcelli Papae secundi sororem. Eximia pietate et castissimis moribus ornatus, duodeviginti annorum
5 adulescens societatem Iesu Romae ingressus est, in eaque usque ad mortem religiosarum virtutum omnibus exemplo fuit. Post philosophiae curriculum Florentiam primum missus, tum Montem Regalem,

---

1. **Politianus** ... Robert was the son of Vincenzo Bellarmini, the chief magistrate in the Tuscan town of Montepulciano, south of Siena, and Cynthia Cervini, the sister of the able Cardinal Marcello Cervini, who ruled for one month in 1555 as Marcellus II. Robert was educated at the local Jesuit school, where he was highly regarded for his outstanding scholastic record and deep piety. His father wanted him to be a doctor but finally consented to his entry into the Society of Jesus in 1560.

6. **virtutum omnibus exemplo**; a double dative; cf. 6.14n. Renowned for his brilliance, Robert was also beloved for his spiritual qualities, especially his cheerfulness and simplicity.

8. **Florentiam missus.** Because of ill-health (which attended him through life), he was sent back to his native Tuscany, where he taught rhetoric and Latin poetry for a year.

Montem Regalem. cf. 26.20. Told to instruct the students there in Cicero and Demosthenes, Bellarmine set himself to the task of learning Greek for the first time, succeeded in

Patavium et Lovanium, magistri et contionatoris
10 munere nondum sacerdos mirifice functus est. Lovanii praeterea sacerdotio auctus, theologiam ita docuit, ut theologus per Europam clarissimus iam tum haberetur.

Romam revocatus, theologicam controversiarum

keeping a lesson ahead of his students. Later at Louvain, he learned Hebrew and wrote a simplified grammar of the language.

9. **Patavium.** The Jesuit provincial sent Bellarmine to the University of Padua in 1567 for his theological training. St. Francis Borgia, the Superior General, transferred him to Louvain in 1569 to finish his studies and also to counteract the dangerous teachings on grace and free will of Michael Baius, who in 1570 became Dean of the Faculty. After his ordination in 1570, Robert lectured on the *Summa* of St. Thomas, being the first Jesuit to do so, and studied thoroughly the Fathers of the Church. (Later in life he helped in an edition of Ambrose's works for Sixtus V (1585-1590).)

contionatoris. Even before his ordination, Bellarmine had shown he was a born orator, and his sermons—in Latin— were popular. Being of small stature, he used to stand on a stool in the high pulpits to make himself seen and heard.

14. **controversiarum disciplinam.** For eleven years, 1576-1587, Bellarmine taught the course of Controversy which had been founded by the Jesuits to deal specifically with the current Protestant theological teachings. From this course came his most important work, the *Disputations on Controversies of the Christian Faith Against the Heretics of this Time,* a work of enormous erudition in which he drew upon his knowledge of the Scriptures, the Fathers, and the Councils of the Church. Required to search through the very writings of the Protestant theologians to find his material, Bellarmine labored to be fair-minded in his exposition of opposing views. Even three hundred years later, the work was still declared to be the most com-

ST. ROBERT BELLARMINE. An engraving.
Courtesy, Radio Times Hulton Picture Library

disciplinam in collegio Romano tradidit, ubi etiam vitae spiritualis magister constitutus, angelicum iuvenem Aloisium per sanctitatis semitas moderatus est. A Clemente Papa octavo, frustra reluctans, in Patrum Cardinalium numerum cooptatus et paulo post consecratus episcopus, Capuanam archidioece-

plete defence of Catholic teaching yet published. The work was recognized all over Europe as the outstanding challenge to Protestant theology, and lectures and sermons were given to answer it. (At Oxford, where Queen Elizabeth had ordered courses refuting the work, one minister spoke against Bellarmine every Sunday night for seven years.) But the book attracted far more friends than foes, and was credited with the conversion and return of countless souls.

15. **collegio Romano.** The Roman College was founded by St. Francis Borgia, Ignatius' successor as general of the Jesuits, c. 1580. For three hundred years the Jesuits staffed this famous international college on the same property given to them in 1582 by Gregory XIII. But in 1870 the new Italian government expelled them, and the present Gregorian University near-by is its successor. Bellarmine was appointed spiritual director in 1588 and rector in 1592. He was superior of the Naples province of the Society 1594-95.

17. **Aloisium;** St. Aloysius Gonzaga (1568-1591), who died from a disease contracted while nursing the sick. Bellarmine assisted at his death-bed, later successfully promoted his beatification.

18. **in...Cardinalium numerum.** He was appointed, to his own great dismay, by Clement VIII (1592-1605), who declared that the Church did not have his equal in learning. At Clement's request, Bellarmine wrote two catechisms, one of which is still used. He also served on the Commission that edited the new version of the Clementine Vulgate ordered by the Council of Trent, and wrote its preface.

20. **Capuanam.** Robert was a central figure in the famous

sim triennium sanctissime rexit. Quo munere deposito, integerrimus ac fidelissimus summi Pontificis consiliarius in Urbe degit, usque prope octogenarius, die decima septima Septembris, anno millesimo sex-
25 centesimo vigesimo primo, pie in Domino quievit. Praeter controversiarum volumina multa alia praeclare scripsit, inter quae aureus catechesis libellus exstat insignis. Fortissimum hunc catholicae veritatis propugnatorem Pius undecimus Pontifex maxi-
30 mus in Sanctorum numerum retulit atque universalis Ecclesiae Doctorem declaravit.

controversy *De Auxiliis* between the Jesuits and the Dominicans concerning the interrelation of grace and free will. Bellarmine's position, eventually adopted, was that the debate should not be decided dogmatically, but left open for future discussion. But Clement was determined on a definition and when Capua fell vacant, he had Bellarmine appointed to it. (1602)

21. **sanctissime rexit.** The scholar put down his books and for the next three years occupied himself with pastoral visitations, preaching, and a revitalization of the life of his diocese along the lines laid down by Trent.

23. **in Urbe degit.** Clement died in 1605 and the new Pope Paul V (1605-1621) called Bellarmine to Rome, where as head of the Vatican Library and member of almost every Congregation, he took a prominent part in important ecclesiastical affairs.

27. **catechesis**; genitive case.

30. **in Sanctorum numerum.** Bellarmine's cause was immediately introduced, and in 1627 he passed the first stage and won the title Venerable. But his beatification was held up—until 1923—because of opposition from some quarters to some of his teachings, e.g., on papal authority in temporal matters. Pius XI (1922-1939) canonized him in 1930, and in 1931 declared a Doctor of the Church the saint whom a contemporary Cardinal had called "the Athanasius or the Augustine of our time."

Oratio

Deus, qui ad errorum insidias repellendas et Apostolicae Sedis iura propugnanda, beatum Robertum Pontificem tuum atque Doctorem mira eruditione et virtute decorasti, eius meritis et intercessione concede ut nos in veritatis amore crescamus, et errantium corda ad Ecclesiae tuae redeant unitatem. Per Dominum nostrum.

30. ST. JOHN BAPTIST DE LA SALLE

May 15   1651-1719

   Ioannes Baptista de la Salle Rhemis claro genere ortus, puer adhuc moribus et factis in sortem Domini se vocandum et sanctimoniae laude honestandum portendit. Adulescens in Rhemensi academia
5 litteras ac philosophicas disciplinas didicit; quo tempore, etsi ob animi virtutes et alacre ingenium ac suave omnibus carus esset, ab aequalium tamen societate abhorrebat, ut solitudini addictus facilius Deo vacaret. In clericalem militiam iam pridem
10 cooptatus, sexto decimo aetatis anno inter Rhemenses canonicos ascriptus est. Lutetiam Parisiorum, theologiae in Sorbonica universitate daturus operam,

   1. **claro genere ortus.** Both his parents were of the nobility, his father's ancestry going as far back as the ninth century. Despite his aristocratic background and fortune, however, de la Salle's entire life was spent in the service of the lower classes.
   3. **se ... portendit,** 'indicated that he deserved to be called to the lot of the Lord and honored with praise for holiness'.
   9. **iam pridem cooptatus.** de la Salle had already been tonsured. His father wanted his eldest son to study law and continue the family tradition, but John Baptist insisted that he was called to serve the Church. In 1667 he became a canon of the cathedral chapter (cf. 6.39n.) at Rheims, while he continued his seminary studies at the Collège des Bons Enfants.
   12. **daturus,** 'in order to give'; the future active participle used to express purpose.

contendit, atque in Sulpicianum seminarium ascitus
est. At brevi parentibus orbatus, domum regredi
coactus, fratres educandos suscepit; quod, scientiarum interim sacrarum studia non intermittens, optimo cum fructu praestitit, uti exitus comprobavit.

Sacerdotio demum auctus, qua praestanti fide
animique ardore primum ad aram fecit, eisdem toto
vitae tempore Sacris est operatus. Interea, salutis
animarum studio incensus, totum in earumdem utilitatem sese impendit. Sororum a Iesu infante, puellis

13. **Sulpicianum seminarium.** After receiving a Master of Arts degree from the college, in 1670 de la Salle entered the Seminary of Saint-Sulpice. This seminary, destined to become famous, had been founded in 1642 by Jean-Jacques Olier (1608-1657). The seminarians studied theology at the Sorbonne, which had been founded by Robert de Sorbon in the thirteenth century as part of the University of Paris.

14. **parentibus orbatus.** His mother died July, 1671. When his father died the following April, de la Salle left Saint-Sulpice and returned to Rheims to assume responsibility for his brothers and sisters. While setting the family business in order, he accepted the advice of his spiritual adviser and fellow-canon, Nicolas Roland, and was ordained to the subdiaconate, June, 1672. Four years later he was ordained a deacon, at which time he in vain sought permission to resign his office as canon and devote himself to parish work. In 1678 he was ordained to the priesthood.

18. **qua ... operatus**, 'with what outstanding faith and ardor of spirit he first celebrated at the altar, with the same sentiments he offered the Holy Sacrifice all his life'. **operatus** is used in the special sense of performing what is due to God, i.e., sacrifice. **Sacris** is an ablative of means. **Fecit** is used in the same sense. cf. Verg. *Ecl.* 3,77; Hor. *Od.* 3,14,6.

22. **Sororum ... regimen suscepit.** On his death-bed Ni-

ST. JOHN BAPTIST DE LA SALLE. A portrait attributed to Pierre Léger.

educandis institutarum, regimen suscepit; easque
non modo prudentissime est moderatus, sed ab ex-
cidio vindicavit. Hinc porro animum advertit ad
pueros de plebe religione bonisque moribus informandos. Atque in hoc quidem illum suscitaverat
Deus, ut scilicet, nova in Ecclesia sua religiosorum
hominum familia condita, puerorum, praesertim
pauperum, scholis perenni efficacique ratione consuleret. Demandatum vero a Dei providentia munus
per contradictiones plurimas magnasque aerumnas

colas Roland had entrusted to his care the Congregation of
the Sisters of the Child Jesus, which he had established in 1670.
These sisters were engaged in the conduct of a girls' orphanage
and school, and thus de la Salle was first drawn into what would
be his life work, Christian education of the young.

25. **animum advertit ad pueros ... informandos.** In 1679
he helped Adrian Nyel who had come to Rheims to open a free
elementary school for poor boys. Two schools were started and
de la Salle soon became more and more interested in this work.
But the situation of the teachers particularly attracted him and
by helping them both in and out of class, he was drawn into
closer association with them. He eventually invited them to
live in his own house, but this first step resulted in great dis-
appointment, as of the seven teachers, five soon departed. But
de la Salle waited patiently, and soon other men came who
formed the nucleus of a new institute. To make himself level
with his teachers, he resigned his canonical office and its sti-
pend in 1683, and in 1684 gave away all his money to the poor.

27. **in hoc ... ut scilicet ... scholis ... consuleret**, 'for this
purpose, namely that ... he might care for schools....'.

32. **per contradictiones ... aerumnas.** In its first two
decades, the institute had a difficult time surviving. Not only
was it plagued with deaths and defections, but law-suits brought
by hostile secular teachers obliged the founder to close all his

feliciter implevit, fundata fratrum sodalitate, quam a Scholis christianis nuncupavit.

35 Adiunctos igitur sibi homines in gravi opere et arduo apud se primum suscepit. Tum aptiori in sede constitutos disciplina sua optime imbuit iis legibus sapientibusque institutis quae postea a Benedicto decimo tertio sunt confirmata. Ex demissione animi
40 ac paupertatis amore primum canonicatu se abdicavit, omniaque sua bona in pauperes erogavit; quin etiam serius, quod frustra saepius tentaverat, fundati a se instituti regimen sponte deposuit. Nihil tamen

schools and houses in Paris. And in 1702, because of complaints of undue severity towards the novices, he even found himself deposed for a time by the Archbishop of Paris.

34. **a Scholis christianis**, '(Brothers) of the Christian Schools'. (cf. 22.1n.) In 1684 de la Salle formed the group of teachers associated with him into a religious community. In 1690 the death just prior to ordination of a very promising candidate convinced him that the advancement of this person had not been God's will, and so he determined that in the future no Brother should ever become a priest and that no priest should ever become a Brother. Education was to be their sole work. The rule is still in effect.

38. **a Benedicto decimo tertio**. Before his death in 1719, de la Salle completed the revision of his Rule, but he never lived to see it approved. In 1725, six years later, Benedict XIII gave formal approbation to the new Congregation and its rule.

40. **canonicatu se abdicavit**, 'he resigned his canonical office'. *abdico* in this sense is used with a reflexive and the ablative.

43. **regimen sponte deposuit**. In 1717, two years before his death, de la Salle determined to resign and called a general chapter to have a superior general elected to succeed him. He spent the remaining years of his life at the novitiate in Rouen, writing

interim de fratrum sollicitudine remittens deque
scholis ab eo pluribus iam locis apertis, impensius
Deo vacare coepit. Assidue ieiuniis, flagellis aliisque
asperitatibus in se ipsum saeviens, noctes orando
ducebat; donec virtutibus omnibus conspicuus, praesertim oboedientia, studio divinae voluntatis implen-
dae, amore ac devotione in apostolicam Sedem;
meritis onustus, sacramentis rite susceptis, obdormivit in Domino annos natus duo de septuaginta.
Eum Leo decimus tertius Pontifex maximus Beatorum catalogo inseruit; novisque fulgentem signis anno iubilaei millesimo nongentesimo Sanctorum
honoribus decoravit. Pius vero duodecimus omnium
magistrorum pueris adulescentibusque instituendis
praecipuum apud Deum caelestem Patronum constituit.

several educational and religious works, teaching the novices, and putting his Rule into final form.

45. **scholis ... apertis**. Free elementary schools for the poor had been opened not only in Rheims, but in Paris and in many cities of France: Rouen, Chartres, Grenoble, Avignon, Boulogne, Marseilles, and other places. In addition to these schools, a novitiate was begun in 1685; training colleges for teachers were founded in Rheims (1684), Paris (1699), and Saint-Denis (1709); in Rouen two important and successful institutions were begun, one a tuition boarding-school on the secondary level, and a school for delinquent boys. From such origins there grew up the present world-wide organization, the largest teaching order in the Church, ranging from the primary level to the university. In the United States, the Congregation has over two thousand brothers in five provinces.

59. **caelestem Patronum**. Pius XII so declared him in 1950. Not only had de la Salle provided a system of education for the

Oratio

Deus, qui ad christianam pauperum eruditionem et ad iuventam in via veritatis firmandam, sanctum Ioannem Baptistam confessorem excitasti, et novam per eum in Ecclesia familiam collegisti, concede propitius ut eius intercessione et exemplo, studio gloriae tuae in animarum salute ferventes, eius in caelis coronae participes fieri valeamus. Per Dominum nostrum.

neglected poor of his own day, but his creative pedagogical ideas, ranging from study programs on the primary level to the establishment of teachers' colleges, were a major contribution to modern education. Further, many other religious orders of teaching-Brothers founded in the nineteenth century, owed much of their inspiration to his aims, methods, and ideals.

31. ST. GREGORY VII

May 25   c. 1023-1085

    Gregorius Papa septimus, antea Hildebrandus, Suanae in Etruria natus, doctrina, sanctitate, omnique virtutum genere cum primis nobilis, mirifice universam Dei illustravit Ecclesiam. Cum parvulus
5 ad pedes fabri, ligna edolantis, iam litterarum inscius luderet, ex reiectis tamen segmentis illa Davidici elementa oraculi: *Dominabitur a mare usque ad mare,* casu formasse narratur, manum pueri ductante Numine; quo significaretur eius fore amplissi-

    1. **Hildebrandus.** The name indicates some Lombard connection, but of the saint's ancestry nothing certain is known except that he was of peasant stock. His name (Hellebrand) signified to his friends 'a bright flame', to his enemies 'a brand of hell'.

    4. **parvulus,** 'as a little boy'.

    5. **ad pedes fabri.** The authority for this story is Cardinal Baronius (cf. 32.16n.), who identifies the *faber* as Gregory's father; *patris* came to be dropped out, apparently to cover the Pontiff's humble origins. cf. *Acta Sanctorum,* May vol. 6, p. 104; 110. For a similar idealization of a saint's infancy and boyhood, see 22.4n.

    7. **oraculi.** *Psalm* 71,8.

    8. **formasse narratur,** 'he is said to have formed...'

    9. **Numine.** See H. J. Rose, *Religion in Greece and Rome,* pp. 160-174 for a fascinating account of the history of the word and its significance.

        quo significaretur; relative clause of purpose, 'that thereby it might be signified that...'

10 mam in mundo auctoritatem. Romam deinde profectus, sub protectione sancti Petri educatus est. Iuvenis, Ecclesiae libertatem a laicis oppressam ac depravatos ecclesiasticorum mores vehementius dolens, in Cluniacensi monasterio, ubi sub regula

    11. **educatus est.** Hildebrand was educated in the monastery of St. Mary on the Aventine Hill in Rome, where his uncle was abbot. In this monastery, influenced as it was by the Cluny reform, Hildebrand first absorbed the ideals of Church reform which was his main occupation in life.

    12. **Ecclesiae libertatem ... oppressam.** The reference is to the custom of lay investiture.

    13. **depravatos mores ...** The twin stain of simony and incontinence among the clergy. cf. 0.54n. The Church in the tenth and eleventh century had reached its lowest point. Later as Supreme Pontiff in 1075 Gregory wrote to the abbot of Cluny: "Wherever I turn my eyes, to the west, to the north, or to the south, I find everywhere bishops who have obtained their office in an irregular way, whose lives and conversation are strangely at variance with their sacred calling; who go through their duties not for the love of Christ but from motives of worldly gain. There are no longer princes who set God's honor before their own selfish ends, or who allow justice to stand in the way of their ambition." (*Reg.* 2,49; *P.L.* 148,400)

    14. **Cluniacensi monasterio.** This famous Benedictine monastery was founded in 909 by the Duke of Aquitaine and in its first centuries of existence had remarkable saints as its abbots. A strict form of the rule of St. Benedict was introduced, which was spread by a radically new system of central government. The abbey incorporated monasteries already in existence and founded new ones, and all of them became dependent on the motherhouse, for their abbots were all subjects of the abbot of Cluny, and were indeed his own nominees. Every profession required Cluny's sanction and every monk had to spend some time in

sancti Benedicti austerioris vitae observantia eo tempore maxime vigebat, monachi habitum induens, tanto pietatis ardore divinae maiestati deserviebat, ut a sanctis eiusdem coenobii patribus prior sit electus. Sed divina providentia maiora de eo disponente, in salutem plurimorum Cluniaco educatus Hildebrandus, abbas primum monasterii sancti Pauli extra muros Urbis electus ac postmodum Romanae Ecclesiae cardinalis creatus, sub summis Pontificibus Leone nono, Victore secundo, Stephano nono, Nicolao secundo et Alexandro secundo, praecipuis muneribus et legationibus perfunctus est; sanctissimi et purissimi consilii vir a beato Petro Damiano nuncupatus. A Victore Papa secundo legatus a latere in

Cluny itself. While the organization was foreign to Benedictine tradition, the monks of Cluny were always regarded as Benedictines.

16. **monachi habitum induens** ... Hildebrand was professed at Rome, not Cluny. The date is not known.

18. **prior sit electus.** cf. *Acta Sanctorum*, ibid., p. 104, but this is regarded as not at all likely. cf. ibid., p. 106.

24. **Leone nono.** St. Leo IX (1048-1054) appointed him supervisor of the monastery of St. Paul's Outside the Walls, which he reformed and restored to its former austerity. Hildebrand was not elected abbot (1. 17), but his exact position is unknown. cf. *Acta Sanctorum*, ibid., p. 113: *praelatus est*. Leo also made Hildebrand a cardinal and financial administrator of the Papal States. Before serving Leo, Hildebrand had been chaplain and secretary to Gregory VI (1045-1046), a former teacher of his at the Lateran Seminary. For the other Pontiffs, see Peter Damian 6.

28. **Victore Papa secundo.** Finding that the people and clergy of Rome were intent on electing him after the death of

ST. GREGORY VII ACCEPTS THE SUBMISSION
OF HENRY IV. Painting by Federico Zuccari (1540-1609).
Vatican Picture Gallery

Galliam missus, Lugduni episcopum, simoniaca labe
30 infectum, ad sui criminis confessionem miraculo adegit. Berengarium in concilio Turonensi ad iteratam haeresis abiurationem compulit. Cadaloi quoque schisma sua virtute compressit.

Mortuo Alexandro secundo, invitus et maerens
35 unanimi omnium consensu decimo Kalendas Maii,

Leo, Hildebrand set out for Germany and eventually succeeded in having his personal candidate nominated by the Holy Roman Emperor, who was subsequently elected and took the name Victor (1055-1057). During this and subsequent pontificates, Hildebrand continued to exercise a dominant influence.

30. **ad confessionem miraculo adegit.** The bishop, not identified, denied his simony and was ordered by Gregory to recite the *Gloria Patri etc.* The bishop began confidently but was unable to pronounce the name of the Holy Ghost. Beginning a second time, he could not pronounce the name of the Son, and on the third try failed to go beyond the word *gloria*. The bishop then threw himself at Gregory's feet and confessed that he had wrongly acquired his see. cf. *Acta Sanctorum*, p. 114.

31. **Berengarium.** The Eucharistic teachings of this theologian (999-1088) were condemned by several councils between 1050 and 1080, and though Berengarius later retracted his submissions, he finally died reconciled to the Church. His teaching that the substance of bread did not change into the Body of Christ constituted the first major controversy regarding the Real Presence in ten centuries, and led to the later (Fourth Lateran Council, 1215) definition of the doctrine of Transubstantiation. Hildebrand presided as legate at the Council of Tours in 1055.

32. **Cadaloi.** cf. 6.57n.

35. **decimo Kalendas Maii** == April 22, 1073. After Hildebrand's acclamation by the people, he was duly elected by the College of Cardinals, according to the new regulations of Nicholas II (cf. 6.56n.).

ST. GREGORY VII 213

anno Christi millesimo septuagesimo tertio, summus
Pontifex electus, sicut sol effulsit in domo Dei. Nam
potens opere et sermone, ecclesiasticae disciplinae
reparandae, fidei propagandae, libertati Ecclesiae
40 restituendae, exstirpandis erroribus et corruptelis
tanto studio incubuit, ut ex Apostolorum aetate nullus Pontificum fuisse tradatur, qui maiores pro Ecclesia Dei labores molestiasque pertulerit, aut qui
pro eius libertate acrius pugnaverit. Aliquot provin-
45 cias a simoniaca labe expurgavit. Contra Henrici imperatoris impios conatus, fortis per omnia athleta,

38. **ecclesiasticae disciplinae reparandae**... In the March immediately following his election, the First Lenten Synod ordered that all clergy who had obtained their positions by simony or were living incontinent lives should cease to exercise their ministry. Like similar (and largely unsuccessful) decrees passed by previous synods, this one was greeted by the clergy in Europe with violent resistance, general indifference, and open defiance. But Gregory followed up his decrees by sending legates empowered to depose any immoral or simoniacal ecclesiastic.

39. **libertati Ecclesiae restituendae.** In 1075 a second Roman synod excommunicated any person, even if they were emperor or king, who should confer an investiture in connection with any ecclesiastical office. It was the first outright prohibition of lay investiture.

45. **Henrici imperatoris.** The Synod of 1075 had cited the Holy Roman Emperor Henry IV (1056-1106) to appear in Rome to answer to charges of investiture. The Diet of Worms the following January retorted by declaring Gregory deposed. Gregory replied by excommunicating Henry and all his ecclesiastical supporters, and released his subjects from their oath of allegiance.

46. **athleta**; cf. 11.36n.

impavidus permansit seque pro muro domui Israel
ponere non timuit; ac eumdem Henricum, in pro-
fundum malorum prolapsum, fidelium communione
50 regnoque privavit atque subditos populos fide ei
data liberavit.

Dum Missarum solemnia perageret, visa est viris
piis columba e caelo delapsa, umero eius dextro in-
sidens, alis extensis caput eius velare; quo significa-
55 tum est Spiritus Sancti afflatu, non humanae pru-
dentiae rationibus, ipsum duci in Ecclesiae regimine.
Cum ab iniqui Henrici exercitu Romae gravi ob-
sidione premeretur, excitatum ab hostibus incendium

47. **seque pro muro...**, 'he did not fear to set himself as a wall for the house of Israel'; i.e., the new Israel, the Church of Christ.

52. **visa est columba...velare**, 'a dove was seen to cover...' One day two *rustici* attended his Mass and one of them '*velut in exstasim raptus*' had the vision described here. cf. *Acta Sanctorum*, p. 116. The story would identify Gregory as a second Gregory the Great. cf. 9.56n.

viris, dative of agency with the passive.

57. **Henrici exercitu**...In 1077 Henry had submitted to Gregory, in one of the most famous events of medieval history, by begging absolution for three days in the snow outside the castle of the Countess Matilda at Canossa. By 1080, however, Gregory was forced to renew the excommunication when Henry threatened to have the excommunicated Archbishop of Ravenna elected anti-Pope. The same year saw the death in battle of Henry's rival for the German throne and his march into Italy. He succeeded in capturing Rome three years later, in 1084.

58. **incendium...exstinxit**. The fire was started by Henry to draw off defenders from their positions, but Gregory ordered

signo crucis exstinxit. De eius manu tandem a Roberto Guiscardo duce Northmanno ereptus, Cassinum se contulit, atque inde Salernum ad dedicandam ecclesiam sancti Matthaei Apostoli contendit. Cum aliquando in ea civitate sermonem habuisset ad populum, aerumnis confectus in morbum incidit, quo se interiturum praescivit. Postrema morientis Gregorii verba fuere: "Dilexi iustitiam et odivi iniquitatem; propterea morior in exsilio." Innumerabilia sunt quae vel fortiter sustinuit vel multis coactis in Urbe synodis sapienter constituit; vir vere

all the soldiers to their posts and checked the fire by making the sign of the Cross. cf. *Acta Sanctorum* p. 112 and 144.

59. Roberto Guiscardo. The Normans had invaded southern Italy earlier in the century and had resisted all attempts to dislodge them. Eventually, to 'legalize' their position, they made themselves the vassals of the Holy See, and in this capacity they responded to the plea of the besieged Gregory. But as they were more interested in sacking the Holy City than in rescuing the Pope, they were driven out by an enraged populace, and Gregory was forced to go with them as his sole protectors.

61. Salernum. The Normans under Giuscard had taken possession of Salerno, the last Lombard principality, in 1075. Its cathedral was built by Guiscard and dedicated by Gregory to St. Matthew, whose relics according to tradition are preserved in the crypt.

66. Dilexi iustitiam...cf. *Acta Sanctorum*, p. 138. cf. *Ps.* 44,8

69. vir vere sanctus... "Although he was not particularly prepossessing in manner, appearance, or voice, he was a man of indomitable will and genuine spirituality. He was always the priest, the ascetic, the truly holy man. But he also knew how and when to act with great boldness. With him, deeds, not words, counted." (Hayes, Baldwin, Cole, *History of Europe*, p. 198)

70 sanctus, criminum vindex, et acerrimus Ecclesiae defensor. Exactis itaque in pontificatu annis duodecim, migravit in caelum anno salutis millesimo octogesimo quinto, pluribus in vita et post mortem miraculis clarus; eiusque sacrum corpus in cathedra-
75 li basilica Salernitana est honorifice conditum.

Oratio

Deus, in te sperantium fortitudo, qui beatum Gregorium Confessorem tuum atque Pontificem pro tuenda Ecclesiae libertate, virtute constantiae roborasti, da nobis eius exemplo et intercessione omnia
80 adversantia fortiter superare. Per Dominum nostrum.

Gregory was beatified by Gregory XIII in 1584, after the reforming council of Trent, and canonized by Benedict XIII in 1728.

32. ST. PHILIP NERI

May 26   **1515-1595**

Philippus Nerius piis honestisque parentibus Florentiae natus, ab ipsa ineunte aetate non obscura dedit futurae sanctitatis indicia. Adulescens ampla patrui hereditate dimissa Romam se contulit, ubi
5 philosophia ac sacris litteris eruditus, totum se Christo dicavit. Ea fuit abstinentia ut saepe ieiunus triduum permanserit. Vigiliis et orationibus intentus,

    1. **parentibus.** Philip was one of four children of Francesco Neri, a notary of Florence. His mother died when he was very young.
    4. **patrui hereditate.** At sixteen Philip was sent to an uncle who owned a business near Monte Cassino, who was so pleased with him that he determined to make him his heir. But after a time Philip found his surroundings uncongenial. During one of his many retreats to a mountain chapel belonging to the monks, he had a mystical experience, which he later spoke of as his 'conversion', and set out for Rome.
      Romam se contulit. Philip arrived in Rome in 1533 and found lodging with a Florentine family whose sons he undertook to tutor. In 1535, after two years spent largely as a hermit, he entered the University of the Sapienza to study philosophy, and studied theology with the Augustinians. Three years later he suddenly terminated his studies, sold his books and began his life-long apostolate among the people of Rome.

septem Urbis ecclesias frequenter visitans, apud coemeterium Callisti in caelestium rerum contempla-
10 tione pernoctare consuevit. Sacerdos ex oboedientia factus, in animarum salute procuranda totus fuit, et in confessionibus audiendis ad extremum usque diem perseverans, innumeros paene filios Christo peperit. Quos verbi Dei cotidiano pabulo, sacramentorum
15 frequentia, orationis assiduitate aliisque piis exercitationibus enutriri cupiens, Oratorii congregationem instituit.

8. **septem Urbis ecclesias.** Phiilp's favorite devotion grew into the specially indulgenced Seven Church Walk, to St. Peter's St. Paul's Outside the Walls, St. Sebastian's, St. John Lateran, the Holy Cross in Jerusalem, St. Lawrence's, St. Mary Major.

10. **Sacerdos ... factus.** For seventeen years Philip had lived as a layman, but in 1551 he yielded to his confessor and was ordained a priest. He went to live at the church of San Girolamo della Caritá, where his apostolate was characterized by long sessions in the confessional where he was skillful in reading the hearts of men.

11. **totus fuit,** 'he applied himself wholly to ...'

14. **Quos ... enutriri cupiens,** 'Desiring to nourish these men ...'

16. **Oratorii congregationem.** In 1575 the organization of the group that had grown around Philip was approved by Gregory XIII (1572-1585), and assigned the church of St. Maria in Vallicella, later called the Chiesa Nuova. The new congregation was composed of secular priests who shared a common life and spiritual exercises under obedience, but were strictly forbidden to take vows or renounce property. The rule of the Oratory was not formally drawn up until seventeen years after Philip's death and was then approved by Paul V (1605-1612) in 1612. Today there are some fifty oratories in Europe and the United States. One of the most famous is the Oratory in England

ST. PHILIP NERI. Statue by Alessandro Algardi
(1595-1654). S. Maria in Vallicella (Chiesa Nuova),
Rome. Courtesy, Alinari

Caritate Dei vulneratus languebat iugiter tantoque cor eius aestuabat ardore, ut cum intra fines suos contineri non posset, illius sinum, confractis atque elatis duabus costulis, mirabiliter Dominus ampliaverit. Sacrum vero faciens aut ferventius orans, in aera quandoque sublatus, mira undique luce fulgere visus fuit. Egenos et pauperes

which was established by Cardinal Newman in 1847, two years after his conversion. Of the immediate disciples of Philip, the best known is the famous church historian Cardinal Baronius (1538-1607), whose monumental *Annales Ecclesiastici* (up to 1198) was the direct result of the assignment given him by Philip to preach the history of the Church. (cf. 27.27n.)

20. illius sinum ... ampliaverit. This extraordinary phenomenon happened on Pentecost, 1544, when Philip was praying in the catacombs of St. Sebastian (not St. Callistus, 1. 9, a mistake of early biographers). A ball of fire seemed to enter into his mouth and lodge in his breast, and this brought on violent paroxysms and caused a large swelling to appear on his side, the size of a man's fist. Ever after Philip was subject to shaking-fits and palpitation of the heart whenever he performed any intense spiritual exercise, but the swelling itself never gave him any pain. (cf. *Acta Sanctorum,* May vol. 6, p. 462-3; 523) After his death his body was examined by doctors and it was found that two ribs had been broken and curved to form an arch to make room for the saint's dilated heart. Several medical treatises were written shortly afterwards on the palpitations and the fractured ribs. (cf.. the following texts used in Philip's Mass: *Rom.* 5,5; *Ps.* 38,4; 118,32)

22. Sacrum ... faciens, 'When celebrating Mass ...' (cf. 30.18n)

23. mira ... fulgere. cf. *Acta Sanctorum,* May vol. 6, p. 585. The biography written by the Oratorian Gallonio, a companion of Philip's, contains the incidents, and many more, referred to generally in this biography.

25 omni caritatis officio prosequebatur; dignus qui et
    Angelo in specie pauperis eleemosynam erogaret, et
    dum egentibus noctu panem deferret in foveam
    lapsus, inde pariter ab Angelo incolumis eriperetur.
    Humilitati addictus, ab honoribus semper abhorruit,
30 atque ecclesiasticas dignitates, etiam primarias, non
    semel ultro delatas constantissime recusavit.
       Prophetiae dono fuit illustris, et in animorum
    sensibus penetrandis mirifice enituit. Virginitatem
    perpetuo illibatam servavit, idque assecutus est ut
35 eos qui puritatem colerent, ex odore, qui vero secus,
    ex foetore dignosceret. Absentibus interdum ap-
    paruit, iisque periclitantibus opem tulit; aegrotos
    plurimos et morti proximos sanitati restituit; mor-
    tuum quoque ad vitam revocavit. Caelestium spiri-
40 tuum et ipsius Deiparae Virginis frequenter fuit
    apparitione dignatus, ac plurimorum animas, splen-
    dore circumfusas, in caelum conscendere vidit.
    Denique anno salutis millesimo quingentesimo nona-
    gesimo quinto octavo Kalendas Iunias, in quem

   25. dignus qui... erogaret,... eriperetur; Relative clauses of purpose: 'a man worthy to give..., to be taken out...'
   30. dignitates... recusavit. In 1590 a close follower became Gregory XIV (1590-1591) and tried to make Philip accept the red hat. Clement VIII (1592-1605) tried and failed also.
   35. eos... dignosceret, 'he could recognize from their pleasant odor those who practiced purity; from their unpleasant odor, those who did otherwise.'
   44. octavo Kalendas Iunias = May 25. Strictly, the name of the month should be in the form of an adjective, as here. cf. 2.17n.
       in quem diem, 'the day on which...'; for the incorpora-

45 diem inciderat festum Corporis Christi, Sacro maxima spiritus exsultatione peracto ceterisque functionibus expletis, post mediam noctem, qua praedixerat hora, octogenarius obdormivit in Domino; quem Gregorius decimus quintus miraculis clarum in
50 Sanctorum numerum retulit.

Oratio

Deus, qui beatum Philippum Confessorem tuum Sanctorum tuorum gloria sublimasti, concede propitius ut cuius solemnitate laetamur, eius virtutum proficiamus exemplo. Per Dominum nostrum.

tion of the antecedent into the relative clause, see 22.54n., and line 47, **qua praedixerat hora.**

45. **Sacro ... peracto,** 'after Mass had been celebrated...'; cf. 22n.

49. **Gregorius XV** (1621-1623) canonized the 'Apostle of Rome' in 1622, together with the 'Apostle of the Indies', St. Francis Xavier (1506-1552), whom Philip had once longed to follow to India, but had been told, "Your Indies are in Rome."

33. ST. BEDE THE VENERABLE

May 27   672/3-735

Beda presbyter Girvi in Britanniae et Scotiae finibus ortus, septennis sancto Benedicto Biscopio abbati Wiremuthensi educandus traditur. Monachus deinde factus, vitam sic instituit, ut dum se artium

1. **Girvi.** Bede was born in what would shortly become the territory of the monastery of Jarrow, as he himself relates in the last chapter of his most important work, the *Ecclesiastical History of the English People*. This is practically the sole source for details of his life. cf. *P.L.* 95, 288-289.

2. **Benedicto Biscopio.** St. Benedict Biscop (c. 628-690) founded the twin monasteries of St. Peter at Wearmouth (674) and St. Paul at Jarrow (682). As a result of the several journeys he made to Rome, he was able to build up a remarkable library, which made Bede's historical and patristic work possible. Benedict also engaged the cantor of St. Peter's in Rome to supervise the chant and ceremonies at the monasteries, and in other ways helped to link the new Christianity and monasticism of Northumbria with the traditions of the Continent.

4. **vitam sic instituit** ... Bede writes, "I have spent the whole of my life within that monastery (Jarrow), devoting all my pains to the study of the Scriptures; and amid the observance of monastic discipline and the daily charge of singing in the church, it has ever been my delight to learn or teach or write." Only a few visits outside the monastery are recorded. One of them, in 733, was to his former pupil Archbishop Egbert of York (d. 766), whose famous school produced the illustrious Alcuin (735-804), who in turn established a school for

et doctrinarum studiis totum impenderet, nihil umquam de regulari disciplina remitteret. Nullum fuit doctrinae genus in quo non esset diligentissime versatus. Sed praecipua illi cura fuit divinarum Scripturarum meditatio; quarum sententiam ut plenius assequeretur, Graeci Hebraicique sermonis notitiam est adeptus. Tricesimo aetatis anno abbatis sui iussu sacerdos initiatus, statim suasore Acca Hagulstadensi episcopo sacros explanare libros aggressus est, in quo sanctorum Patrum doctrinis adeo inhaesit, ut nihil proferret nisi illorum iudicio comprobatum, eorumdem etiam fere verbis usus. Otium perosus semper, ex lectione ad orationem transibat ac vicissim ex oratione ad lectionem; in qua adeo animo inflammabatur, ut saepe inter legendum et docendum lacrimis perfunderetur. Ne autem rerum fluxarum curis distraheretur, delatum abbatis munus constantissime detrectavit.

Scientiae ac pietatis laude Bedae nomen sic

Charlemagne at the Carolingian court in 781. Thus the scholarship of these Anglo-Saxon monks became responsible for what has been called the Carolingian renaissance.

12. **Acca Hagulstadensi.** St. Bede dedicated several of his works to St. Acca (c. 660-742), who in 709 became bishop of Hexham, succeeding St. John of Beverly who had ordained Bede to the priesthood. The monastery of Hexham had been founded by St. Wilfrid of York in 674 and made a bishopric for the surrounding territory in 678.

15. **ut nihil ... comprobatum**, 'that he put forth nothing except what was approved by the teaching of the Fathers, even using almost the very words of the same (Fathers)'. cf. 27.7n.

ST. BEDE. Miniature from the twelfth century manuscript of his **Life of St. Cuthbert.** British Museum. Courtesy, Trustees of the British Museum.

brevi claruit, ut sanctus Sergius Papa de eo Romam
arcessendo cogitaverit; quo diffficillimis scilicet,
quae de rebus sacris exortae erant, quaestionibus
definiendis conferret operam. Emendandis fidelium
moribus, fidei vindicandae atque asserendae libros
plures conscripsit, quibus tantam sui apud omnes
opinionem fecit, ut illum sanctus Bonifatius episcopus et martyr Ecclesiae lumen praedicaverit; Lanfrancus, Anglorum doctorem; concilium Aquisgranense, doctorem admirabilem dixerit. Quin eius
scripta eo adhuc vivente publice in ecclesiis lege-
bantur. Quod cum fieret, quoniam ipsum sanctum

24. **Sergius** (687-701) had several other associations with the Church in England: he baptized the king of the West Saxons (689); restored St. Wilfrid to his see at York; and consecrated Willibrord (695) and sent him to preach to the Frisians (in the modern Netherlands).

25. **quo ... conferret operam**; relative clause of purpose: 'in order that there he might help...'

30. **Bonifatius** (c. 675-755), born Winfrid, was renamed by Gregory II (715-731) who consecrated him bishop in 722, after having authorized him to preach to his Saxon cousins east of the Rhine. Having converted and organized the German tribes, he died a martyr at the hands of pagan savages in 755. He is revered as the Apostle of Germany. cf. 21.49n.

31. **lumen praedicaverit.** cf. *Acta Sanctorum*, May vol. 6, p. 711: *vice candelae; fulgere concessit ut candela; candela Ecclesiae quam illuxit Spiritus Sanctus.*

Lanfrancus. cf. 19.11n.

32. **concilium Aquisgranense** in 835. During the ninth century many councils were held in this important Carolingian capital.

minime appellare liceret, Venerabilis titulo efferebant; qui deinde veluti proprius secutis etiam temporibus semper habitus est. Eius autem doctrinae eo vis efficacior erat, quod vitae sanctimonia
40 religiosisque virtutibus confirmabatur. Quam ob rem discipulos, quos multos et egregios imbuendos habuit, studio et exemplo non litteris modo atque scientiis sed etiam sanctitate fecit insignes.

Aetate demum et laboribus fractus, gravi morbo
45 correptus est. Quo cum amplius quinquaginta dies detentus esset, consuetum orandi morem Scripturasque interpretandi non intercepit; eo namque tempore Evangelium Ioannis in popularium suorum

    36. **minime ... liceret**, i.e., since he was still alive.

          Venerabilis. This term, not seldom used when referring to distinguished religious, seems to have become peculiar to Bede within two generations after his death. The title is used by Alcuin; and the Council of Aachen in 835 described the saint as *venerabilis et modernis temporibus doctor admirabilis Beda*. The title is one which has always clung to him, even after his canonization in 1899, when the Venerable Bede became St. Bede the Venerable. A striking testimony to the extent of his reputation is the fact that he is the only Englishman named by Dante in the *Divina Commedia*. (*Par.* 10,131, where Bede is mentioned in company with Albert the Great, Aquinas, Isidore of Seville, *et al.*)

    37. **qui ... habitus est**, 'and this he was considered ...'

    41. **discipulos ... insignes ...** 'the many excellent pupils he had under instruction, he made outstanding by his zeal and example, not only in literature and other subjects, but also in holiness.

    45. **amplius quinquaginta...** *quam* is usually omitted after *amplius* before numbers; 'for more *than* fifty days'.

usum Anglice vertit. Cum autem in Ascensionis
praeludio instare sibi mortem persentiret, supremis
Ecclesiae sacramentis muniri voluit. Tum sodales
amplexatus atque humi super cilicio stratus, cum
illa verba ingeminaret, *Gloria Patri et Filio et
Spiritui Sancto,* obdormivit in Domino. Eius corpus,
suavissimum, uti fertur, spirans odorem, sepultum
est in monasterio Girvensi, ac postea Dunclinum
cum sancti Cuthberti reliquiis translatum. Eum
tamquam Doctorem a Benedictinis aliisque religio-
sis familiis ac dioecesibus cultum, Leo decimus
tertius ex sacrorum Rituum Congregationis consulto
universalis Ecclesiae Doctorem declaravit, et festo

54. **obdormivit...** One of Bede's own disciples wrote a moving account of Bede's last sickness and death, which reveals the love felt for the saint by the members of his community. cf. *Acta Sanctorum,* p. 713.

57. **Cuthberti.** The tomb of the revered prior, later bishop, of the monastery at Lindisfarne (founded 635 by St. Aidan), was famous for extraordinary miracles. At the end of the tenth century, his incorrupt remains were interred in a new shrine at Durham, and a century later were transferred to the present cathedral. A biography of St. Cuthbert (c. 635-687) was written by Bede.

59. **dioecesibus cultum.** The cult of St. Bede had been maintained at York and elsewhere in northern England through the Middle Ages.

61. **Ecclesiae Doctorem.** Cardinal Wiseman and the English bishops had in 1859 petitioned the Holy See to declare Bede a Doctor of the Church, and had specially referred to the words of the Council of Aachen. The title was bestowed in 1899 by Leo XIII.

ipsius die Missam et Officium de Doctoribus ab omnibus recitari decrevit.

Oratio

Deus, qui Ecclesiam tuam beati Bedae Con-
65 fessoris tui atque Doctoris eruditione clarificas, concede propitius famulis tuis, eius semper illustrari sapientia et meritis adiuvari. Per Dominum nostrum.

34. ST. AUGUSTINE OF CANTERBURY

May 28   † 604?

Augustinus, Romae in Lateranensi coenobio monachus, a Gregorio Magno cum sociis monachis fere quadraginta in Angliam missus est anno quingentesimo nonagesimo septimo, ut gentes illas ad
5 Christum converteret. Erat eo tempore rex Ethel-

    1. **in Lateranensi coenobio**. No details are known about Augustine's life before his mission to the Anglo-Saxon people of England, except the fact that he was a monk and later Prior in the monastery of St. Andrew in Rome. cf. 9.4. Pope St. Gregory had himself long entertained the desire to evangelize the English, and five years after his election he turned to the monastery he had founded and governed for many years, for the missionary band to accomplish his purpose. The figure of Gregory is from the start as important as Augustine's in the Christianizing of the Anglo-Saxons. The main sources for the history of the mission are St. Bede's *Ecclesiastical History* (1, 23-34; 2,2-3), and the letters of Gregory the Great with whom Augustine maintained an extensive correspondence.
    5. **Ethelbertus** (522-616) inherited the Kingdom of Kent in 560 and in twenty years was overlord of Britain almost as far north as York. His political importance was enhanced by his marriage to the daughter of the Frankish king of Paris. Ethelbert allowed his Christian wife to retain her own chaplain, Bishop Luidhard, and put at her disposal an old Roman church dedicated to St. Martin in Canterbury, his capital. But neither the king's tolerance nor his wife's example nor her chaplain's presence

bertus, in Cantio potentissimus, qui audita adventus
Augustini causa eum cum sociis Cantuariam, sui
regni metropolim, invitavit, ibique manendi et
Christum praedicandi facultatem eidem liberaliter
10 concessit. Quare sanctus vir prope Cantuariam oratorium exstruxit, ubi ipse aliquamdiu consedit atque
apostolicam vivendi rationem cum suis aemulatus est.
　Caelestis doctrinae praedicatione plurimis fir-
15 mata miraculis ac vitae exemplo, sic insulanos illos
demulsit, ut eorum plerosque ad christianam fidem
perduxerit ac demum regem ipsum, quem cum innumero suorum comitatu sacro fonte lustravit, summa cum laetitia Berthae, regiae uxoris, quae
20 christiana erat. Olim in Natali Domini, cum decem

nor the Celtic bishops to the west succeeded in converting the
pagan Anglo-Saxons. That would have to wait upon Gregory's
Italian monks.
　6. **audita adventus ... causa.** Ethelbert first ordered the
party to wait on the off-shore island of Thanet, then came himself the twelve miles from Canterbury to greet Augustine and
offer him the hospitality of the kingdom. It was the spring of
597 and marked the end of the long journey which had begun
in June of the previous year.
　12. **apostolicam ... rationem.** The monks established the
observance of the Benedictine rule and then quietly began to
preach.
　17. **regem ipsum.** The king was impressed by Augustine's
unworldly character and doctrine, and after a period of instruction was baptized on Pentecost, a few months after Augustine's
arrival. The speed of his conversion and his subjects' indicated
that the past remissness was being swiftly corrected and atoned
for.

millibus et amplius baptismum in alvea fluminis Eboraci contulisset, quotquot ex iis morbo aliquo affecti erant, cum animae salute, corporis quoque sanitatem recepisse memoriae proditum est. Iussu
25 Gregorii ordinatus episcopus, sedem Cantuariae instituit in ecclesia Salvatoris a se erecta, in qua monachos operis sui subsidiarios collocavit; et sancti Petri monasterium, quod postea et a suo nomine dictum est, in suburbanis construxit. Idem Gregorius
30 usum pallii cum facultate ecclesiasticae hierarchiae

21. **fluminis Eboraci.** The ceremony probably took place not far from the mouth of the Medway River near Canterbury.

25. **ordinatus episcopus.** Soon after Ethelbert's conversion, Augustine returned to France and sought episcopal consecration from the bishop of Arles, south of Avignon, and immediately thereafter returned to Kent. Following the king's conversion, more than ten thousand of his subjects were baptized the following Christmas, but Ethelbert's policy was to compel no one to embrace Christianity. For his service to the Church he is revered as a saint in several English dioceses; his name is listed in the Roman Martyrology; and until the time of Henry VIII a light was kept burning before his tomb in the church of St. Peter (cf. *Acta Sanctorum*, May vol. 6, p. 435-437.)

26. **in ecclesia Salvatoris a se erecta.** Augustine rebuilt and consecrated a church that had originally been built by early Roman Christians (cf. 1.9). This church continued in existence as the Cathedral until it was destroyed by fire in 1067. Work on the new (now Anglican) Cathedral was begun by Lanfranc (cf. 19.11n.) in 1070.

30. **usum pallii.** Augustine received the pallium in 601, on the return from Rome of two associates who had been sent to tell the Pope of the success of the mission and to ask for new missionaries. Augustine was also given authority over all the bishops of Britain.

SCENES FROM THE LIFE OF ST. AUGUSTINE.
Miniature from the Breviary of the Duke of
Bedford (1424). Bibliothèque Nationale Paris

in Anglia instituendae ei concessit; quo novam etiam operariorum manum misit, nempe Mellitum, Iustum, Paulinum et Rufinianum.

Dispositis eius ecclesiae rebus, synodum habuit
35 Augustinus cum episcopis atque doctoribus veterum

32. **Mellitum**. St. Mellitus in 604 was consecrated bishop of London, thereby restoring the hierarchy to the old Roman-Briton see which had been wiped out by the invasions of the Saxons during the fifth century. Mellitus succeeded in converting the king of the East Saxons.

Iustum. St. Justus was consecrated first bishop of the new see of Rochester in 604. The Cathedral there was founded by Ethelbert and dedicated to St. Andrew, from whose monastery in Rome both Augustine and Justus had come.

33. **Paulinum**. Another Roman monk from St. Andrew's, St. Paulinus labored in Kent until 625 when he was consecrated by St. Justus, then the fourth Archbishop of Canterbury, and sent with the sister of the king of Kent who was marrying the king of Northumbria. Paulinus converted King (and later St.) Edwin in 627 and established his see at York.

34. **synodum ... cum episcopis ... veterum Britonum**. Augustine met, at an unknown date, with the Celtic Bishops of south-eastern Britain in an attempt to secure uniformity in church practice and cooperation in the conversion of the Anglo-Saxons. The origins of the Celtic rite of these bishops are very obscure because of the lack of ancient testimony, but the rite differed from the Roman rite in the manner of calculating the date of Easter, the form of the tonsure, and an unspecified difference in the administration of Baptism. The existence of the different rite is not surprising as there were several rites in Europe and at this very time the Irish St. Columbanus (543-615) was establishing in France, Germany and even Italy monasteries following the Celtic rite. Augustine's first conference, held at Malmesbury near the Severn in western England, failed as the Celtic bishops refused to yield. A second meeting, attended by

Britonum qui in Paschae celebratione aliisque ritibus ab Ecclesia Romana iamdudum dissidebant. Sed cum eos neque apostolicae Sedis auctoritate neque miraculis movere posset ut discidio cessarent,
40 prophetico spiritu eis excidium praenuntiavit. Denique maximis pro Christo exantlatis laboribus, miraculis clarum, cum Mellitum Londinensi ecclesiae praefecisset, Iustum Roffensi, suae Laurentium, in caelum migravit septimo Kalendas Iunias Ethelber-

only seven of the bishops who came with their 'most learned' men, headed by the abbot of the monastery of Bangor, likewise failed, as Augustine's lack of tact further alienated the bishops.

39. **neque miraculis**... Augustine succeeded, where the Celtic bishops had failed, in restoring sight to a blind man. cf. *Acta Sanctorum,* May vol. 6, p. 385; Bede, *H.E.* 2,2.

40. **excidium praenuntiavit.** Because the bishops refused to cooperate with him in the conversion of their conquerors, Augustine declared," If you will not have peace with the brethren, you shall have war from your enemies, and if you will not preach the Way of Life to the English, you shall suffer the punishment of death at their hands." Some ten years later the monks of Bangor were put to death by Ethelfrid of Northumbria, who defeated the Britons at Chester in 613, thus fulfilling, in the minds of the people, the prophecy of Augustine. cf. *Acta Sanctorum,* p. 386.

43. **Laurentium.** One of the original band of missionaries, St. Lawrence had been sent to Rome with the news of the conversion of Ethelbert (cf. 30n.) and had returned with the pallium and more workers for Augustine. In 604 Augustine consecrated him to be his successor. Lawrence died in 619 after having suffered through a temporary pagan reaction following Ethelbert's death in 616.

44. **septimo Kalendas Iunias**=May 26, the date Augustine's feast is observed in England. The year is not given by

45 to regnante ac sepultus est in monasterio sancti Petri, quod exinde Cantuariensium antistitum et aliquot regum conditorium fuit. Eius cultum ferventi studio prosecutae sunt Anglorum gentes ac Leo decimus tertius Pontifex maximus eius Officium et Missam
50 ad universam extendit Ecclesiam.

Oratio

Deus, qui Anglorum gentes praedicatione et miraculis beati Augustini Confessoris tui atque Pontificis, verae fidei luce illustrare dignatus es, concede ut ipso interveniente errantium corda ad veritatis
55 tuae redeant unitatem, et nos in tua simus voluntate concordes. Per Dominum nostrum.

St. Bede, but an ancient tradition says he died the same year as Gregory the Great. (cf. *H.E.* 2,3; *P.L.* 95,85c)

35. THE QUEENSHIP OF MARY

May 31

Cur beatissimam Virginem Mariam Reginae nomine, Damascenum, Athanasium aliosque secuti, non compellemus, cuius et pater, David rex inclutus, et filius, Rex regum Dominusque dominantium sine
5 fine imperans, laudem in Scripturis praestantissimam tenent? Regina est insuper si cum illis conferatur quibus veluti regibus caeleste regnum cum Christo Rege summo contigit, utpote illius coheredibus et in eodem veluti throno, ut Scriptura loquitur, cum
10 illo collocatis. Regina est etiam nulli electorum

The text is from St. Peter Canisius' *De Maria Virgine Incomparabili et Dei Genetrice Sacrosancta*, bk. 5, ch. 13. It will be found in the *Summa Aurea de Laudibus Beatissimae Virginae Mariae* (Migne 1862), vol. 9, 150; 407.

1. **Cur ... non compellemus**, 'Why do we not address...?' The subjunctive is deliberative.

3. **et pater ... et filius**; subjects of **tenent**. Mary, like Joseph, was descended from King David. cf. *Lk*. 1,32; *Rom*. 1,3; 2 *Tim*. 2,8. (The genealogies of Jesus, *Mt*. 1,1-17; *Lk*. 3, 23-31, are traced through Joseph as Christ's legal father, since descent on the female side was irrelevant in law.)

8. **illius coheredibus**; cf. *Rom*. 8,17

9. **in eodem veluti throno**; cf. *Apoc*. 3,22; *Mt*. 19,28; 1 *Cor*. 6,2-4.

10. **Regina est ...**, 'As Queen, she is....'

secunda, sed simul angelis et hominibus tanto praelata dignius, quo nihil illa sublimius ac sanctius esse potest, quae sola cum Deo Patre Filium habet communem, et quae supra se Deum et Christum tantum,
15 infra se vero reliqua videt omnia.

Magnus Athanasius perspicue dixit: "Mariam non modo Deiparam sed etiam Reginam et Dominam proprie vereque censeri, quandoquidem Christus, ex ipsa matre Virgine natus, Deus et Dominus idem-
20 que Rex maneat." De hac igitur Regina dictum illud Psalmographi interpretatur: *Astitit Regina a dextris tuis in vestitu deaurato*. Non ergo solum caeli sed et caelorum Regina recte dicitur Maria, utpote mater Regis angelorum, Regisque caelorum et amica
25 et sponsa. A te vero, augustissima Regina eademque fidissima Mater Maria, quam sine fructu pie nullus implorat et cui mortales omnes beneficiorum memoria sempiterna devincti sunt, etiam atque etiam re-

11. tanto ... quo; ablatives of degree of difference; quo= ut eo, a result clause; '... but has been raised so far above both angels and men together, that nothing can be more exalted or holy than she'.

13. **Filium habet communem**, 'has a common Son', or has the Son in common'.

16. **Athanasius**; Serm. in Annuntiationem Deiparae, 13 *P.G.* 28, 935, 938; opera spuria)

19. **idemque Rex**, 'and likewise King ...'; so also **eademque**, line 25.

21. Psalmographi; ψαλμος , psalm; γραφω , to write; cf. *Ps.* 44,10.

22. **caeli sed et caelorum Regina**. The distinction between the singular and the plural is vague. But see *Eccl.* 16,18; 3 *Kg.* 8,27; Aug., *Conf.*, 12,2.

THE CORONATION OF THE VIRGIN. Painting by Diego Velázquez (1590-1660). **Prado Museum, Madrid**

verenter oro et obsecro, ut hoc qualecumque
observantiae erga te meae testimonium ratum et
gratum habere velis, utque oblati muneris exiguitatem studiosa offerentis voluntate metiri ac tuo
praepotenti Filio comprobare digneris.

Oratio

Concede nobis, quaesumus, Domine, ut qui
solemnitatem beatae Mariae Virginis Reginae nostrae celebramus, eius muniti praesidio, pacem in
praesenti et gloriam in futuro consequi mereamur.
Per Dominum nostrum.

29. hoc qualecumque ... testimonium, 'this evidence, whatever it is worth'. Lines 22-30 will be found at the conclusion of the book, and so by *hoc* Canisius means his entire five-volume work.

30. ratum ... velis, 'that you consent to consider (this evidence) accepted and pleasing'. (= to accept and be pleased with.)

MAPS

11. *Latin Book*

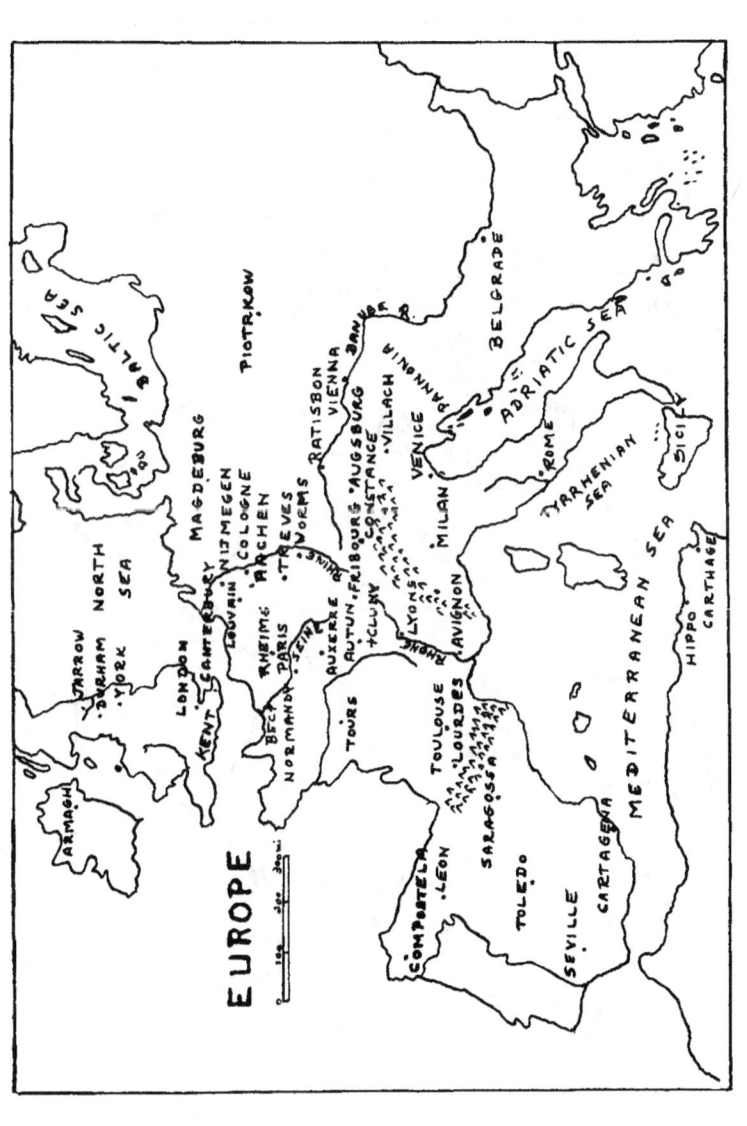

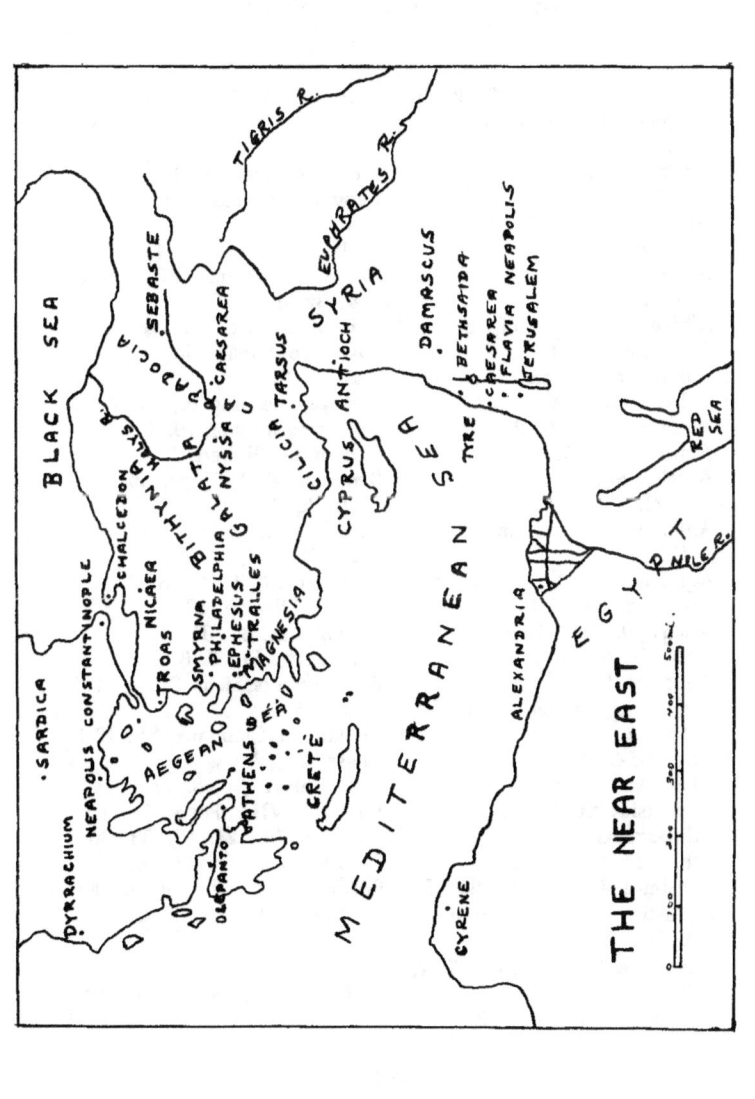

INDEX TO THE NOTES

Aachen, council of, 33. 36, 61
Acephali, 14. 52; 16. 32
Adamites, 15. 34
Adrian I, Pope, 14. 48
Agatha, St., 3
Agnoetae, 9. 30. see also Monophysites
Albert the Great, St., 8. 30; 33. 36
Albigensians, sect of, 8. 12
Alcuin, 33. 4, 36
Alexander II, Pope, 6. 57, 60; 19. 8; 31. 24
Alexandria, 4. 19; 20. 12; 24
Ambrose, St., 25. 8; 29. 9
Anselm, St., 19
Antioch, 1. 1
Antoninus Pius, Emperor, 18. 17, 19
Aquileia, 17. 3
Arab civilization, 14. 10
Arians, 9. 31; 11. 23; 16. 9; 24. 5; 27. 14
Arius, 24. 5
Armenians, union with the, 15. 27
Artemis, 4. 35
Assisi, 15. 8
Athanasius, St., 24
Athenagoras, 18. 17
Attila, 17. 2
Augsburg Confession, 21. 35
Augustine, St., of Canterbury, 9. 30; 34
Augustine, St., of Hippo, 7. 1; 25
Augustus, Emperor, 7. 2; 19. 1

Avignon, 17. 34; 23. 39

Baius, Michael, 29. 9
Bangor, monastery of, 34. 34, 40
Bari, council of, 19. 47
Baronius, Cardinal, 27. 27; 31. 4; 32. 16
Bartholomew, St., 28. 3
Basil the Great, St., 11. 40; 27. 3, 37
Basilica, meaning of, 5. 77
Bec, monastery of, 19. 8
Bellarmine, Robert, St., 29
Benedict XIII, Pope, 22 27; 30. 38; 31. 69
Benedict XIV, Pope, 17. 42; 22. 36
Benedict, St., 9. 4; 13; 27. 6
Benedict Biscop, 33. 2
Berengarius, 31. 31
Bernadette, St., 5. 6
Bernardine of Siena, St., 15. 11, 18, 35
Bernard of Clairvaux, St., 12.1
Blaise, St., 2
Bonaventure, St., 8. 49
Boniface VIII, Pope, 5. 81
Boniface, St., 21. 49; 33. 30
Brothers, Christ's, 28. 36
Brothers of the Christian Schools, 30. 34, 45

Cadalous, anti-pope, 6. 57; 31. 32

Caesaro-papism, 14. 42
Callistus III, Pope, 15. 38
Camaldolese, Order of, 6. 29; 9. 4
Canons, Chapters of, 6. 40; cf. 30. 9, 40
Canterbury, 19. 11, 27; 34. 5
Cardinal, meaning of, 9. 8; 26. 19
Cartagena, 16. 1
Carthage, 7. 2; 16. 1
Cassino, see Monte Cassino
Castile, 16. 63
Catacombs, 17. 31; 32. 20
Catechisms, 11. 10; 21. 44; 29. 18
Catherine Labouré, St. 5. 1
Catherine of Siena, St., 23
Catholic Epistles, the, 28. 50
Celestine I, St., Pope, 4. 27; 10. 16; 17. 1
Celtic Rite, 34. 34
Centuriators of Magdeburg, 21. 43
Chalcedon, Council of, 17. 23
Chant, Gregorian, 9. 50
Charlemagne, 33. 4
Charles Borromeo, St., 26. 26
Charles of Anjou, 15. 4
Claudius, Emperor, 13. 3
Clement IV, Pope, 8. 55
Clement V, Pope, 23. 39
Clement VII (Avignon), 23. 45
Clement VIII, Pope, 29. 8, 20; 32. 30
Clement XI, Pope, 26. 49
Clement XIV, Pope, 22. 36
Clement of Alexandria, 20. 5
Cluny, monastery of, 31. 11, 14

Cologne, 21. 7
Compostella, 16. 43
Constance, Council of, 15. 22, 33
Constans, Emperor, 24. 29, 38
Constantine, Emperor, 17. 34; 24. 8, 27
Constantine V, Emperor, 14. 39
Constantinople, Council of, 11. 59; 27. 14
Constantius, Emperor, 11. 23, 29. 32; 25; 24. 29, 38
Cornelius, Pope, 4. 18; 17. 31
Crescens, Cynic philosopher, 18. 25
Crusades, the, 12. 1; 15. 38; 19. 44
cuius regio, eius religio, 21. 32
Cuthbert, St., 33. 57
Cyril of Alexandria, St., 4; 20. 12
Cyril of Jerusalem, St., 11
Damascus, 14. 10
Dante, 33. 36
Daphne, 1. 42
Decius, Emperor, 3. 3
Diocletian, Emperor, 2.3; 9. 31
Discipline, the, 6. 73
Discipline of the Secret, 11. 17
Dominic St., 8. 12; Third Order of, 23. 2
Donatists, 9. 31
Durham, 33. 57

Egbert, Archbishop of York, 33. 4
Ephesus, Council of, 4. 35
Ethelbert, King of Kent, 34. 5, 25

Eucharist, doctrine of, 11. 17; 18. 40; 31. 32
Eugenius III, Pope, 12. 1
Eusebius, Arian Bishop, 24. 4, 29
Eutyches, monophysite, 17. 21
Eutychians, 17. 21

Fabian, Pope, 4. 18
Felicitas, St., 7
Ferdinand I of Castile, 16. 63
Filioque Controversy, 19. 47
Florence, Council of, 8. 59; 15. 26
Fossa Nuova, monastery of, 8. 61, 67
Francis Borgia, St., 29. 8, 15
Francis of Assisi, St., 15. 8; 23. 28
Francis Xavier, St., 32. 49
Fraticelli, 15. 22
Frederick II, Emperor, 8. 2, 11, 15
Frederick III, Emperor, 15. 23
Free-will and grace, controversy over, 29. 8, 20

Genseric, 17. 17
Germain of Auxerre, 10. 13
Gonzaga, Aloysius, St., 29. 17
Gospel of the Nazarenes, 1. 11
Grace and free will, controversy over, 29. 8, 20
Gregory the Great, St., Pope, 9; 13. 1; 27. 2; 34. 1, 44
Gregory II, Pope, 33. 30
Gregory III, Pope, 14. 5
Gregory VI, Pope, 31. 25

Gregory VII, Pope, 6. 46; 19. 30; 31
Gregory X, Pope, 8. 59
Gregory XI, Pope, 23. 38. 39
Gregory XIII, Pope, 21. 20; 29. 15; 31. 69;
Gregory XIV, Pope, 32. 30
Gregory XV, Pope, 12. 1; 32. 49
Gregory of Nazianzus, St., 27
Gregory of Nyssa, St., 11. 40
Guiscard, Robert, 31. 59

Hadrian, Emperor, 18. 19
Henry IV, Emperor, 6. 58; 31. 46
Herluin, abbot of Bec, 19. 8
Hexham, monastery of, 33. 12
Hildebrand. See Gregory VII
Holy Name of Jesus, 15. 11
Holy Spirit, procession of, 19. 47, 48
Honorius III, Pope, 15. 8
Honorius IV, Pope, 23. 2
Huns, the, 17. 2
Hussites, 15. 33

Iconoclasm, 14
Ignatius of Antioch, St., 1; 18. 28
Ignatius of Loyola, St., 21. 3
Immaculate Conception, dogma of, 5. 1
Innocent IV, Pope, 8. 27
Innocent XIII, Pope, 16. 63
Interdict, 23. 33
Isidore of Seville, St., 16; 33. 36
Islamism, 14. 10

James the Greater, St., Apostle, 16. 44
James the Less, St., Apostle, 28
Jarrow, monastery of, 33. 1, 2
Jerome, St., 1. 1; 20. 1; 28. 20
Jerusalem, Council of, 28. 29
John XXII, Pope, 8. 66; 15. 22
John XXIII, Pope, 26. 19
John Baptist de la Salle, St., 30
John Chrysostom, St., 27. 12, 37
John Damascene, St., 14
John of Capistrano, St., 15
Joseph, St., 12
Jovian, Emperor, 11. 29; 24. 53
Jubilee, 5. 81
Julian the Apostate, Emperor, 4. 7; 11. 29; 53; 24. 44, 53; 27. 4
Julius I, Pope, 24. 29
Justin Martyr, St., 18
Justin II, Emperor, 9. 3
Justinian, Emperor, 6. 1; 13. 31

Lanfranc, 19. 11, 23; 33. 31; 34. 26
Laura, meaning of, 14. 23
Lay investiture, 6. 54; 19. 38, 51; 31. 13, 46
Leander, St., 9. 19; 16. 3
Leo the Great, Pope 10. 26; 17
Leo IV, Pope, 16. 49
Leo IX, Pope, 31. 24
Leo XII, Pope, 6. 87
Leo XIII, Pope, 4. 49; 8. 72; 11. 64; 33. 61

Leo III, Emperor, 14. 4
Leo IV, Emperor, 14. 48
Lepanto, battle of, 22. 13; 26. 34
Lérins, monastery of, 10. 13
Lindisfarne, monastery of, 33. 57
Lombards, the, 9. 3, 8; 13. 25; 31. 62
London, diocese of, 34. 32
Lourdes, 5
Luther, 21. 2
Lyons, Second Council of, 8. 59; 15. 26

Manichaeans, 25. 6
Marcus Aurelius, Emperor, 18. 19
Mark, St., Evangelist, 20
Martin V, Pope, 15. 22; 23. 45
Martin of Tours, St., 10. 2; 13. 19
Maurice, Emperor, 9. 21, 40
Melanchthon, 21. 35
Messiah, meaning of, 28. 4
Milan, 25. 7
Mohammed, 14. 10
Monica, St., 25
Monophysites, 9. 31; 14. 52; 17.21
Monothelites, 14. 52
Monte Cassino, monastery of, 6. 73; 8. 9; 13. 19

Naples, Kingdom of, 15. 4
Nathanael, 28. 3
Nero, Emperor, 28. 48
Nestorians, 4. 23; 17. 21
Nestorius, 4. 18, 23, 28

Newman, Cardinal, 22. 52; 24. 54; 32. 16
Nicaea, Council of, 11. 23; 24. 4, 54; 27. 14
Nicaea, Second Council of, 14. 48
Nicholas II, Pope, 6. 57; 31. 25
Nicholas V, Pope, 15. 23
Nijmegen, 21. 1
Normans, the, 15. 4; 31. 59
Novatian 4. 18
numen, 31. 9

Oratory, Congregation of the, 32. 16
Origen, 20. 12; 27. 6
Ostia, 6. 48
Otsrogoths, the, 9. 3; 13. 27
Ottoman Turks. see Turks

Padre Pio, 23. 28
Pallium, the, 9. 32; 34. 30
Pannonia, 17. 14
Papal States, the, 8. 15; 15. 4; 31. 4
Papias, 20. 5
Passionists, 22. 36
Patrick, St., 10
Paul III, Pope, 21. 16
Paul IV, Pope, 26. 16
Paul V, Pope, 29. 23; 32. 16
Paul of the Cross, St., 22
Peace of Augsburg, 21. 33
Pelagius II, Pope, 9. 8
Perpetua, St., 7; 18. 28
Peter, St., Apostle, 20. 1, 2, 7; 28. 1
Peter Canisius, St., 21; 35. 1

Peter Damian, St., 6
Peter Lombard, 14. 64; 19. 26
Philip, St., Apostle, 28
Philip Neri, St., 32
Philo, 20. 16
Pius I, Pope, 18. 46
Pius II, Pope, 23. 50
Pius IV, Pope, 21. 16, 26. 20
Pius V, St., Pope, 8. 72; 21. 43 24. 54; 26
Pius VI, Pope, 22. 36
Pius VII, Pope, 5. 1
Pius IX, Pope, 5. 1; 12. 1; 21. 73; 22. 55
Pius XI, Pope, 29. 30
Pius XII, Pope, 30. 50
Pliny the Younger, 1. 3
Polycarp, St., 1. 5; 18. 28; 20. 6
Pomposa, monastery of, 6. 30
Popes, election of, 6. 57; 9. 20; 31. 28
Priesthood, treatises on, 27. 12
Pudens, 18, 46

Ravenna, 6. 1
Reccared, King of the Visigoths, 9. 31; 16. 9, 14
Robert Bellarmine, St., 29
Rochester, Diocese of, 34. 32
Romuald, St., 6. 29

sacramentum, 12. 19
Saracens, 16. 58
Sardica, Council of, 24. 29
Schism, Great Western, 15. 18; 23. 45
Scholasticism, 8. 30; 14. 64; 19. 26, 58

Index to the Notes

Scythia, 28. 11
Septimius Severus, Emperor, 7. 1
Sergius, Pope, 33. 24
Seven Church Walk, 32. 8
Sicilies, Kingdom of the Two, 15. 4
Siena, 23. 1
Simony, 6. 55; 31. 13, 31, 38
Sixtus V, Pope, 26. 19; 29. 9
Society of Jesus, 21. 3
Sorbonne, the, 30. 13
Station Church, 9. 49
Stephen IX, Pope, 6. 46, 57; 31. 20
Stigmata, 23. 28
Sulpician Seminary, 30. 13

Taborites, 15. 34
Tatian, 18. 17; 46
Tertullian,, 7. 1; 10. 24
Theodoric, Emperor, 6. 1
Theodosius the Great, Emperor, 11. 34; 27. 14
Theopaschites, 14. 53
Thomas Aquinas, St., 8; 14. 64; 19. 26; 33. 36
Tiberius Constantine, Emperor, 9. 10
Titus, Emperor, 11. 53
Toledo, Councils of, 9. 26; 16
Totila, 9. 3; 13. 31
Trajan, Emperor, 1. 3; 7. 1
Trent, Council of, 14. 48; 21. 16; 26. 26; 29. 18, 21

Turks, 15. 29, 43; 22. 11; 26. 29

Urban II, Pope, 19. 45
Urban IV, Pope, 8. 51
Urban V, Pope, 8. 67
Urban VI, Pope, 23. 45

Valens, Emperor, 11. 32; 24. 54
Valentinian I, Emperor, 11. 32
Valentinian II, Emperor, 17. 34
Valentinian III, Emperor, 17. 6
Vandals, the, 10. 4; 16. 9; 17. 17
Venice, 15. 54; 17. 3; 20. 23
Vespasian, Emperor, 18. 1
Victor II, Pope, 31. 28
Visigoths, the, 9. 31; 16. 9, 58; 17. 2; 14. 10
Vulgate, the Clementine, 29. 18

Wearmouth, monastery of, 33. 2
Wilfrid of York, St., 33. 12, 24
William Rufus, King of England, 19. 29, 41
William the Conqueror, 19. 11, 36

York, diocese of, 34. 33

VOCABULARY OF PROPER NAMES AND PLACES

Acca - ae m, Acca
Acephali - orum m, Acephalites, members of a Monophysite sect.
Adamiti - orum m, Adamites
Aegyptum - i n, Egypt
Africa - ae f, Africa
Agnoitae - arum m, Agnoetae
Agricolaus - i m, Agricolaus
Albertus - i m, Albert
Alexander - dri m, Alexander
Alexandria - ae f, Alexandria in Egypt; also, Alessandria in N. Italy: **Alexandrinus** - a - um, of Alexandria
Aloisius - i m, Aloysius
Ambrosius - i m, Ambrose
America - ae f, America
Andreas - ae m, Andrew
Anglia - ae f, England: **Angli** - orum, the English
Anselmus - i m, Anselm
Antiochia - ae f, Antioch in Syria: **Antiochensis** - e, and **Antiochenus** - a - um, of Antioch.
Antoninus (- i) Pius (- i) m, Antoninus Pius
Aphrodisia - ae f, Aphrodisia
Apollo - inis m, Apollo
Aquilanus - a - um, of Aquila in Italy
Aquileia - ae f, Aquileia in N. Italy
Aquinas - atis, of Aquino in Italy

Aquisgranensis - e, of Aix-la-Chapelle or Aachen in Germany
Armachanus - a - um, of Armagh in Ireland
Armenia - ae f, Armenia: **Armeni** - orum m, the people of Armenia
Arius - i m, Arius: **Arianus** - a - um, Arian: **Ariani** - orum m, Arians
Arsenius - i m, Arsenius
Assisiensis - e, of Assisi in Italy
Athanasius - i m, Athanasius
Athenae - arum f, Athens in Greece
Attila - ae m, Attila
Augustanus - a - um, of Augsburg in Germany
Augusta (- ae) Praetoria (- ae), Aosta in NE Italy
Augustus (mensis), the month of August
Augustodunensis - e, of Autun in France
Avellanensis - e, of Avellano in Italy: **Avellanitae** - arum m, Avellanites
Avenio - onis f, Avignon in France

Barensis - e, of Bari in S. Italy
Basilius - i m, Basil
Beccensis - e, of Bec in Normandy

252

Vocabulary 253

Beda - ae m, Bede
Belgium - i n, Belgium
Bellarmini - orum m, the Bellarmine family
Benedictus - i m, Benedict; B. Biscopius, B. Biscop
Benedictini - orum m, members of the Order of St. Benedict
Berengarius - i m, Berengarius
Bernardinus - i m, Bernardine
Bertha - ae f, Bertha
Bethsaida - ae f, Bethsaida in Palestine
Blasius - i m, Blaise
Bonifatius - i m, Boniface
Bononia - ae f, Bologna in Italy
Boschum - i n, Bosco near Alessandria in N. Italy
Braulio - onis m, Braulio
Britannia - ae f, Britain; **Brito** - onis m, a Britain

Cadalous - i m, Cadalous
Caelestinus - i m, Celestine
Caesaraugustanus - a - um, of Saragossa in Spain
Callistus - i m, Callistus
Calphurnius - i m, Calpurnius
Camaldulenses - ium m, members of the Camaldolese Order.
Cantium - i n, Kent in SE England
Cantuaria - ae f, Canterbury in SE England; **Cantuariensis** - e, of Canterbury
Cappadocia - ae f, Cappadocia in Asia Minor; **Cappadox** - ocis m, a Cappadocian

Capua - ae f, Capua in Italy; **Capuanus** - a - um, of Capua
Carthaginiensis - e, of Cartagena in Spain
Carolus - i m, Charles
Cassinates - um m, the monks of Monte Cassino
Cassinum - i n, Cassino in Italy
Castella - ae f, Castile in Spain
Castellatium - i n, Castellazzo near Alessandria in N. Italy
Catana - ae f, Catania in Sicily; **Catanenses** - ium, the people of Catania
Catharina - ae f, Catherine
Centuriatores - um m, Centuriators
Chalcedonensis - e, of Chalcedon in Asia Minor
Cilicia - ae f, Cilicia in Asia Minor
Cistercienses - ium m, members of the Cistercian Order
Clemens - entis m, Clement
Cluniacensis - e, and **Cluniacus** - a - um, of Cluny, a monastery in France
Colonia (- ae) **Agrippina** (- ae), Cologne in Germany
Conchessa - ae f, Concessa
Constans - antis m, Constans
Constantinopolis - is f, Constantinople; **Constantinopolitanus** - a - um, of Constantinople.
Constantinus - i m, Constantine; **Constantinianus** - a - um, of Constantine,

Constantinian
Constantius - i m, Constantius
Cornelius - i m, Cornelius
Cosmas - ae m, Cosmas
Crescens - entis m, Crescens; Cynicus, C. the Cynic
Cuthbertus - i m, Cuthbert
Cynthia - ae f, Cynthia; C. Cervini, of the Cervini family
Cyrillus - i m, Cyril

Damianus - i m, Damian
Damascus - i m, Damascus in the Near East; **Damascenus** - a - um, of Damascus, Damascene
Daphniticus - a - um, of Daphne
Davidicus - a - um, of David
December - bris (mensis), the month of December
Decius - i m, Decius
Demetria - ae f, Demetria
Diocletianus - i m, Diocletian
Dioscurus - i m, Dioscurus
Dominicus - i m, Dominic
Donatistae - arum, Donatists
Dunclinum - i n, Durham in England
Dunum - i n, Down, a county in Ireland

Eboracum - i n, York in England
Echinades - um f, Echinades Islands, modern Curzolari Islands, near the Gulf of Lepanto in Greece

Enetus - i m, Enet
Ephesinus - a - um, of Ephesus in Asia Minor; **Ephesii** - orum m, the people of Ephesus
Ermemberga - ae f, Hermenberga
Ethelbertus - i m, Ethelbert
Etruria - ae f, Etruria, later Tuscany, in Italy; **Etruscus** - a - um, Etruscan; Tuscan
Eugubina - ae f, Gubbio in Italy
Eulalius - i m, Eulalius
Europa - ae f, Europe
Eutyches - is m, Eutyches
Eutychius - i m, Eutychius; Eutychiani - orum m, Eutychians, followers of Eutychius

Falconius - i m, Falconius
Faventia - ae f, Faënza near Ravenna in Italy; **Faventini** - orum m, the people of Faënza
Februaris (mensis), the month of February
Felicitas - atis f, Felicitas
Ferdinandus - i m, Ferdinand
Flavia (- ae) Neapolis (- is) f, Flavia Neapolis, modern Nablus, in Palestine
Florentia - ae f, Florence in Italy; **Florentini** - orum m, the people of Florence; Florentinus - a - um, of Florence
Florentina - ae f, Florentina
Fons (Fontis) Avellana (- ae),

Vocabulary

Fonte Avellana in Italy
Fossa (- ae) Nova (-ae) f, Fossa Nuova, a monastery south of Rome
Franciscus - i m, Francis; F. Salesius, F. de Sales
Fraticelli - orum m, the Fraticelli, (lit., little brothers), a group among the Franciscans
Fratres Minores, the Friars Minor.
Fribergum - i n, Fribourg in Switzerland
Fridericus - i m, Frederick
Fulgentius - i m, Fulgentius

Galatae - arum m, the people of Galatia in Asia Minor
Gallia - ae f, France
Gavum - i n, the Gave, a river near Lourdes
Gelria - ae f, the Netherlands
Gensericus - i m, Genseric
Germania - ae f, Germany; **Germanus** - a - um, German
Ghisleri - orum m, the Ghisleri family
Girvum - i n, Jarrow, a monastery in N. England; **Girvensis** - e, of Jarrow
Gordianus - i m, Gordian
Gothi - orum m, the Goths
Graecus - a - um, Greek; **Graeci** - orum m, the Greeks
Gregorius - i m, Gregory
Gundulphus - i m, Gundulph

Hagulstadensis - e, of Hexham, an abbey in England
Hebraei - orum m, the Jews; **Hebraicus** - a - um, Hebrew
Helvetii - orum m, the people of Switzerland
Henricus - i m, Henry
Herluinus - i m, Herluin
Herodianus - a - um, of Herod
Hibernia - ae f, Ireland; **Hiberni** - orum m, the people of Ireland
Hierapolis - is f, Hierapolis in Phrygia
Hieronymus - i m, Jerome
Hierosolyma - ae f, and **Hierusalem**, indecl. n, Jerusalem; **Hierosolymi** - orum m, the people of Jerusalem; **Hierosolymitanus** - a - um, of Jerusalem
Hilario - onis m, Hilarion
Hildebrandus - i m, Hildebrand
Hispalis - is f, Seville in Spain; **Hispalensis** - e, of Seville
Hispania - ae f, Spain; **Hispanus** - a - um, Spanish
Hunni - orum m, the Huns
Hussiti - orum m, Hussites

Iacobus - i m, Jacob; James
Iconomachi - orum m, Iconoclasts
Idus - uum f, the Ides, the 15th of March, May, July, Oct., the 13th of the other months.
Ignatius - i m, Ignatius
Ildefonsus - i m, Ildephonsus
Insubria - ae f, Insubria, later Lombardy, in N. Italy

Ioannes - is m, John
Ioseph, indecl. m, Joseph
Isauricus - a - um, Isaurian, from Isauria in central Asia Minor
Isidorus - i m, Isidore
Israel, indecl. m, Israel
Italia - ae f, Italy
Iudaei - orum m, the Jews
Iulianus - i m, Julian
Iulius - i m, Julius
Iunius (mensis), the month of June
Iustinus - i m, Justin

Kalendae - arum f, the Kalends, the first day of the month

Ladislaus - i m, Ladislaus
Landulphus - i m, Landulph
Lanfrancus - i m, Lanfranc
Lateranensis - e, pertaining to the Lateran
Latinus - a - um, Latin
Leander - dri m, Leander
Legio - onis f, Leon in Spain
Leo - onis m, Leo
Liguria - ae f, Liguria in N. Italy
Lovanium - i n, Louvain in Belgium
Lucius (- i) **Aurelius** (- i) **Commodus** (- i) m, Lucius Aurelius Commodus
Ludulphus - i m, Ludulph
Lugdunum - i n, Lyons in France
Lutetia - ae f, Lutetia, the capital of the Parisii; later Paris

Lutherus - i m, Luther

Macedonius - i m, Macedonius
Magdeburgensis - e, of Magdeburg in Germany
Magnesiani - orum m, the people of Magnesia in Asia Minor
Maius (mensis), the month of May
Marcus (- i) **Antoninus** (- i) **Verus** (- i) m, Marcus Antoninus Verus
Manichaei - orum m, the Manichaeans
Marcellus - i m, Marcellus
Marcus - i m, Mark
Maria - ae f, Mary
Martinus - i m, Martin
Martius (mensis), the month of March
Matthaeus - i m, Matthew
Mauritius - i m, Mauritius; Maurice
Maximianus - i m, Maximian
Maximus - i m, Maximus
Mediolanum - i n, Milan in N. Italy; Mediolanensis - e, of Milan
Mellitus - i m, Mellitus
Mincius - i m, the Mincio, a river in N. Italy
Monica - ae f, Monica
Monothelitae - arum m, Monothelites
Mons (Montis) **Regalis** (- is), Mondovi in NE Italy
Mons (Montis) **Argaeus** (- i) m, Mount Argaeus in Asia Minor

Mons (Montis) Argentarius (- i) m, Monte Argentaro in Italy
Mosaicus - a - um, of Moses; Mosaic

Nathanael, indecl. m, Nathanael
Nazianzus - i m, Nazianzus in Cappadocia; Nazianzenus - a - um, of Nazianzus
Neapolis - is f, Naples in Italy; Neapolitanus - a - um, of Naples
Nepesinus - a - um, of Nepi in Italy
Nestorius - i m, Nestorius; Nestoriani - orum m, Nestorians; Nestorianus - a - um, of Nestorius; Nestorian
Nicaenus - a - um, of Nicaea in Asia Minor
Nicolaitae - arum m, Nicolites
Nicolaus - i m, Nicolaus
Nonae - arum f, the Nones, the ninth day before the Ides, i.e., the fifth day of every month except March, May, July, Oct., when it is the seventh.
Northmannus - i m, a Norman
Nova (- ae) Carthago (- inis) f, Cartagena in Spain
Novatus - i m, Novatus; used by some Greek authorities for Novatian.
Novati - orum m, the Reformers
November - bris (mensis), the month of November

Noviomagus - i m, Nijmegen in the Netherlands
Nursia - ae f, Norcia in Italy

Oriens - entis m, the East, the Orient
Ostia - ae f, Ostia in Italy; Ostiensis - e, of Ostia; Ostia Tiberina, Ostia on the Tiber

Padus - i m, the Po, river in Italy
Palaestina - ae f, Palestine
Pannonia - ae f, Pannonia
Panormitani - orum m, the people of Palermo in Sicily
Parisium - i n, Paris in France; Parisii - orum m, the Parisii, a Gallic people on the Seine River.
Patricius - i m, Patrick
Patavium - i n, Padua in N. Italy
Paulinus - i m, Paulinus
Paulus - i m, Paul
Pelagius - i m, Pelagius
Peligni - orum m, the Peligni, a people of central Italy
Perpetua - ae f, Perpetua
Perusium - i n, Perugia in Italy
Petra (- ae) Pertusa (- ae), Pietra Pertusa, a monastery near Ravenna
Petricoviensis - e, of Piotrkow in Poland
Petrus - i m, Peter; P. Damianus, Peter Damian; P. Canisius, P. Canisius
Philadelphii - orum, the people

of Philadelphia in Asia Minor
Philippus - i m, Philip; **P. Nerius**, P. Neri
Philo - onis m, Philo
Phrygia - ae f, Phrygia in Asia Minor
Pisae - arum f, Pisa in Italy
Pius - i m, Pius
Politianus - a - um, of Montepulciano in Italy
Polycarpus - i m, Polycarp
Pomposianus - a - um, of Pomposa, a monastery near Ravenna
Priscus - i m, Priscus
Pudens - entis m, Pudens

Quintianus - i m, Quintianus
Quirinalis - is (collis) m, the Quirinal hill in Rome

Ratisbonensis - e, of Ratisbon in Germany
Ravenna - ae f, Ravenna in Italy; **Ravennas** - atis, pertaining to Ravenna; **Ravennates** - um m, the people of Ravenna
Reccardus - i m, Reccared
Reginaldus - i m, Reginald
Revocatus - i m, Revocatus
Rhemi - orum m, Rheims, chief town of the Remi of ancient Gaul; **Rhemensis** - e, of Rheims
Robertus - i m, Robert; **R. Guiscardus**, R. Guiscard; **R. Bellarminus**, R. Bellarmine
Roffensis - e, of Rochester in England
Roma - ae f, Rome; **Romanus** - a - um, Roman, **Romani** - orum m, the Romans
Romualdus - i m, Romuald
Rufinianus - i m, Rufinian
Rusticus - i m, Rusticus

Sabas - ae m, Sabas
Salernum - i n, Salerno in Italy; **Salernitanus** - a - um, of Salerno
Saraceni - orum m, the Saracens; **Saracenus** - a - um, Saracen
Sardicensis - e, of Sardica, modern Sofia, in Bulgaria
Sasimi - orum m, the people of Sasima in Cappadocia
Saturninus - i m, Saturninus
Satyrus - i m, Satyrus
Scaurus - i m, Scaurus
Scotia - ae f, Scotland, the land of the Scots in N. Britain
Scythia -ae f, Scythia; southern Russia
Sebaste -es f, Sebaste in Armenia
Secundulus -i m, Secundulus
Selimus -i m, Selim
Senensis -e, of Siena in Italy
Sergius - i m, Sergius
Severianus - i m, Severian
Severus - i m, Severus
Sicilia -ae f, Sicily
Silvinus -i m, Silvinus
Smyrna -ae f, Smyrna in Asia Minor; **Smyrnaeus** -a -um, of Smyrna
Sorbonicus -a -um, pertaining

to the Sorbonne
Statielli -orum m, the Statielli family
Stephanus -i m, Stephen
Suana -ae f, Sovana in Italy
Subalpinus -a -um, at the foot of the Alps; Piedmont in Italy
Sublacus -i m, Subiaco in Italy
Sulpicianus -a -um, of the Sulpicians
Sutrinus -a -um, of Sutri in Italy
Syagrius -i m, Syagrius
Syria ae f, Syria

Tarbiensis -e, of Tarbes in France
Tarsus -i f, Tarsus in Cilicia
Taurunensis -e, of Taurunum opposite Belgrade
Thaboriti -orum m, Taborites, a Hussite sect
Theodora -ae f, Theodora
Theodosius -i m, Theodosius
Theopaschitae -arum m, Theopaschites
Theophilus -i m, Theophilus
Theutonicus -a -um, Teutonic (Teutonia, a province of Germany)
Theuzon -onis m, Theuzo
Thomas -ae m, Thomas
Tiberius (-i) **Constantinus** (-i) m, Tiberius Constantine
Timotheus -i m, Timothy
Titus -i m, Titus
Toletanus -a -um, of Toledo in Spain
Tolosa -ae f, Toulouse in France
Totila -ae m, Totila
Traianus -i m, Trajan
Trallenses -ium m, the people of Tralles in Asia Minor
Treviri -orum m, the people of Treves or Trier in Germany
Tridentinus -a -um, of Trent in Italy
Turca -ae m, a Turk
Turonensis -e, of Tours in France
Tyrrhenum (-i) Mare n, the Tyrrhenian Sea, west coast of Italy
Tyrus -i f, Tyre in the Near East

Ultonia -ae f, Ulster, a province in Ireland
Urbanus -i m, Urban
Urbinas -atis, of Urbino in Italy
Uvada -ae f, Ovada near Genoa in Italy
Valens - entis m, Valens
Vaticanus -a -um, pertaining to the Vatican
Veliternus -a -um, of Velletri in Italy
Venetiae -arum f, Venice in N. Italy
Victor -oris m, Victor
Villacum -i n, Villach in Austria
Vincentius -i m, Vincent
Willelmus -i m, William
Wiremuthensis -e, Wearmouth, a monastery at Durham, England

GENERAL VOCABULARY

a, ab, prep. w. abl., *from; by*
abbas - atis m, *an abbot*
abdico 1, *to renounce, reject*
abdo 3 - didi - ditum, *to conceal, hide*
abduco 3, *to take away, lead away*
abeo, *to depart, leave*
aberro 1, *to wander away, deviate from*
abhorreo 2, *to shrink back from*
abicio 3 (iacio), *to throw away, abandon*
abiectus - a - um, *wretched*
abiuratio - onis f, *a renunciation*
aboleo 2, *to destroy, abolish*
abripio 3 (rapio), *to drag off, snatch away*
abscindo 3 - scidi - scissum, *to tear off*
absolvo 3 - solvi - solutum, *to free; to complete, finish*
absens - entis, *absent*
abstergeo 2, *to wipe off*
abstinentia - ae f, *self-denial; a refraining from*
abstineo 2 - tinui - tentum, *to keep away from, hold back from*
abstuli; see aufero
absum, *to be away, be far from*
abusus - us m, *a misuse, abuse*
ac and atque, conj., *and*
academium - i n, *a school*
accedo 3, *to approach, come near*

accelero 1, *to quicken, hasten*
accendo 3 - cendi - censum, *to kindle, inflame, excite*
acceptus - a - um, *welcome, agreeable to; from*
accipio 3 (capio), *to receive, take; to hear*
accomodatus - a - um, *suitable to, adapted to; from*
accomodo 1, *to fit, make suitable*
accuso 1, *to accuse*
acer - cris - cre, *sharp, keen*
acerbus - a - um, *bitter, painful*
acetum - i n, *vinegar*
acquisitus - a - um, *acquired*
actio - onis f, *an action, doing; deeds*
acta - orum n, *a record of proceedings*
acutus - a - um, *sharp, pointed*
ad, prep. w. acc., *to, at; for the purpose of*
adaugeo 2 - auxi - auctum, *to magnify*
addico 3, *to give over, dedicate*
addo 3 - didi - ditum, *to bring to; to inspire; to add*
adduco 3, *to draw to, to bring to*
adeo, adv., *so, so much*
adeo, *to approach, come to, visit*
adhibeo 2 (habeo), *to use, employ; to bring one thing to another; to invite*; with adv., *to treat*

260

General Vocabulary

adhuc, adv., *still*
adigo 3 (ago), *to drive to, force to*
adimpleo 2, *to fulfill*
adipiscor - ipisci - eptus 3 dep., *to obtain*
adiungo 3 - iunxi - iunctum, *to join to*
adiuvo 1, *to aid, help*
administer - tri m, *an assistant*
administro 1, *to manage, direct*
admirabilis - e, *worthy of wonder, approval*
admiratio - onis f, *wonder, astonishment*
admiror 1 dep., *to marvel, wonder*
admoveo 2, *to bring to, move to, apply*
adnitor - niti - nisus or nixus 3 dep., *to strive, exert oneself*
adoro 1, *to adore, worship*
adsum, *to be present, stand by, help* (w. dat.)
adulescens - entis, *young; a young person*
adulescentia - ae f, *youth*
aduro 3, *to set fire to*
adustus - a - um, *burnt*
advenio 4, *to come, arrive*
adventus - us m, *an arrival*
adversarius - i m, *an adversary*
adversor 1 dep., *to oppose, resist*
adverto 3 - verti - versum, *to turn to;*
animum adverto (animadverto) *to turn one's attention to, observe*
adversus, prep. w. acc., *against*

advoco 1, *to summon*
advolvo 3 - volvi - volutum, *to roll to*
aedes - is f, *a building, a church;* in pl., *a house*
aedicula ae f, *a small church*
aedifico 1, *to build*
aeger - gra - grum, *sick, ill;* aegre, adv., *with vexation, with difficulty;* aegre ferre, *to be annoyed at*
aegrotus - a - um, *sick*
aemulor 1 dep., *to try to equal, emulate*
aemulus - i m, *a rival*
aequalis - is, *of the same age, contemporary*
aer aeris m, *the air*
aerumna - ae f, *hardship, hard labor, toil*
aestuo 1, *to burn, be hot*
aetas - atis f, *age, time of life*
aeternus - a - um, *eternal*
affectus - us m, *a feeling, emotion*
affero, *to bring to bear, apply*
afficio 3 (facio), *to work upon, touch, inflict upon*
affligo 3 - fixi - fixum, *to fasten to*
affirmo 1, *to assert as true*
afflatus - us m, *a breathing on; inspiration*
affligo 3 - flixi - flictum, *to knock about, mistreat*
afflo 1, *to blow on, breathe on, inspire*
affor 1 dep., *to address*
ager agri m, *field, land*
aggredior 3 dep., (gradior), *to approach; undertake; attack*

agito 1, *to vex, harry, trouble*
agnosco 3 - novi - nitum - *to recognize, acknowledge*
ago agere egi actum, *to drive, lead; to do;* (quintum) annum agere, *to be in one's (fifth) year;*
aio, (*defective*), *to say, affirm*
ala - ae f, *a wing*
alacer - cris - cre, *quick, lively*
algidus - a - um, *cold*
alibi, adv., *elsewhere*
alienus - a - um, *that which belongs to another; strange*
alimentum - i n, *food, sustenance*
aliquamdiu, adv., *for some time*
aliquando, adv., *at some, at one time, once*
aliqui aliquae aliquod, *some*
aliquis aliquid, *someone, something*
aliquot, indecl., *some, several*
alius - a - ud, *other, another*
allego 3, *to choose, select*
alloquor 3 dep., *to address, speak to*
allicio 3 - lexi - lectum, *to entice*
alo 3 alui alitum, *to nourish*
altare - aris n, *an altar*
alter - tera - terum, *another; a second*
altus - a - um, *high; deep*
alumnus - i m, *a foster-child; pupil*
alveus - i m, *the bed of a river*
amens amentis, *mad, insane*
amica - ae f, *a friend, one dear to*

amicus i m, *a friend, one dear to*
amor - oris m, *love*
amphitheatrum, - i n, *an amphitheatre*
amplector - plecti - plexus sum 3 dep., *to embrace*
amplexo 1, *to embrace*
amplificator - oris m, *one who enlarges*
amplifico 1, *to enlarge, magnify, increase*
amplitudo - inis f, *greatness, scope*
amplius, adv., *more*
amplus - a - um, *large, spacious, generous*
amputo 1, *to cut off; amputate*
an, conj., *whether; or*
ancilla - ae f, *a servant, handmaid*
angelicus - a - um, *angelic*
angelus - i m, *an angel*
Anglice, adv., *in English*
anima - ae f, *soul, life;* animam agere, *to be in death agony*
animus - i m, *soul, mind, spirit*
annuntiatio - onis f, *annunciation*
annuntio 1, *to announce, proclaim*
annuo 3 - nui - nutum, *to assent to, agree to*
annus - i m, *a year*
annuus - a - um, *yearly, annual*
ante, adv., and prep. w. acc., *before*
antea, adv., *formerly, before*
antelucanus - a - um, *pertain-*

ing to the time before dawn
antequam, conj., *before*
antiquus - a - um, *ancient*
antistes - stitis m, *a bishop*
aperio 4 aperui apertum, *to open, lay bare, expose*
apertus - a - um, *open, manifest*
apologia - ae f, *a defence, explanation*
apostata - ae m, *an apostate*
apostolicus - a - um, *apostolic; pertaining to the apostles, or the Holy See*
apostolus - i m, *an apostle*
appareo 2 - ui, *to appear, be manifest*
apparitio - onis f, *an apparition, appearance*
appellatio - onis f, *a name, title*
appello 1, *to address, appeal to; to name, entitle*
appeto 3, *to make for, attack*
applico 1, *to apply, devote oneself to*
apprehendo 3, *to take hold of, arrest*
aptus - a - um, *suited, appropriate*
apud, prep. w. acc., *near, at, with; before, in the presence of*
aqua - ae f, *water*
ara - ae f, *an altar*
arbitratus - us m, *a decision, choice, will*
arbitror 1 dep., *to think, judge*
arcesso 3 - ivi - itum, *to summon*
archiconfraternitas - atis f, *an arch-confraternity*

archidioecesis - eos and - is f, *an archdiocese*
archiepiscopatus - us m, *the office of an archbishop*
ardens - entis. *burning, passionate*
ardor - oris f, *eagerness, ardent desire, love*
arduus - a - um, *difficult*
arma - orum n, *soldiers, military power*
arrideo 2 - risi - risum, *to smile upon*
arrogantia - ae f, *arrogance*
arrogo 1, *to usurp, claim presumptuously*
ars artis f, *occupation, practise, skill;* ars magica, *magic*
artus - a - um, *narrow, difficult*
arx arcis f, *a castle, citadel*
ascendo 3 - scendi - scensum, *to go up, ascend*
Ascensio - onis f, *the Ascension*
asceterium - i n, *a hermitage*
ascisco 3 ivi - itum, *to receive, admit to a certain position*
ascribo 3, *to enroll*
aspectus - us m, *appearance, aspect*
asper - era - erum, *rough, harsh*
asperitas - atis f, *austerity, severity*
assecla - ae m, *a follower*
assequor 3 dep., *to attain, reach*
assero 3 - serui - sertum, *to declare, assert*
assertor - oris m, *an asserter, defender*
assideo 2 (sedeo), *to stand beside, to aid, assist* (w. dat.)

assiduitas - atis f, *constant repetition*
assiduus - a - um, *constant, continuous*
assigno 1, *to assign*
assumo 3, *to take up, accept, choose as worthy*
asto 1, astiti, *to stand beside, stand near*
astringo 3, *to bind, confine*
at, conj., *but*
ater atra atrum, *black*
athleta - ae m, *a wrestler, contender*
atque and **ac**, conj., *and*
atrocitas - atis f, *cruelty*
attingo 3 - tigi - tactum, *to touch, attain*
auctor - oris m, *cause, author*
auctoritas - atis f, *authority*
audacia - ae f, *boldness, temerity*
audeo 2 ausus sum, *to dare*
audio 4, *to hear*
auditor - oris m, *a hearer, student*
aufero, *to take away*
aufugio 3, *to flee away, escape*
augeo 2 auxi auctum, *to increase, enlarge, grow, enrich with, furnish with*
augmentum - i n, *an increase*
augustus - a - um, *majestic*
aureus - a - um, *golden*
austeritas - atis f, *severity, strictness*
austerus - a - um, *severe, strict*
aut, conj., *or, or even;* aut . . . aut, *either . . . or*
autem, conj., *but, however, moreover*

aviditas - atis f, *strong desire, longing*
avidus - a - um, *longing for, eager for;* **avide**, adv., *eagerly*

balneum - i n, *a bath*
baptisma - atis n, *baptism*
baptizo 1, *to baptize*
barbarus - a - um, *barbarian, foreign*
basilica - ae f, *a basilica*
beatitudo - inis f, *happiness, bliss*
beatus - a - um, *blessed*
bellum - i n, *war*
bene, adv., *well;* comp., melius; superl., optime.
benedictio - onis f, *a blessing*
benedico 3, *to bless*
benefacio 3, *to do good to, be kind to* (w. dat.)
beneficentia - ae f, *magnanimity, charity*
beneficium - i n, *a favor, kind deed*
benignus - a - um, *kind, friendly*
bestia - ae f, *a beast*
bibo 3 bibi bibitum, *to drink*
biennium - i n, *a period of two years*
bini - ae - a, *two, a pair, double*
bis, adv., *twice*
blanditia - ae f, *flattery, cajolery*
blandus - a - um, *gentle, soothing*
bonus - a - um, *good;* comp., melior, melius, superl., op-

timus - a - um; **bona** - orum n, *goods, possessions*
bracchium - i n, *the arm*
brevis - e, *short;* **brevi** (*tempore*), *in a short time*

caedes - is f, *slaughter*
caedo 3 cecidi caesum, *to strike, cut to pieces*
caeles - itis, *a dweller in heaven*
caelestis - e, *pertaining to heaven, heavenly, of heaven*
caelitus, adv., *from heaven*
caelum - i n, *heaven*
caeremonia - ae f, *ceremony, rite*
caeruleus - a - um, *dark blue*
calamitas - atis f, *misfortune, loss*
caleo 2 - ui, *to be warm, hot*
calipha - ae m, *a caliph, sultan*
callum - i n, *a callus*
calumnia - ae f, *a false accusation*
camelus - i m, *a camel*
camera - ae f, *a room, chamber*
candeo 2 - ui, *to glow with heat*
candor - oris f, *sincerity, candor*
canis - is c, *a dog*
canon - onis m, *a norm, rule, canon; the Canon of the Mass*
canonicus - a - um, *canonical, pertaining to the rules of the Church*
canonicus - i m, *a canon, a member of a cathedral chapter*

canonizatio - onis f, *canonization, declaration of sainthood*
canticum - i n, *a song, canticle*
cantus - us m, *a song*
capio 3 cepi captum, *to lay hold of, seize*
capitalis - e, *pertaining to the head or to life, as capital punishment*
captivitas - atis f, *captivity*
capto 1, *to lay hold of, seek, desire*
caput - itis n, *the head*
carbo - onis m, *burning wood, coals*
carcer - eris m, *a prison*
cardinalis - is m, *a cardinal*
cardinalatus - us m, *the rank of a cardinal*
careo 2 - ui, *to be without, be free from* (w. abl.)
caritas - atis f, *love, charity*
carnifex - ficis m, *an executioner, tormentor*
caro carnis f, *flesh*
carus - a - um, *dear, beloved*
castigatio - onis f, *punishment*
castimonium - i n, *chastity*
castitas - atis f, *chastity*
castrum - i n, *a castle, fortress*
castus - a - um, *chaste*
casu, abl., *by chance*
catalogus - i m, *list of names, catalogue*
catechesis - is f, *religious instruction, a book of religious instruction*
catechismus - i m, *a catechism*
catechumenus - a - um, *one under instruction, a catechumen*

cathedra - ae f, *a chair; episcopal office*
cathedralis - e, *pertaining to a bishop's see; episcopal*
catholicus - a - um, *catholic, universal*
causa - ae f, *a cause, reason;* causa abl., *on account of, for the sake of* (w. gen.)
cedo 3 cessi cessum, *to go, proceed; fall to the lot of; to withdraw from, give up* (w. abl.)
celeber - bris - bre, *famous, renowned*
celebratio - onis f, *celebration*
celebro 1, *to celebrate, make known, praise*
censo 2 censui censum, *to be of an opinion, to account, appraise*
centies, adv., *one hundred times*
cereus - a - um, *waxen;* cereus i m, *a wax taper, candle*
cerno 3 crevi certus, *to see, perceive*
certatim adv., *emulously, eagerly*
certus - a - um, *certain, definite*
ceterus - a - um, *the other, the rest*
cesso 1, *to cease, stop*
ceu, adv., *as, like*
chartula - ae f, *a small piece of paper*
Christianus - a - um, *a Christian*
Christus - i m, *the Anointed One, the Messiah, Christ*
Christifidelis - e, *a believer in Christ, one faithful to Christ, a Christian*
cibus - i m, *food*
cicatrix - icis f, *a scar, mark*
cilicium - i n, *a coarse garment, hairshirt*
cinis - eris m, *ashes;* Dies Cinerum, *Ash Wenesday*
circiter, adv., *about*
circum, prep. w. acc., *round, around*
circumcisio - onis f, *circumcision*
circumfundo 3 (²fundo), *to surround*
circumventio - onis f, *a circumvention by stratagem, deceit*
cisterna - ae f, *a cistern*
civis - is c, *a citizen, fellow citizen*
civitas - atis f, *a city*
clam, adv., *secretly*
clareo 2, *to be illustrious, distinguished*
clarifico 1, *to make illustrious*
clarus - a - um, *clear, distinct; distinguished, illustrious*
classis - is f, *a fleet*
clericalis - e, *of the clergy*
clericus - i m, *a cleric, clergyman, priest*
clerus - i m, *the clergy*
cliens, - entis m, *a client*
clivus - i m, *a slope, a rise of ground*
coadiutor - oris m, *a helper, assistant*
coaevus - a - um, *of the same age*

coalesco 3 - alui - alitum, *to unite, grow together*
coemeterium - i n, *a cemetery*
coenobium - i n, *a cloister*
coepio 3 coepi coeptum, *to begin*
cogito 1, *to think, reflect*
cognomen - inis n, *a name*
cognomentum - i n, *a name*
cognosco 3 - gnovi - gnitum, *to get to know*
cogo 3 - coegi coactum (ago), *to compel; to collect together*
coheres - edis, c, *a fellow-heir, co-heir*
colaphus - i m, *a blow*
collabor 3 dep., *to fall down, collapse*
collatio - onis f, *a collection; a contribution*
collaudo 1, *to praise greatly*
collegium - i n, *an educational institution, a college*
colligo 3 (lego), *to gather together;* se **colligere**, *to compose oneself*
collis - is m, *a hill*
colloco 1, *to place, settle*
colloquium - i n, *a conversation, discussion*
colluceo 2, *to shine on all sides*
colo 3 colui cultum, *to honor, pay reverence to, worship; practise; tend*
color - oris m, *a color*
columba - ae f, *a dove*
columen - inis n, *a support, pillar*
columna - ae f, *a pillar, column*
comedo - esse - edi - esum, *to eat up*

comes - itis m, *a count*
comitatus - us m, *a retinue, train*
commartyr - yris m, *a fellow martyr*
commendo 1, *to entrust, commit to one's care; to recommend*
commentatio - onis f, *a reflection, meditation*
comminuo 3 - ui - utum, *to break into small pieces*
commisceo 2 - miscui - mixtum, *to unite;*
committo 3, *to entrust, commit*
commoror 1 dep., *to remain, linger*
commoveo 2, *to stir up*
¹ **communio** 4, *to strengthen, fortify*
² **communio** - onis f, *a participation, communion*
communis - e, *common, general*
comparo 1, *to liken, compare; to bring together*
¹ **compello** 3 *to drive, force*
² **compello** 1, *to address, call*
comperio 4 - peri - pertum, *to discover, find out*
complano 1, *to level, make level*
complector - plecti - plexus 3 dep., *to embrace, include*
compleo 2 - plevi - pletum, *to fill out, accomplish, perform*
comploro 1, *to lament loudly*
complures - plura, *several, very many*
compono 3, *to put together, compare; form, arrange*

comprehendo 3, - prehendi - prehensum, *to capture, arrest; embrace*
comprimo 3 - pressi - pressum, *to press together, squeeze*
comprobo 1, *to establish, prove; approve, recommend*
conatus - us, m, *an effort, an undertaking*
concedo 3 - cessi - cessus, *to grant, vouchsafe; withdraw, retire*
conceptus - us m, *conception*
concido 3 - cidi - cisum, *to strike down, cut down*
concilio 1, *to unite, bring together, win over*
concilium - i n, *a council, assembly*
concino 3 - cinui, *to sing together*
concipio 3 - cepi ceptum, *to conceive, devise*
concito 1, *to stir up, excite*
concordia - ae f, *harmony, union*
concors - cordis, *of one mind, agreeing*
conculco 1, *to trample under foot, despise*
concupiscentia - ae f, *concupiscence, lust*
concursus - us m, *a crowd, assemblage*
condemno 1, *to condemn*
condo 3 - didi - ditum, *to build, found; to put away, place; to bury*
conditorium - i n, *a burial place, crypt*
confero, *to bestow, give; to compare;* se **conferre**, *to betake oneself to, go to*
confessio - onis f, *an acknowledgment, confession*
confessor - oris m, *a confessor*
confestim, adv., *immediately*
conficio 3 - feci - fectum (facio), *to finish; exhaust, weaken;* **conficere librum**, *to write a book*
confingo 3 - finxi - fictum, *to fabricate, invent, forge*
confirmo 1, *to make firm, confirm, ratify*
confiteor - eri - fessus sum 2 dep., *to acknowledge, confess*
confluo 3 - fluxi, *to flock together*
confractio - onis f, *breakage, the act of breaking*
confringo 3 (frango), *to break to pieces*
confuto 1, *to silence; refute*
congregatio - onis f, *a congregation*
conicio 3 (iacio), *to throw; to conjecture; to surmise, infer*
coniungo 3 - iunxi, - iunctum, *to join, unite*
connumero 1, *to number with, reckon among*
conor 1 dep., *to try, attempt*
conquiro 3 - quisivi - quisitum, *to seek for, search for*
consanguineus - a - um, *related by blood, a relative*
conscendo 3 -scendi - scensum, *to ascend, go up*
conscius - a - um, *privy to, cognizant of, aware of*

General Vocabulary 269

conscribo 3, *to write, compose; enroll*
consecro 1, *to consecrate*
consensus - us m, *an agreement, general consent*
consentaneus - a - um, *consistent with, consonant with* (w. dat.)
consentio 4, *to agree, harmonize*
consequor 3 dep., *to attain, obtain*
consido 3 - sedi, *to settle, sit down*
consiliarius - i m, *an adviser*
consilium - i n, *advice, counsel, resolution, plan*
consisto 3 - stiti - stitum, *to stop, halt*
consolator - oris m, *a consoler*
conspectus - us m, *a view, sight*
conspicio 3 - spexi - spectum, *to behold, see, understand*
conspicuus - a - um, *remarkable, illustrious*
conspiro 1, *to plot*
constans - antis, *firm, unchanging;* constanter adv., *steadfastly*
constantia - ae f, *firmness, perseverance*
constituo 3 - stitui - stitutum, *to decide, establish, decree, appoint, halt*
constitutio - onis f, *an arrangement, disposition*
constringo 3 - strinxi - strictum, *to bind fast*
construo 3 - struxi - structum, *to construct, build*

consuesco 3 - suevi - suetum, *to accustom oneself;* in perf., *I am accustomed*
consuetudo - inis f, *a custom*
consuetus - a - um, *accustomed, usual*
consulo 3 - lui, *to take care of, have regard for* (w. dat.)
consultum - i n, *a decision, decree*
consumo 3, *to spend, wear out, consume, destroy*
consummatus - a - um, *perfect, of the highest degree*
consurgo 3 - surrexi - surrectum, *to rise up*
contagio - onis f, *an infection, contagion*
contego 3 - texi - tectum, *to cover*
contemno 3 - tempsi - temptum, *to despise, scorn*
contemplatio - onis f, *contemplation, meditation*
contemptus - us m, *disdain, contempt*
contendo 3 - tendi - tentum, *to exert oneself; to hasten*
contentus - a - um, *satisfied, contented*
contero 3 - trivi - tritum, *to rub away, wear away, destroy*
contexo 3 - texui - textum, *to weave together*
continentia - ae f, *chastity, purity, continence*
contineo 2, *to surround, shut in, restrain;* continens - entis, *self-controlled, continent*
contingo 3 - tigi - tactum, *to*

befall, happen, come up
continuo, adv., *immediately, at once*
continuus - a - um, *uninterrupted*
contio - onis f, *a sermon*
contionator - oris m, *a preacher*
contionor 1 dep., *to speak publicly, preach*
contra, prep. w. acc., *against*
contradictio - onis f, *an objection*
contrarius - a - um, *opposite*
contremisco 3 - tremui, *to tremble violently*
contritio - onis f, *act of wearing away, destroying* (contero)
controversia - ae f, *a controversy*
convenio 4 *to come together, gather*
conventus - us m, *a group, gathering, council, diet*
conversatio - onis f, *manner of life, conduct*
conversio - onis f, *a conversion*
converto 3 - verti - versum, *to turn around, turn towards, convert*
convinco 3 - vici - victum, *to prove erroneous, prove mistaken*
convivium - i n, *a meal, banquet*
coopto 1, *to elect, choose*
copia - ae f, *abundance;* in pl., *troops, forces*
copiosus - a - um, *plentiful, abundant*

cor cordis n, *the heart*
coram, adv., *openly, publicly;* as prep. w. abl., *in the presence of*
corona - ae f, *a crown; a rosary, chaplet*
corono 1, *to crown*
corporeus - a - um, *physical, material*
corpus - oris n, *a body*
corripio 3 - ripui - reptum, *to overcome, lay hold of*
corruo 3 - rui, *to fall down*
corrumpo 3 - rupi - ruptum, *to corrupt*
corruptus - a - um, *corrupt*
costulum - i n, *a rib*
cotidianus - a - um, *daily*
cotidie, adv., *daily, every day*
creator - oris m, *creator, maker*
creber - bra - brum, *repeated numerous*
credo 3 - didi - ditum, *to believe; to entrust;* **credens** - entis, *a believer*
credulus - a - um, *believing easily* (w. dat.)
creo 1, *to make, create*
cresco 3 crevi cretus, *to grow increase*
crimen - inis n, *a fault; an accusation*
criminor 1 dep., *to charge, accuse*
cruciatus - us m, *torture, torment*
crucifigo 3 - fixi - fixum, *to crucify*
crudelis - e, *cruel*
crudelitas - atis f, *cruelty*
cruentus - a - um, *bloody*

crus cruris n, *the leg*
crux crucis f, *a cross*
cubiculum - i n, *a room*
culpa - ae f, *a fault*
cultor - oris m, and **cultrix** - icis f, *a worshipper* (colo)
cultus - us m, *worship, devotion; care, attention*
cum conj., *when, since;* as prep. w. abl., *with*
cumulo 1, *to heap up, pile on, magnify*
cunctus - a - um, *all, the whole*
cupio 3 cupivi or - ii - itum, *to desire, long for*
cura - ae f, *care, anxiety, concern*
curo 1, *to care for; see to a thing being done; to cure, heal*
curriculum - i n, *course of studies*
cursus - us m, *course, direction*
custodio 4, *to guard*
custos - odis m, *a guard*

daemon - onis m, *an evil spirit, a devil*
daemonium - i n, *a spirit*
damno 1, *to condemn*
deauratus - a - um, *adorned with gold, golden*
debeo 2 - ui - itum, *to owe, ought*
decerno 3, *to decide, decree*
decerto 1, *contend, fight*
decet 2 - uit, *it is proper, fitting*
declaro 1, *to declare, proclaim*

decoro 1, *to beautify, adorn, honor*
decretum - i n, *a decree*
decus - oris n, *adornment, honor, glory*
dedicatio - onis f, *dedication*
dedico 1, *to dedicate*
deditus - a - um, *given to, devoted to*
deduco 3, *to lead forth, conduct, bring*
defendo 3 - fendi - fensum, *to ward off, defend, protect*
defensio - onis f, *a defender*
defensor - oris m, *a defender*
defero, *to bring, carry, offer*
deficio 3 - feci - fectum, *to fail, become weak; to cease, forsake* (w. abl.)
definio 4, *to define, interpret, settle*
definitio - onis f, *definition, definitive interpretation*
defungor 3 dep., *to finish; to die*
deglutio 4, *to swallow down*
dego 3 degi, *to live*
deicio 3 (iacio), *to cast out, eject*
dein and **deinde**, adv., *then, afterwards*
deinceps, adv., *one after another, successively*
Deipara - ae f, *the Mother of God*
delabor 3 dep., *to fall down, glide down*
delego 1, *to transfer, assign, delegate*
delibero 1, *to weigh carefully*
deligo 3 (lego), *to choose,*

select
delitesco 3 - litui, *to conceal oneself, lie hid*
demando 1, *to entrust, commit*
demens - entis, *out of one's mind, insane*
demissio - onis f, *humility*
demissus - a - um, *hanging down; modest, unassuming*
demitto 3, *to send down, let down*
demo 3 dempsi demptum, *to take away*
demulceo 2 - mulsi, *to soften, win over*
demum, adv., *at last, finally*
denique, adv, *finally, at last*
dens dentis m, *a tooth*
denuntio 1, *to accuse publicly, denounce*
deosculor 1 dep., *to kiss warmly*
depello 3, *to drive away, remove*
deploro 1, *to lament, bewail*
depono 3, *to put down, lay aside*
deposco 3 - poposci, *to demand, ask for*
depravo 1, *to corrupt, deprave;* **depravatus** - a - um, *corrupt, depraved*
deprecor 1 dep., *to entreat for, beg for*
deprehendo 3 - prehensi - prehensum, *to catch*
derelinquo 3, *to forsake, abandon*
descendo 3 - scendi - scensum, *to go down*
descisco 3 - scivi - scitum, *to break away from*
describo 3, *to write down; describe*
deservio 4, *to serve zealously* (w. dat.)
desiderium - i n, *a desire, longing*
desidero 1, *to long for*
desino 3 - sii - situm, *to cease*
desisto 3 - stiti - stitum, *to cease, leave off*
despero 1, *to despair;* **desperatus** - a - um, in pass. sense, *despaired of*
desponso 1, *to betroth*
destino 1, *to appoint, fix*
destituo 3 - stitui - stitutum, *to desert, forsake; to deprive of* (w. abl.); **destitutus** - a - um, *robbed of, destitute of*
desudo 1, *to sweat violently, exert oneself*
desum, *to fail, be wanting*
desumo 3, *to take out, select*
deterreo 2, *to frighten away, deter*
detineo 2, *to keep in custody, hold back*
detrecto 1, *to decline, refuse*
detrudo 3 - trusi - trusum, *to thrust down, push aside*
deturbo 1, *to drive off, eject*
Deus - i m, *God*
deverto 3, *to turn aside to a lodging, to stay with*
devexus - a - um, *moving downwards, sinking*
devincio 4, *to bind fast*
divinco 3, *to conquer completely*
devoro 1, *to devour*

devotio - onis f, *devotion*
dexter - tera - terum and - tra - trum, *right, on the right hand*
diabolicus - a - um, *diabolical*
diabolus - i m, *a devil*
diaconus - i m, *a deacon*
diadema - atis n, *a crown*
[1] **dico** 1, *to consecrate, dedicate*
[2] **dico** 3 dixi dictum *to say; to name, call*
dicto 1, *to dictate*
dictum - i n, *a statement, speech*
dies - ei m, *day; in dies; from day to day, day by day*
differo, *to delay, postpone*
difficilis - e, *difficult*
difficultas - atis f, *difficulty*
diffundo 3, *to spread out, extend*
dignitas - atis f, *high worth, high rank*
digno 1, *to consider worthy*
dignor 1 dep., *to consider worthy* (w. abl.), *to deign to*
dignosco 3 - novi, *to recognize*
dignus - a - um, *worthy* (w. gen., abl.)
dilanio 1, *to tear to pieces*
diligens - entis, *careful, attentive*
diligo 3 (lego), *to love, esteem highly*
dilucidus - a - um, *clear, plain*
dimidius - a - um, *a half*
dimitto 3, *to let go*
dimoveo 2, *to move apart, take away*
dioecesis - is f, *a district, diocese*
direptio - onis f, *a plundering, pillaging*
diripio 3 -ripui - reptum, *to pillage, lay waste*
dis ditis, *rich*
discedo 3, *to depart, go away*
discidium - i n, *disagreement, difference, quarrel, discord*
disciplina - ae f, *that which is taught: subjects, study, discipline*
discipulus - i m, *a disciple, follower*
disco 3 didici, *to learn*
discrimen - inis n, *a crisis, danger*
disertus - a - um, *eloquent, clear, distinct*
dispensatorius - a - um, *pertaining to a steward or manager*
dispono 3, *to arrange, dispose, set in order*
disputatio - onis f, *argumentation*
disputo 1, *to argue, debate*
dissero 3 - serui - sertum, *to discuss, treat of*
dissideo 3 (sedeo), *to be separated, to dissent, be at variance*
distinguo 3 - stinxi - stinctum, *to distinguish, set off, adorn;* **distinctus** - a - um, *adorned;* **distincte**, adv., *clearly, distinctly*
distraho 3, *to draw away*
distribuo 3 - tribui - utum, *to divide, distribute*
diu, adv., *for a long time*

diurnus - a - um, *pertaining to the day time, daily*
diuternus - a - um, *lasting for a long time*
diversus - a - um, *different, diverse*
divido 3 - visi - visum, *to divide, separate*
divinitas - atis f, *divinity*
divinitus, adv., *by divine inspiration*
divinus - a - um, *divine*
divisio - onis f, *a division, act of dividing, pulling apart*
divortium - i n, *a divorce, separation*
do dare dedi datum, *to give*
doceo 2, *to teach*
doctor - oris m, *a teacher, doctor*
doctrina - ae f, *schooling, instruction, teaching; learning*
doctus - a - um, *learned*
documentum - i n, *example, proof*
dogma - atis n, *doctrine, teaching*
dogmaticus - a - um, *dogmatic, pertaining to official teaching*
doleo 2, *to be in pain, grieve*
dolor - oris f, *pain*
domesticus - a - um, *pertaining to the household*
domicilium - i n, *a residence*
domina - ae f, *mistress, lady*
dominicus - a - um, *belonging to the Lord;* **Dies Dominicus,** *Sunday*
dominor 1 dep., *to rule, be master of* (w. dat.)

dominus - i m, *lord, master*
domus - us f, *a house, home;* **domum,** *homewards*
donec, conj., *until*
dono 1, *to grant, bestow, present*
donum - i n, *a gift*
dubito 1, *to doubt; to hesitate to*
dubium - i n, *a doubt*
duco 3 duxi ductum, *to lead; to prolong*
ducto 1, *to lead, draw, guide*
dum, conj., *until; while*
duplex - plicis, *double, two-fold;* **dupliciter,** adv., *in a two-fold manner*
durities - ei f, *hardness*
durus - a - um, *hard, difficult*
dux ducis m, *a leader, guide*

e, ex, prep. w. abl., *out of, from*
ecclesia - ae f, *a church*
ecclesiasticus - a - um, *ecclesiastical*
eculeus - i m, *a torture-rack*
edico 3, *to declare, announce*
edictum - i n, *a decree*
edo 3 - didi - ditum, *to put forth; cause, bring about*
edoceo 2, *to teach*
edolo 1, *to hew*
[1] educo 1, *to bring up, educate*
[2] educo 3, *to lead out*
effero, *to raise up, lift up; proclaim*
efficax - acis, *effective*
efficio 3 (facio), *to make, to bring it about*

efflo 1, *to breathe forth*
effugio 3, *to escape, free from*
effulgeo 2, *to shine forth*
effundo 3, *to pour out*
effutio 4, *to babble, chatter*
egenus - a - um, *needy, destitute*
egeo 2, *to want, be in need;* egens - entis, *needy*
egredior - gredi - gressus 3 dep., *to go out*
egregius - a - um, *excellent, extraordinary;* egregie, adv., *admirably, excellently*
eicio 3 (iacio), *to cast out, drive out*
eiuro 1, *to deny on oath*
elabor 1 dep., *to glide away, slip away*
electio - onis f, *choice, election*
electus - a - um, *chosen, selected;*
  electi - orum m, *the elect*
eleemosyna - ae f, *alms*
elementum - i n, *an element, first principle;* pl., *physical elements*
elido 3 - lisi - lisum, *to strike, thrust*
eligo 3 (lego), *to choose, select*
elimino 1, *to expel, eliminate*
eloquens - entis, *eloquent*
elucubro 1, *to compose at night; to compose with great labor*
emendatio - onis f, *correction*
emendo 1, *to free from errors, correct, improve*
emetior - metiri - mensus sum, *to pass through; measure out, bestow*
emico 1, - micui - micatum, *to shine forth, be conspicuous*
emineo 2, *to stand out;* eminens - entis, *outstanding*
emitto 3, *to send forth, let go, free; to utter*
emo 3 emi emptum, *to buy, purchase*
emolumentum - i n, *advantage, gain*
enarro 1, *to narrate, tell*
enim, conj., *indeed, for*
eniteo 2, *to shine forth, be conspicuous*
enitor - niti - nisus or nixus 3 dep., *to strive, struggle; to bring forth;*
enixe, adv., *eagerly, strenuously*
enucleate, adv., *clearly, plainly*
enutrio 4, *to nourish*
[1] eo ire ivi and ii itum, *to go*
[2] eo, adv., *there, in that place; on that account* (abl. of *is*)
episcopalis - e, *episcopal, pertaining to a bishop*
episcopatus - us m, *episcopacy, office of a bishop*
episcopus - i m, *a bishop*
epistula - ae f, *a letter*
erectus - a um, *intent on, directed to* (erigo)
erga, prep. w. acc., *towards, in relation to*
ergo, adv., *therefore, accordingly*
erigo 3 - rexi - rectum, *to set up, raise up*
eripio 3 - ripui - reptum, *to*

snatch away, rescue
erogo 1, *to pay out, give*
erro 1, *to wander, stray from the right path*
error - oris m, *an error, mistake*
erudio 4, *to instruct, educate*
eruditio - onis f, *learning, knowledge*
erumpo 3 - rupi - ruptum, *to burst forth*
et, conj., *and;* adv., *also, even*
ethnicus - a - um, *heathen, non-Christian*
etiam, conj. and adv., *also, even;* etiam atque etiam, *again and again*
etymologia - ae f, *etymology*
Eucharistia - ae f, *the Eucharist*
evado 3 - vasi - vasum, *to go out; to turn out, result*
evangelicus - a - um, *evangelical*
evangelista - ae m, *an evangelist, author of one of the Gospels*
evangelium - i n, *a Gospel*
eveho 3 - vexi - vectum, *to carry up; promote, advance*
evenio 4, *to come forth; to happen, occur*
everto 3, *to overthrow, destroy*
evoco 1, *to call up, call forth*
ex, prep. with abl., *from, out of, of*
exagito 1, *to harass*
exantlo 1, *to exhaust, bear to the end*
exardeo 2, *to blaze up*
exaudio 4, *to hear favorably, listen to*

excello 3, *to excel, be outstanding*
excessus - us m, *an excess, superabundance*
excidium - i n, *destruction, ruin*
excipio 3 - cepi - ceptum, *to take out, rescue; except; receive, welcome*
excito 1, *to rouse, stir, excite*
excolo 3, *to tend carefully; ennoble*
exemplar - aris n, *a pattern, ideal*
exemplum - i n, *an example*
exeo, *to go out, come out*
exerceo 2, *to exercise, employ; work at, practise*
exercitatio - onis f, *practise, exercise*
exercitium - i n, *exercise, practise*
exercitus - us, m, *an army*
exhibeo 2, *to show, display*
exigo 3 - egi - actum, *to complete* (of time)
exiguitas - atis f, *smallness*
exiguus - a - um, *small, little*
eximius - a - um, *extraordinary, outstanding*
eximo 3 (emo), *to take out, free, release*
exinde, adv., *thereupon, then; from there, thence*
existimo 1, *to consider, regard*
exitus - us m, *end, finish, outcome*
exopto 1, *to desire, long for*
exorior 4 dep., *to rise up, appear, come forward*
exorno 1, *to adorn, make eminent*

General Vocabulary 277

expedio 4 - ivi and - ii - itum, *to disentangle, set free, set straight*
expeditio - onis f, *an expedition*
expello 3, *to drive out*
experior - periri - pertus sum 4 dep., *to experience, feel*
expeto 3, *to seek after, demand*
expiatio - onis f, *expiation, atonement*
explano 1, *to explain, make clear*
expleo 2 - plevi - pletum, *to complete*
explico 1, *to explain, interpret*
exploro 1, *to investigate, search out;* **exploratus** - a - um, *certain, sure*
expono 3, *to set forth, explain*
exporto 1, *to carry out*
exprimo 3 - pressi - pressus, *to portray, exhibit*
expurgo 1, *to cleanse, purify*
exquiro 3 (quaero), *to seek out, ask*
exsequor 3 dep., *to follow to the end, accomplish*
exsilium - i n, *exile*
exspectatio - onis f, *expectation*
exspecto 1, *to look for, count upon*
exstatis - is f, *ecstasy*
exstinguo 3 - stinxi - stinctum, *to put out, extinguish*
exstirpo 1, *to root out*
exsto 1, *to stand out*
exstruo 3 - struxi - structum, *to build up*
exsul - sulis c, *an exile*

exsulo 1, *to be banished; to live in exile*
exsultatio - onis f, *a rejoicing, exultation*
extendo 3, *to extend*
exterior - ius, *outer, exterior*
extermino 1, *to drive out, remove*
externus - a - um, *external, outside, foreign*
extra, adv., and prep. w. acc., *outside of, except for*
extremus - a - um, *of the highest degree; extreme, last,* ad extrema, *to the end*

faber - bri m, *a carpenter*
facies - ei f, *form, outward appearance*
facilis - e, *easy*
facilitas - atis f, *ease, facility*
facio facere feci factum, *to make, do;*
factio - onis f, *a party, group, faction*
factor - oris m, *a maker*
factum - i n, *a deed, act, fact*
facultas -atis f, *means, resources, power*
fallax - acis, *deceptive, fallacious*
falsus - a - um, *spurious, false*
fama ae f, *report, reputation*
familia - ae f, *household, group, family*
familiaris - is c, *a close friend*
familiariter, adv., *familiarly, intimately*
famulor 1 dep., *to serve*
famulus - i m, *a servant*

fauces - ium f, *the throat*
fautor - oris m, *a partisan, devoted follower*
fax facis f, *a torch*
febris - is f, *a fever*
fecundo 1, *to enrich, render fruitful*
fel fellis n, *gall*
felix - icis, *fruitful, successful*
femina - ae f, *a woman*
fenestra - ae f, *a window*
fere, adv., *almost, nearly*
ferme, adv., *almost, nearly*
feria - ae f, *a day in the week*
fero ferre tuli latus, *to bear, carry; to report, speak of;* fertur, *men say, it is said;* prae se ferre, *to show, manifest*
ferox - ocis, *wild, fierce*
ferreus - a - um, *of iron*
fervens - entis, *ardent, fervent;*
ferventer, adv., *ardently*
fervor - oris m, *ardor*
festum - i n, *a feast*
festus - a - um, *festive*
fictus - a - um, *false, feigned*
fides - ei f, *faith; pledge, promise; protection*
fidelis - e, *faithful, honest, conscientious;* fideliter, adv., *faithfully*
fidus - a - um, *faithful, trusty*
filia - ae f, *a daughter*
filiolus - i m, dimin. of filius
filius - i m, *a son, child*
fimbria - ae f, *edge, hem of a garment*
finis - is m, *end;* in pl., *borders, territory*
fio fieri factus sum, *to become; happen*
firmitas - atis f, *strength, firmness*
firmo 1, *to strengthen, make secure*
flagellum - i n, *a whip, scourge*
flagitium - i n, *a shameful deed*
flagro 1, *to blaze, burn;* flagrans - antis, *burning*
flamma - ae f, *a flame*
fleo 2 flevi fletum, *to weep*
fletus - us m, *a weeping, bewailing*
floreo 2, *to flourish, be in high repute;* florens - entis, *flourishing, blooming*
floresco 3, *to begin to flourish, blossom*
flumen - inis n, *a river, stream*
fluvius - i n, *a stream, river*
¹ fluxus - a - um, *fleeting, unstable*
² fluxus - us m, *a flowing, a flow*
foetor - oris m, *a bad smell*
fons fontis m, *a spring, source, waters of baptism*
foris, adv., *outside, from without*
forma - ae f, *figure, image, form*
formo 1, *to fashion, form*
fors, abl. forte, f., *chance*
fortis - e, *brave, courageous;* fortiter, adv., *bravely*
fortitudo - inis f, *courage, strength*
forum - i n, *a public square, forum*
fovea - ae f. *a pit, ditch*
foveo 2 fovi fotum, *to foster, support*

fragilis - e, *weak, fragile*
fragrans - antis, *sweet-smelling*
frango 3 fregi fractum, *to break, subdue*
frater - tris m, *a brother*
fraternus - a - um, *of a brother, fraternal*
fraus fraudis f, *a deception*
frequens - entis, *frequent, constant;* frequenter adv., *often*
frequentia - ae f, *frequency*
frequento 1, *to celebrate; to visit often, attend*
frigesco 3, *to become cold*
fructus - us m, *fruit, profit*
frumentum - i n, *grain*
fruor frui fructus sum 3 dep., *to enjoy* (w. abl.)
frustra, adv., *in vain*
fugo 1, *to drive away*
fugio 3, fugi fugitum, *to flee*
fulgeo 2, *to shine;* fulgens - entis, *shining, brilliant*
fulgor - oris m, *brightness, glory*
functio - onis f, *duty, business*
fundamentum - i n, *a foundation*
¹ fundo 1, *to found, establish*
² fundo 3 fudi fusum, *to pour forth*
fundus - i m, *an estate*
fungor fungi functus sum 3 dep., *to perform, carry out* (w. abl.)
funus - eris n, *a burial, funeral*
furor - oris m, *fury, madness, anger*
fustus - is m, *a club, cudgel*
futurus a - um, cf. sum

gaudeo 2, *to rejoice*
gaudium - i n, *joy*
gelu - us, n, *frost, icy-cold*
gemitus - us m, *a sigh, groan*
generalis - e, *general, universal*
generosus - a - um, *noble, noble-hearted*
genetrix - icis f, *a mother*
gens gentis f, *a nation, people;* Gentes - ium, *non-Jews, Gentiles*
genu - us n, *the knee;* flexis genibus, *on bended knee*
genuflecto 3 - flexi - flexum, *to genuflect*
genus - eris n, *family, birth, descent, race, kind, class*
gero 3 gessi gestum, *to carry on, conduct, manage; wear*
gestio 4, *to be excited, joyful*
gesto 1, *to wear*
gestus - us m, *a gesture*
gladium - i n, *a sword*
globus - i m, *a round ball*
gloria - ae f, *glory*
gloriosus - a - um, *glorious*
gradior gradi gessus sum 3 dep., *to walk, go, make one's way*
grandis - e, *great, large*
grassor 1 dep., *to go about, move around; rage*
gratia - ae f, *favor, grace;* gratiam reddere, *to express thanks*
gratus - a - um, *pleasing, acceptable*
gravis - e, *heavy, weighty, serious;* graviter, adv., *grievously, harshly*
gravitas - atis f, *weight, im-*

portance, power
gravo 1, *to burden, weigh down*
grex gregis m, *a flock*
guberno 1, *to govern*
guttur - uris n, *the throat*

habeo 2, *to have, hold; consider*
habitaculum - i n, *a dwelling place*
habitus - us m, *garb, dress, habit*
haeresis - is and eos f, *a heresy*
haereticus - i m, *a heretic*
harena - ae f, *sand, sandy ground*
haud, adv., *not, not at all*
haurio 4 hausi haustum, *to draw, derive*
hebdomada - ae f, *a week*
hereditas - atis f, *inheritance*
[1] hic haec hoc, *this*
[2] hic, adv., *here*
hierarchia - ae f, *hierarchy*
hilaris - e, *cheerful*
hinc, adv., *from here, hence; from this cause*
homo - inis m, *a man*
honesto 1, *to adorn, dignify, honor*
honestus - a - um, *honorable, respected*
honor - oris m, *honor; an office, position*
honorifice, adv., *with honor, in a respectful manner*
honoro 1, *to honor, show honor to*
hora - ae f, *an hour*

horarius - a - um, *pertaining to an hour*
hortatus - us m, *an encouragement, urging*
hortor 1 dep., *to encourage, urge*
hospitium - i n, *lodging, hospitality*
hostia - ae f, *a victim*
hostis - is m, *an enemy*
huc, adv., *to this place, hither*
huiusmodi, *of this kind, of such of kind*
humanitas - atis f, *humaneness*
humanus - a - um, *human, pertaining to human beings*
humilis - e, *humble, mean;* humiliter, adv., *humbly*
humilitas - atis f, *humility*
humus - i f, *the ground, earth*
hymnus -i m, *a hymn, song*

iaceo 2 iacui, *to lie*
iacio 3 ieci iactum, *to lay*
iacto 1, *to throw, fling about*
iam, adv., *now, already;* iam diu, iam dudum, iam pridem, *now for a long time*
ibi, adv., *there, at that place*
ibidem, adv., *in the same place*
ictus - us m, *a blow, stroke*
idcirco, adv., *for that reason*
idem eadem idem, *the same*
ideo, adv., *therefore, for that reason*
idolum - i n, *an idol*
idoneus - a - um, *suitable, fitting*
ieiunium i n, *fast, abstinence*
ieiuno 1, *to fast*

igitur, adv., *then, accordingly*
igneus - a - um, *fiery, of fire*
ignis - is m, *fire*
ignominia - ae f, *disgrace, degradation*
ignosco 3 - novi - notum, *to forgive* (w. dat.)
ignotus - a - um, *unknown*
illabor 3 dep., *to die down, diminish*
illaesus - a - um, *uninjured, unhurt*
ille illa illud, *he, she, it; that*
illecebra - ae f, *an allurement*
illibatus - a - um, *unblemished, undiminished*
illic, adv., *there, in that place*
illo, adv., *to that place, there*
illustratio - onis f, *an illumination, enlightenment*
illustris - e, *brilliant, illustrious*
illustro 1, *to illumine; render famous, renowned*
imago - inis f, *an image, representation (statue, picture)*
imber imbris m, *rain*
imbuo 3 - ui - utum, *to steep, saturate; instruct;* **imbutus** - a - um, *instructed in*
imitatio - onis f, *an imitation*
imitor 1 dep., *to imitate*
immaculatus - a - um, *immaculate, free of stain*
immensus - a - um, *immense;* in immensum, *to an immense height*
immersus - a - um, *plunged in, immersed in*
immoror 1 dep., *to stay, remain in*

immunis - e, *stainless, free from*
immuto 1, *to change, altar*
impavidus - a - um, *undaunted, undismayed*
impello 3, *to drive on, urge on*
impendeo 2, *to hang over, threaten* (w. dat.)
impendo 3 - pendi - pensum, *to expend, spend*
impense, adv., *urgently, pressingly*
imperator - oris m, *a commander-in-chief, emperor*
imperatum - i n, *a command*
imperium - i n, *power, command; the Empire*
impero 1, *to order, command* (w. dat.)
impeto 3, *to assail, attack*
impetro 1, *to obtain by asking*
impietas - atis f, *wickedness, ungodliness*
impiger - gra - grum, *unslothful, active*
impius - a - um, *godless, irreverent*
impleo 2 - plevi - pletum, *to fulfill, perform*
imploro 1, *to beg, beseech*
impono 3, *to lay upon, impose*
impudens - entis, *shameless*
impudentia - ae f, *effrontery*
impugno 1, *to attack, assail*
in, prep. w. abl., *in, on, among;* w. acc., *to, into, towards, against*
incedo 3, *to walk, proceed*
incendium - i n, *a fire, conflagration*
incendo 3, - cendi - censum, *to set on fire*

inceptum - i n, *an enterprise, undertaking*
incessabilis - e, *unceasing*
incido 3 - cidi - casum, *to fall*
incipio 3 - cepi - ceptum, *to begin*
inclaresco 3 - clarui, *to become famous*
includo 3 - clusi - clusum, *to shut in, confine*
inclutus - a - um, *glorious, renowned*
incola - ae m, *an inhabitant*
incolumis - e, *uninjured, safe*
incolumitas - atis f, *preservation, safety*
incommodum - i n, *misfortune, trouble*
incorporalis - e, *without a body*
incorruptus - a - um, *not corrupted, untainted*
incredibilis - e, *unbelievable*
incrementum - i n, *growth, increase*
incumbo 3 - cubui cubitum, *to apply oneself to, concentrate upon* (w. dat.)
inde, adv., *from there, then*
indefessus - a - um, *unwearied*
indeficiens - entis, *unfailing*
indicium - i n, *a sign, evidence*
¹ **indico** 1, *to disclose, make known*
² **indico** 3, *to proclaim, announce*
indigens - entis, *in need, destitute*
indigne, adv., *impatiently, indignantly*
indubitanter, adv., *with certainty, unquestioningly*
induco 3, *to bring in, introduce*
indulgentia - ae f, *pardon, indulgence*
indulgeo 2 - dulsi, *to grant, allow* (w. dat.)
induo 3 - dui - dutum, *to put on, clothe*
industria - ae, f, *diligence;* ex industria, *on purpose*
inedia - ae f, *starvation*
ineo, *to come in;* ab ineunte aetate, *from youth*
inexhaustus - a - um, *untired*
infans - antis, *an infant*
infantia - ae f, *infancy*
infantulus - a - um, dimin. of *infans*
infectus - a - um, *poisoned, tainted*
infero, *to bring or carry in, to bring on, inflict*
infestus - a - um, *hostile*
infidelis - is m, *an unbeliever, an infidel*
infinitus - a - um, *endless, countless*
infirmitas - atis f, *weakness*
infirmus - a - um, *sick, weak*
inflammo 1, *to set on fire*
influo 3, - fluxi - fluxum, *to flow in*
informo 1, *to instruct, educate*
infra, prep. w. acc., *below, beneath*
infractus - a - um, *unbroken*
infusus - a - um, *infused*
ingemino 1, *to redouble, repeat*
ingenium - i n, *character; ability*

ingens - entis, *vast, huge, prodigious*
ingenuus - a - um, *frank, open, ingenuous*
ingero 3, *to throw*; se ingerere, *to rush*
ingredior - gredi - gressus sum 3 dep., *to enter*
inhaereo 2 - haesi - haesum, *to stick in, cleave to, cling to*
inicio 3 (iacio), *to throw in*
inimicia - ae f, *enmity*
inimicus - i m, *a foe, enemy*
iniquitas - atis f, *wickedness*
iniquus - a - um, *unrighteous, unjust, sinful*
initio 1, *to initiate*
initium - i n, *a beginning*
iniuria - ae f, *injustice, wrong*
innocentia - ae f, *innocence, sanctity*
innotesco 3 - notui, *to become known*
innoxius - a - um, *unhurt, unharmed*
innumerus - a - um, *countless*
inopia - ae f, *poverty, indigence*
inquam, *I say*
inquino 1, *to stain, corrupt*
inquisitio - onis f, *investigation, inquisition*
inquisitor - oris m, *investigator, inquisitor*
insatiabilis - e, *insatiable*
inscius - a - um, *ignorant, not knowing* (w. gen.)
insector 1 dep., *to attack, harass*
insequor 3 dep., *to pursue*
insero 3 - serui - sertum, *to introduce, enroll among* (w dat.)
inservio 4, *to serve*
insidiae - arum f, *a snare, plot, treachery*
insidior 1 dep., *to plot against* (w. dat.)
insido 3 - sedi -sessum, *to sit, perch on*
insigne - is n, *a distinguishing token; mark, sign*
insignio 4, *to distinguish, make prominent*
insignis - e, *distinguished, eminent*
insignitus - a - um, *marked, distinguished*
insisto 3 - stiti, *to follow hard upon, pursue; persist in*
insolesco 3, *to become haughty, insolent*
insolitus - a - um, *unusual, strange*
inspecto 1, *to look on, observe*
instauro 1, *to set up, establish, restore*
instituo 3 - ui -utum, *to establish, ordain; teach*
institutio - onis f, *an established rule, custom; instruction*
institutor - oris m, *a teacher*
institutum - i n, *a practise, custom, institution*
insto 1, - stiti, *to be on hand, impend; insist pressingly*
instruo 3 - struxi - structum, *to instruct, train*
insuetus - a - um, *unusual*
insula - ae f, *an island*
insulanus - i m, *an islander*
insulto 1, *to leap*

insumo 3, *to expend upon*
insuper, *adv., in addition, moreover*
integer - gra - grum, *entire, whole; upright*
integritas - atis f, *integrity, completeness*
intellectus - us m, *the intellect, understanding*
intellegentia - ae f, *understanding, power of understanding*
intendo 3, *to direct one's thoughts to, to apply the mind to*
inter, *prep. w. acc., between, among, in;* inter haec, *meanwhile;* inter orandum, *in prayer*
intercedo 3, *to intercede*
intercessio - onis f, *intercession*
intercessor - oris m, *a mediator, interceder*
intercipio 3 (capio), *to interrupt*
interdictum - i n, *an interdict*
interiu, *adv., by day*
interdum, *adv., occasionally, from time to time*
interea, *adv., meanwhile*
intereo, *to perish, die*
interficio 3 (facio), *to kill*
interim, *adv., meanwhile, in the meantime*
interitus - us m, *destruction, death*
intericio 3 (iacio), *to put between*
intermitto 3, *to interrupt; neglect*
interpres - pretis m, *an interpreter, expounder*
interpretor 1 dep., *to explain, expound, interpret*
interrogo 1, *to question, interrogate*
intersum, *to be present at, take part in*
interventus - us m, *intercession*
intimus - a - um, *close, intimate*
introduco 3, *to bring in*
intueor - tueri - tuitus sum 2 dep., *to gaze at*
intus, *adv., within, inside*
inusitatus - a - um, *unusual, uncommon*
inutilis - e, *useless, unprofitable*
invado 3 - vasi - vasum, *to assail, seize*
invenio 4, *to come upon, find*
invictus - a - um, *invincible, unconquered*
invidia - ae f, *jealousy, ill-will*
invidus - a - um, *envious, jealous*
inviolabilis - e, *inviolable*
invito 1, *to invite*
invitus - a - um, *unwilling*
invoco 1, *to invoke, call upon*
ipse - a - um, *self*
ira - ae f, *wrath, violence*
iratus - a - um, *angry, angered*
irrepo, 3 - repsi - reptum, *to creep in*
irrideo 2 - risi - risum, *to laugh at, jeer at*
irrisio - onis f, *a mocking, derision*
is ea id, *he, she, it; this, that*
iste ista istud, *that*
ita, *adv., so, in such a way*

itaque, adv., *therefore, and so*
iter itineris n, *a journey*
itero 1, *to repeat*
iterum, adv., *again, a second time*
itidem, adv., *likewise, in like manner*
iubeo 2 - iussi - iussum, *to order*
iubilaeus - a - um, *pertaining to a Jubilee, of the Jubilee*
iudex - icis m, *a judge*
iugis - e, *continual, constant;* iugiter, adv., *constantly*
iugum - i n, *a yoke*
iuridicus - a - um, *pertaining to the law, juridical*
ius iuris n, *law;* iura pl., *rights*
iusiurandum - i n, *an oath*
iussu, abl., *by order of*
iustificatus - a - um, *justified*
iustitia - ae f, *justice, rectitude*
iustus - a - um, *fair, right, just*
iuvenilis - e, *youthful*
iuvenis - is, *young, youthful*
iuventa - ae f, *youth*
iuventas - atis f, *youth*
iuvo 1, *to help, assist*
iuxta, prep. w. acc., *according to; near*

labefacto 1, *to weaken, cause to totter*
labes - is f, *a stain, blemish*
¹ labor labi lapsus sum 3 dep., *to fall down, slip*
² labor - oris m, *work, labor, toil*
laboro 1, *to labor, toil*

lacero 1, *to cut to pieces, mangle*
lacrima - ae f, *a tear*
lacrimosus - a - um, *tearful*
lactens - entis, *sucking milk, nursing*
laetifico 1, *to gladden, make joyful*
laetitia - ae f, *joy, delight*
laetor 1 dep., *to take delight in, rejoice in*
laicus - i m, *a layman*
lamina - ae f, *an iron plate*
lampas - adis f, *a torch, light*
langueo 2, *to be faint, weak*
languor - oris m, *faintness, weariness*
lapis - idis m, *a stone*
latebra - ae f, *a hiding-place, retreat*
lateo 2, *to lie hid, be concealed*
¹ latus - a - um, *broad, wide;* late, adv., *widely*
² latus - eris n, *the side*
laura - ae f, *a cloister, monastery*
laus laudis f, *praise, fame*
lavacrum - i n, *a bath, washing*
laxus - a - um, *loose, lax, unrestrained*
lectio - onis f, *a reading*
legatio - onis f, *an embassy, an official mission*
legatus - i m, *a legate, representative*
¹ lego 1, *to send as ambassador*
² lego 3 legi lectum *to read*
lenio 4, *to soothe, pacify*
lenis - e, *smooth, soft;* leniter, adv., *softly, gently*

leo leonis m, *a lion*
leopardus - i m, *a leopard*
lethalis - e, *fatal*
levo 1, *to relieve, alleviate*
lex legis f, *law*
libellum - i n, *a small book*
libenter, adv., *with pleasure, gladly*
liber - bri m, *a book*
liberalis - e, *liberal, pertaining to a gentleman;* liberaliter, adv., *in a manner becoming a gentleman, i.e., in the 'liberal' arts; also, kindly, generously*
libere, adv., *without restraint*
libero 1, *to set free, make free*
libertas - atis f, *freedom*
libet - bere - buit, *it pleases, is agreeable*
libido - inis f, *the lower appetite, desire, lust*
licentia - ae f, *freedom, independence, license*
licet licere licuit, *it is allowed;* licet, conj., *although*
lignum - i n, *wood*
ligo 1, *to bind*
lineus - a - um, *linen, of linen*
lingua - ae f, *tongue, language*
litania - ae f, *a litany*
litterae - arum f, *literature; studies, writings; a letter*
locus - i m, *a place*
longinquus - a - um, *distant, remote*
longus - a - um, *long;* longe, adv., *far, at a distance;* longe lateque, adv., *far and wide*
loquor loqui locutus sum 3 dep., *to speak*
lucrifacio 3, *to gain*
luctor 1 dep., *to struggle, contend*
luctus - us m, *grief, sorrow*
lucubro 1, *to compose at night; compose carefully*
luculenter, adv., *splendidly, brilliantly*
lucus - i m, *a sacred grove*
ludibrium - i n, *scorn, scoffing*
ludo 3 lusi lusum, *to play*
lues - is f, *a calamity*
lumbus - i m, *the loins*
lumen - inis n, *a light*
lustralis - e, *purifying, holy*
lustro 1, *to visit, review; purify*
lux lucis f, *light*

maceratio - onis f, *mortification, fasting, subjection by fasting*
maculo 1, *to stain, defile*
maereo 2, *to be mournful grieve*
magicus - a - um, *pertaining to magic*
magis, compar. adv., *more*
magister - tri m, *a teacher, master*
magnopere, adv., *greatly, very much*
magnus - a - um, *great, large;* comp., maior, maius; superl., maximus - a - um
maior maius, comp. of magnus
maiores - um m, *elders, predecessors, ancestors*
malignus - a - um, *malicious, wicked*

malleus - i m, *a hammer*
malus - a - um, *evil, bad;* comp., peior, peius; superl., **pessimus** - a - um; **mala** - orum n, *evils*
mamilla - ae f, *the breast*
mancipium - i n, *a slave*
mandatum - i n, *a command, order*
mando 1, *to command, order*
manduco 1, *to eat*
maneo 2 mansi mansum, *to stay, remain*
manus -us f, *the hand; a band, group*
mare maris n, *the sea*
maritus - i m, *a husband*
martyr - yris c, *a witness, martyr*
martyrium - i n, *martyrdom*
mater matris f, *a mother*
maternitas - atis f, *motherhood*
maternus - a - um, *motherly, maternal*
maximus - a - um, superl. of **magnus; Pontifex maximus,** *the Supreme Pontiff;* **maxime,** adv., *especially*
medicus - i m, *a doctor*
meditatio - onis f, *contemplation, thinking over*
meditor 1 dep., *to contemplate, consider*
medius - a - um, *middle, in the middle*
melior melius, comp. of bonus
membrum - i n, *a limb of the body*
memini -isse, perf. with present sense, *to remember, call to mind* (w. gen.)
memor - oris, *mindful, grateful*
memorabilis - e, *memorable, worthy of mention*
memoria - ae f, *memory; history, tradition*
mens mentis f, *the mind*
mensis - is m, *a month*
mentio - onis f, *mention;* **mentionem facere,** *to mention*
merces - edis f, *reward, wages*
mereo 2 - ui - itum and **mereor** 2 dep., *to deserve, merit, earn*
mergeo 3 mersi mersum, *to immerse, dip*
merito, adv., *deservedly*
meritum - i n, *merit*
Messias - ae m, *the Anointed One, the Messiah*
methodus - i f, *a method*
metior metiri mensus 4 dep., *to measure*
metropolis - is f, *a chief city*
meus - a - um, *my, mine*
migro 1, *to go, depart*
miles - itis m, *a soldier*
militia - ae f, *military service, warfare*
milliarium - i n, *a mile-stone*
minae - arum f, *threats*
minimus - a - um, superl. of parvus; **minime,** adv., *least of all, not at all*
minister - tri m, *a servant, helper*
ministerium - i n, *ministry*
ministro 1, *to wait upon, serve*
minitor 1 dep., *to threaten* (w. dat.)
minor minus, comp. of parvus

minuo 3 - ui - utum, *to lessen, diminish*
mirabilis - e, *wonderful, extraordinary;* mirabiliter, adv., *in an extraordinary way*
miraculum - i n, *a wonderful thing, a miracle, a wonder*
mirificus - a - um, *wonderful, extraordinary*
mirus - a - um, *wonderful*
miser - era - erum, *miserable, unhappy*
misere, adv., *miserably*
misericordia - ae f, *pity, compassion*
misericors - cordis, *compassionate, merciful;* misericorditer, adv., *mercifully*
miseror 1 dep., *to pity, have compassion*
Missa -ae and Missae -arum f, *the Mass*
mitto 3 misi missum, *to send*
moderator - oris m, *a governor, controller, superior*
moderor 1 dep., *to direct, govern*
modestia - ae f, *propriety, obedience to authority*
modicus - a - um, *limited, moderate*
modo, adv., *just now:* non modo ... sed, *not just ... but also*
modus - i m, *a way, method*
molestia - ae f, *troublesomeness, annoyance*
molior 4 dep., *to contrive, devise, construct, build*
mollis - e, *soft, gentle*
molo 3 - ui - itum, *to grind*

monacha - ae f, *a nun*
monachus - i m, *a monk*
monasterium - i n, *a monastery*
monasticus - a - um, *monastic*
monitum - i n, *counsel, admonition*
monitus - us m, *a warning, admonition*
mons montis f, *a mountain*
monstro 1, *to show, inform*
monumentum - i n, *a memorial, monument*
morbus - i m, *sickness*
mores - um m, *morals, conduct*
morigerus - a - um, *accomodating, compliant*
morior mori mortuus sum 3 dep., *to die;* mortuus - a - um, *dead*
mors mortis f, *death*
mortalis - e, *subject to death; deadly;*
mortalis - is m, *a mortal man, a man*
mos moris m, *a custom, rule, law;* more, abl., *after the manner of* (w. gen.); de more, *in the customary manner*
moveo 2 movi motum, *to move, influence*
mox, adv., *soon, presently*
mulier - eris f, *a woman*
muliercula - ae f, dimin. of mulier: *a contemptible woman*
multitudo - inis f, *a large number, multitude*
multiplex - plicis, *manifold, of many kinds*
multus - a - um, *much, many;*

comp., **plus pluris;** superl., **plurimus** - a - um; **multo,** abl., *by far*
[1] **mundus** - a - um, *clean*
[2] **mundus** - i m, *the world*
munia - orum n, *official duties*
munio 4, *to fortify*
munus - eris n, *an office, function; a gift*
murus - i m, *a wall*
muto 1, *to change, alter*
mysterium - i n, *a mystery, sacred rite*

nam adv., *for*
nancisoor - isci - nactus 3 dep., *to obtain, get*
narro 1, *to make known, relate*
nascor nasci natus sum 3 dep., *to be born*
natalis - e, *pertaining to birth;*
natalis - is (dies), *a birthday*
natalitia - orum n, *a birthday*
natio - onis f, *birth, stock, family, race, people*
nativitas - atis f, *birth, nativity*
naufragium - i n, *shipwreck, ruin, destruction*
navicula - ae f, *a boat*
navigo 1, *to sail*
navo 1, *to do something energetically*
ne, conj., *that ... not*
nec, neque, conj., *and not, nor;* **necnon,** *and also;* **nec ... nec,** *neither ... nor*
necessarius - a - um, *necessary, required*
neco 1, *to kill, slay*
nedum, conj., *not to mention, to say nothing of*
nefarius - a - um, *abominable, impious*
negotium - i n, *business, affairs*
nemo neminis c, *no one*
nempe, adv. *namely; to be sure*
neophytus - a - um, *newly planted;* **neophytus** - i m, *a recent convert*
nepos - otis m, *a nephew*
nequam, indecl.; *worthless, good for nothing;* superl. **nequissimus**
nequidquam, adv., *in vain, to no purpose*
nescio 4 - ivi and - ii - itum, *not to know*
nex necis f, *death, murder*
nihil, indecl., *nothing*
nihilominus, adv., *nevertheless*
nimirum, adv., *verily, truly;* often=emphatic adj., *very*
nisi, conj., *unless, if not; except*
nitor niti nisus sum 3 dep., *to strive, endeavor*
niveus - a - um, *white as snow*
nix nivis f, *snow*
nobilis - e, *noble, distinguished*
nobilito 1, *to make famous, make renowned*
nolo nolle nolui, *to be unwilling, refuse*
nomen nominis n, *a name; account, heading, ground, pretext*
nomino 1, *to name, call, mention*
non, adv., *not*

nondum, *adv; not yet*
nonne, interr. adv., *expecting answer yes*
nos, pl. of ego, *we*
noster - tra - trum, *our, ours*
nota - ae f, *a sign, distinguishing mark*
notitia - ae f, *knowledge*
notus - a - um, *known*
novies, adv., *nine times*
novus - a - um, *new*
nox noctis f, *night;* **noctu,** adv., *by night*
nudus - a - um, *uncovered, bare*
nullus - a - um, *no one, none, not any*
numen - inis n, *the power of God*
numerosus - a - um, *numerous*
numerus - i m, *a number, company; metre*
nummum - i n, *a piece of money, coin*
numquam, adv., *never*
nunc, adv., *now*
nuncupo 1, *to name, call by name*
nuntio 1, *to announce, report*
nuntius - i m, *a messenger, nuncio*
nuper, adv., *recently*
nuptiae - arum f, *a marriage*
nutricius - a - um, *one who rears, nourishes*
nutrix - icis f, *a nurse*
nutus - us m, *a nod, command, will*

ob, prep. w. acc., *because of*

obdormisco 3 - dormivi, *to sleep*
obduco 3, *to draw over, cover*
obduratus - a - um, *hardened*
obeo, *to go to; apply oneself to, perform, underake; to die*
obicio 3 (iacio), *to throw in the way, expose*
obitus - us m, *death*
obiurgatio - onis f, *a rebuke, chiding*
oboedientia - ae f, *obedience*
oborior 4 dep., *to arise, come up*
obruo 3 - rui - rutum, *to cover over, bury*
obscurus - a - um, *unintelligible, obscure*
obsecro 1, *to beseech, implore*
obsequens - entis, *obedient, submissive*
obsequium - i n, *submission, service, obedience*
observans - antis, *attentive, watchful*
observantia - ae f, *observance, devotion*
obsessus - a - um, *beset, harassed*
obsidio - onis f, *a siege*
obsisto 3 stiti - stitum, *to oppose, resist*
obstringo 3 - strinxi -strictum, *to bind*
obtempero 1, *to comply with, submit to* (w. dat.)
obtestor 1 dep., *to implore*
obtineo 2 (teneo), *to grasp, hold, possess, obtain*
obtingo 3 - tigi, *to fall to the lot of*

occultus - a - um, *hidden, secret;* **occulte,** adv., *secretly*
occurro 3 - curri - cursum, *to meet, come in the way* (w. dat.)
octava - ae f, *an octave of prayer*
oculus - i m, *the eye*
odi odisse, *to hate, detest*
odium - i n, *hatred*
odor - oris m, *a smell, odor*
oecumenicus - a - um, *ecumenical, general*
offero, *to offer, present*
officium - i n, *a position, office, service; the Divine Office, the Breviary*
olim, adv., *formerly, once upon a time, once;* also almost as an adj., *former*
omnino, adv., *entirely, wholly*
omnipotens - entis, *all-powerful*
omnis - e, *every, all*
onustus - a - um, *filled with, loaded with*
opera - ae f, *trouble, pains, efforts;* **opera,** abl., *thanks to;* **operam dare,** *to work hard at* (w. dat.)
operarius - i m, *a worker*
operatio - onis f, *labor, work*
operor 1 dep., *to work, perform* (w. dat. and acc.)
opis (gen.; no nom.) f, *help;* in pl, **opes,** opum, *power, resources*
opinio - onis f, *general report, repute*
opertet - tere - tuit, *it behooves, is proper; one should*

oppidani - orum n, *the inhabitants of a town*
oppidum - i n, *a town*
opprimo (premo), *to press down, crush, exstinguish*
oppugno 1, *to attack*
optimus - a - um, superl. of bonus
optio - onis f, *a choice*
opto 1, *to desire, wish for*
opulentia - ae f, *wealth, riches*
opus - eris n, *work, labor*
ora - ae f, *an edge, short-line, border*
oraculum - i n, *a prophecy*
oratio - onis f, *a prayer; language; eloquence*
oratorium - i n, *an oratory, place of prayer*
orbatus - a - um, *bereft of, bereaved of* (w. abl.)
orbis - is m, *anything round;* **orbis terrae** (or **terrarum**), *the world*
ordino 1, *to ordain to the priesthood*
ordo - inis m, *order, arrangement*
orientalis - e, *oriental, eastern*
orior oriri ortus sum 4 dep., *to spring from, be born from*
oriundus - a - um, *springing from, descended from*
oro 1, *to pray*
ornamentum - i n, *an ornament*
ornatus - us m, *an adornment, embellishment*
orno 1, *to adorn, honor*
oro 1, *to beg, pray*
orthodoxus - a - um, *orthodox,*

approved
¹ os oris n, *the mouth*
² os ossis n, *a bone*
osculum - i n, *a kiss*
ostendo 3 - tendi - tentum and - tensum, *to show, display*
otium - i n, *free time, leisure*
ovis - is f, *a sheep*

pabulum - i n, *food*
paene, adv., *nearly, almost*
paenitentia - ae f, *penance, repentance*
palaestra - ae f, *a wrestling school, gymnasium*
palam, adv., *openly, publicly*
pallium i n, *a mantle*
palma - ae f, *a palm, palm-branch*
palpo 1, *to touch*
panis - is m, *bread*
Papa - ae m, *the Pope*
par paris, *equal, like*
parco 3 peperci parcitum, *to spare, refrain from injuring* (w. dat.)
parcus - a - um, *sparing, frugal*
parens - entis c, *a parent*
paries - etis m, *a wall*
pario 3 peperi partum, *to bring forth, produce*
pariter, adv., *likewise*
paro 1, *to prepare, get obtain*
pars partis f, *a part*
particeps - cipis, *a sharer, participant*
partim ... partim, adv., *in part ... in part*
partus - us m, *a birth, childbirth*
parum, adv., *too little, not enough*
parvulus - a - um, *very small, very little*
Pascha - ae f, *Easter*
pasco 3 pavi pastum, *to feed, nourish*
pascuus - i n, *a pasture*
passio - onis f, *passion, suffering*
passus - us m, *a step, stride;* mille passus, *a mile*
pastor - oris m, *a shepherd*
pater - tris m, *a father*
paternus - a - um, *ancestral*
patiens - enis, *patient;* patienter, adv., *patiently*
patientia - ae f, *patience*
patior pati passus sum 3 dep., *to suffer*
patria - ae f, *native land*
patriarcha - ae m, *a patriarch*
patricius - a - um, *patrician, noble*
patro 1, *to perform, accomplish, bring to pass*
patrocinium - i n, *patronage, protection*
patronus - i m, *a patron, protector*
patruus - i m, *an uncle*
paucus - a - um, *few, little*
paulatim, adv., *gradually, little by little*
paulus - a - um, *little, small;* paulo, adv., *by a little*
pauper - eris, *poor*
paupertas - atis f, *poverty*
pax pacis f, *peace*
peccator - oris m, *a sinner*

peccatum - i n, *a sin*
pecten, - inis m, *a comb; any instrument resembling a comb*
pectus -oris n, *the breast*
peior peius, comp. of malus
pellis - is f, *the skin*
pello 3 pepuli pulsum, *to drive, drive away*
pendeo 2 pependi, *to hang*
penes, prep. w. acc., *with, in the presence of, at*
penetralia - um n, *the interior, inmost part*
penetro 1, *to make one's way into, enter, penetrate*
penitus, adv., *thoroughly, completely*
per, prep. w. acc., *through;* **per somnium**, *in sleep*
perago 3, *to carry through, complete, accomplish*
perago 1, *to wander through, travel through*
percontor 1 dep., *to inquire, question*
percrebresco 3 - bui, *to become very well known, to be spread abroad*
percurro 3 - cucurri or - curri - cursum, *to run through*
percutio 3 - cussi - cussum, *to strike, beat*
perditus - a - um, *abandoned, morally lost*
perdo 3 - didi - ditum, *to destroy, ruin, waste, lose*
perduco 3, *to bring over to, bring to; prolong*
pergratus - a - um, *very pleasant, pleasing*

peregrinans - antis, *a pilgrim*
peregrinatio - onis f, *a pilgrimage*
peregrinus - i, *a pilgrim*
perennis - e, *lasting, eternal*
perfectus - a - um, *perfect*
perfero, *to suffer, endure*
perficio 3(facio), *to make perfect, perfect*
perfundo 3 (^{2} fundo), *to steep in, fill with*
perfungor 3 dep., *to perform fully, discharge* (w. abl.)
pergo 3 perrexi perrectum, *to proceed*
perhibeo 2 (habeo), *to assert, maintain, say*
periclitor 1 dep., *to be in danger*
periculum - i n, *danger*
perinde, adv., *in like manner;* **perinde ... ac**, *just as if*
permaneo 2, *to remain, stay, continue in*
permitto 3, *to allow*
permoveo 2, *to move, persuade, influence*
pernocto 1, *to spend the night*
perosus - a - um, *detesting, hating*
perpetior - peti pessus 3 dep., *to endure* (patior)
perpetuus - a - um, *perpetual, unfailing;*
perpetuo, adv., *forever, uninterruptedly*
perrexit, perf. of pergo
persecutio - onis f, *persecution*
persentio 4, *to perceive clearly*
persevero 1, *to persist, continue*

persona - ae f, *a person*
personaliter, adv., *personally, in person*
perspicuus - a - um, *clear, manifest*
persuadeo 2, *to persuade* (w. dat.)
pertaesus - a - um, *sick of, disgusted at* (w. gen.)
pertinax - acis, *tenacious, obstinate*
pertingo 3, *reach to*
pertracto 1, *to handle, lay hold of*
perturbo 1, *to trouble, disturb*
pervenio 4, *to reach, come through to*
pervinco 3 - vici - victum, *to overcome completely*
pervoluto 1, *to unroll, read*
pervulgo 1, *to spread about, make known*
pes pedis m, *the foot*
pestilentia - ae f, *a plague*
peto 3 - ivi and - ii - itum, *to seek, make for, go to*
petra - ae f, *a rock*
petulanter, adv., *pertly, impudently*
philosophia - ae f, *philosophy*
philosophicus - a um, *philosophical*
philosophus - i m, *a philosopher*
pictus - a - um *painted*
piens - entis, *pious*
pietas - atis f, *dutifulness, devotion*
pius - a - um, *dutiful, virtuous, devout*
placatus - a - um, *appeased, pacified*
placeo 2 - ui - itum, *to please* (w. dat.)
placidus - a - um, *quiet, gentle*
plaga - ae f, *a blow*
plane, adv., *clearly, plainly*
plaudo 3 plausi plausum, *to applaud, approve*
plebs plebis f, *the people*
plenus - a - um, *full of, abounding in* (w. abl., gen.); **plene**, adv., *fully, completely*
plerusque - raque - rumque, *very many; the most part*
ploratus - us m, *a weeping, crying*
pluries, adv., *many times*
plus pluris, comp. of multus
plurimus - a - um, superl. of multus
pluvia - ae - f, *rain*
poculum - i n, *a drinking cup*
polleo 2, *to be strong, powerful* (w. abl.)
pondus - eris n, *weight, burden*
pono 3 posui positum, *to set down, place*
pontifex - icis m, *a bishop, pontiff*
pontificatus - us m, *a pontificate*
pontificius - a - um, *pontifical, papal*
popularis - e, *belonging to the same people*
popularis - is m, *a fellow-countryman*
populus - i m, *a people*
porrigo 3 - rexi - rectum, *to*

stretch out, extend, offer
porro, adv., *henceforth, from then on*
porta - ae f, *a gate*
portendo 3 - tendi - tentum, *to indicate, predict, foretell*
porto 1, *to carry*
possibilitas - atis f, *ability, power*
possum posse potui, *to be able, I can*
post, prep. w. acc., *after;* adv., *afterwards*
postea, adv., *afterwards*
postmodum, adv., *soon, presently*
postquam, conj., *after*
postremus - a - um, *last;* **postremo,** adv., *at last*
postridie, adv., *on the next day*
postulatio - onis f, *a petition*
postulo 1, *to ask, demand*
potens - entis, *powerful*
potentia - ae f, *power*
potestas - atis f, *power, authority*
potio - onis f, *a drink*
potissimum, adv., *c h i e f l y, above all*
potius, adv., *rather, preferably*
prae, prep. w. abl., *before, in front of;* **prae se ferre,** *to show, manifest*
praebeo 2 - bui - bitum, *to offer, show, present*
praecellens - entis, *excellent, surpassing*
praeceptor - oris m, *a teacher*
praeceptum - i n, *a rule of conduct, precept*
praecido 3 - cidi - cisum, *to cut off, mutilate*
praecipio 3 cepi - ceptum, *to instruct, advise, command*
praecipito 1, *to hurl down headlong*
praecipuus - a - um, *especial, outstanding, principal;* **praecipue,** adv., *especially, particularly*
praeclarus - a - um, *outstanding*
praeconium - i n, *praise, commendation*
praedicatio - onis f, *preaching*
praedicator - oris m, *a preacher*
[1] **praedico** 1, *to preach, proclaim*
[2] **praedico** 3, *to predict, foretell*
praefero, *to bear in front, show, display*
praeficio 3 (facio), *to set in command, put in charge* (w. dat.)
praefiguro 1, *to prefigure, show beforehand by a symbol*
praegnans - antis, *pregnant*
praelior 1 dep., *to give battle, fight*
praelium - i n, *a battle, fight*
praeludium - i n, *eve, vigil*
praemitto 3, *to send ahead*
praemium - i n, *reward*
praemoneo 2, *to advise, admonish beforehand*
praenuntio 1, *to foretell, announce beforehand*
praeparo 1, *to prepare, make ready*

praepono 3, *to place before, put before, set in charge of*
praepotens - entis, *very powerful*
praesagio 4, *to have a presentiment of, foretell*
praescio 4, *to know beforehand*
praesens - entis, *present, at hand*
praesentia - ae f, *presence*
praesepe - is n, *a crib, manger*
praesertim, adv., *especially*
praeses - idis m, *a governor, superior*
praesidium - i n, *a defense, protection*
praestans - antis, *excellent, distinguished*
[1] **praesto**, adv., *at hand, ready*
[2] **praesto** 1, - stiti - stitum, *to be distinguished, outstanding; keep, preserve, maintain, perform, grant*
praesul - ulis m, *a director, leader*
praesum, *to be in charge of, preside over*
praeter, prep. w. acc., *beyond, in addition to, contrary to*
praeterea, adv., *besides*
praetermitto 3, *to neglect, omit*
praetor - oris m, *a praetor, governor*
praetorius - a - um, *pertaining to a praetor*
precatio - onis f, *prayer*
precor 1, dep., *to pray, beg*
premo 3 pressi pressum, *to press down, weigh down*
presbyter - eri m, *a priest*
pretiosus - a - um, *costly*

prex precis f, *a prayer, entreaty*
pridem, adv., *long ago, long since*
primarius - a - um, *of the first order, distinguished*
primatus - us m, *primacy*
primus - a - um, *first, foremost;* **primo**, abl., *at first;* **primum**, adv., *first, at first;* **in** and **cum primis**, *principally*
princeps - ipis, *first, foremost; a prince, chief*
[1] **prior prius**, (gen. **prioris**) *former, first;* **prius**, adv., *previously, before, first*
[2] **prior prioris** m, *a prior, superior*
pristinus - a - um, *former, previous, earlier*
privatus - a - um, *private*
privilegium - i n, *a privilege*
privo 1, *to deprive of*
pro, prep. w. abl., *for, on behalf of*
probo 1, *to declare something good, judge of something as good; approve, prove;* **probatus** - a - um, *approved*
procedo 3, *to go forth, advance, proceed*
procer - eris m, *a chief, noble, prince*
procuro 1, *to take care of, look after*
prodigium - i n, *a miracle, marvel*
proditor - oris m, *a traitor*
prodo - didi - ditum, *to betray, hand over*
produco 3, *to bring forward*
profectus - us m, *profit, suc-*

cess, advantage
profero, to bring forth, produce
professio - onis f, acknowledgment, profession
proficio 3 (facio), to make progress, advance
proficiscor - ficisci - fectus sum 3 dep., to set out, depart
profiteor - fiteri - fessus sum 2 dep., to acknowledge, profess
profligo 1, to overpower, overcome
profundus - a - um, deep, profound
progredior 3 dep., to advance
prohibeo 2 (habeo), to forbid, prevent
proicio 3 (iacio), to throw forth, fling out
prolabor 1 dep., to fall forward, side forward
proles - is f, offspring, child
prolixe, adv., willingly
promitto 3, to promise
promotor - oris m, one who encourages, a promoter
promoveo 2, to promote foster, advance
promulgo 1, to promulgate, make known
pronuntio 1, to pronounce, declare
propago 1, to spread, extend, propagate
prope, prep. w. acc., near, hard by; adv., near, almost; comp., propius; superl., proxime
propemodum, adv., almost, nearly
propheta - ae m, a prophet
prophetia - ae f, a prophecy
propheticus - a - um, prophetic, prophetical
propitius - a - um, favorable, kind, propitious
propono 3, to propose, put forward
propositum - i n, intention, purpose
proprius - a - um, one's own, personal, peculiar;
propter, prep. w. acc., on account of
propterea, adv., on that account, therefore
propugnator - oris m, a defender
propugno 1, to defend
propulso 1, to repel, drive back
proscribo 3, to condemn, proscribe
prosequor 3 dep., to attend, follow; imitate
prosilio 4 - ui, to leap forth
prosum prodesse profui, to be useful, benefit
protectio - onis f, protection
protego 3 - texi - tectum, to protect
prout, conj., just as, according as
proveho 3 - vexi - vectum, to carry forward, promote
provenio 4, to come forth
providentia - ae f, providence
provincia - ae f, a country
provoco 1, to call forth, provoke

provolvo 3 - volvi - volutum, *to roll forward;* pass, in middle sense, *to throw oneself down*
proximus - a - um, superl. of proprior, *nearest, very close to;* **proximus** - i m, *a neighbor*
prudens - entis, *prudent*
prudentia - ae f, *prudence*
psalterium - i n, *the psalter*
publicus - a - um, *public;*
publice, adv., *publicly, before the public*
pudet pudere, *it shames* (w. gen. of thing causing shame)
pudicitia - ae f, *modesty, chastity*
puella - ae f, *a girl*
puer - i m, *a child, boy*
pugno 1, *to fight*
pulchritudo - inis f, *beauty*
punior 4 dep., *to punish*
purgo 1, *to cleanse, purify*
puritas - atis f, *purity*
purpuratus - a - um, *clad in purple;* **pater purpuratus**, *a Cardinal*
purus - a - um, *pure, spotless*
puto 1, *to consider, think*

qua, abl., *where*
quaero 3 quaesivi quaesitum, *to seek to know, to ask*
quaesitum - i n, *a question*
quaestio - onis f, *an inquiry, investigation, question*
quaeso 3, *to beseech, entreat*
qualis - e, *of what kind, what sort of*
qualiscumque qualecumque, *of whatever kind*
qualitas - atis f, *a distinguishing attribute, title*
quam, adv., *than* (with comparatives); as interrog.: *how*
quamdiu, adv., *as long as*
quamplurimi - ae - a, *very many*
quamvis, conj., *however much, although*
quando, conj., *when*
quandoque, adv., *some times, at times*
quandoquidem, conj., *since*
quantus - a - um, *how great*
quare, adv., *why; therefore* (at beginning of sentences)
quasi, adv., *as if, as though, as it were*
que, conj., *and*
quemadmodum, adv., *in what manner, how*
questus - us m, *a lament, complaint*
qui quae quod, *who, what which*
quia, conj., *because; that*
quidam quaedam quoddam; *a certain*
quidem, adv., *indeed;* **ne... quidem**, *not even*
quies - etis f, *rest, quiet, sleep,*
quiesco 3 - evi - etum, *to rest, sleep; to die*
quilibet quaelibet quodlibet, *any one, anything*
quin, conj., *but that;* adv., *nay more, moreover*
quippe, adv., *of course, you see, in fact*

General Vocabulary

quis quid, *who, what*
quisnam quidnam, *who, what*
quisquam quaequam quidquam *anyone, anything*
quisquae quaequae quidquae, *each, every;* (quinto) quoque anno, *every (fifth) year*
quisquis quaequae quidquid, *whoever, whatever*
quivis quaevis quidvis, *any you please, any kind; all kinds of*
quo adv., *whither*
quoad, adv., *as long as, as far as*
quod conj., *because, that;* quod si, *but if*
quomodo, adv., *how, in what manner*
quomodo ... sic, *just as ... so*
quondam, adv., *at some future time, in some past time, once;* almost as an adj., *former*
quoniam, conj., *since, because*
quoque, adv., *also, too*
quot, adj. pl. indecl., *how many*
quotquot, indecl. num., *how many as, however many; all, every*
quousque, conj., *until*

radians - antis, *gleaming*
radius - i m, *a ray, beam of light*
rapio 3 rapui raptum, *to seize; hurry on*
rarus - a - um, *infrequent*
ratio - onis f, *the reason, intellect, manner, method, way, reason*
ratus - a - um, *confirmed, accepted*
realis - e, *actual, authentic*
rebellio - onis f, *a rebellion*
recedo 3, *to retreat, retire*
recenseo 2 -censui - censum, *to recount, relate*
recipio 3 (capio), *to receive;* se recipere, *to retire, retreat*
recitatio - onis f, *a recitation*
recito 1, *to read, recite*
recolo 3, *to reflect upon*
recreo 1, *to restore to health, revive, refresh*
rectus - a - um, *correct, right*
recuso 1, *to refuse, decline*
redarguo 3 - gui, *to refute, show to be false*
reddo 3 - didi - ditum, *to give back, make, render;* gratiam reddere, *to express thanks*
redeo, *to go back, return*
reduco 3, *to lead back, bring back*
refero, *to enter in a record, enroll; bring back, report, repeat*
reficio 3 (facio), *to restore, refresh*
reformo 1, *to reform*
refulgeo 2 - fulsi, *to shine brightly*
regenero 1, *to fill with new life*
regimen - inis n, *rule, government, guidance*

regina - ae f, *a queen*
regio - onis f, *a region, country*
regius - a - um, *royal*
regno 1, *to reign, rule*
regnum - i n, *a kingdom*
rego 3 rexi rectum, *to rule*
regredior 3 dep., *to go back, retreat*
regula - ae f, *a rule*
regularis - e, *regular, pertaining to the rules of a religious community*
reicio 3 (iacio), *to reject*
relaxo 1, *to slacken, ease, lighten*
religio - onis f, *respect, awe; religion*
religiosus - a - um, *religious, pertaining to religion*
relinquo 3 - liqui - lictum, *to leave behind, abandon*
reliquiae - arum f, *remains, relics*
reliquus - a - um, *remaining, left*
reluctor 1 dep., *to struggle against, resist*
remedium - i n, *a remedy*
remitto 3, *to let go back, relax, give up*
removeo 2, *to move back or away*
reparo 1, *to renew, restore*
repello 3, *to drive back; refute*
reperio 4, repperi repertum, *to find, discover*
repeto 3, *to ask back; repeat*
repleo 2 -plevi - pletum, *to fill;*
repletus - a - um, *filled with* (w. gen., abl.)
repraesento 1, *to exhibit, show, display*
reprimo 3 - pressi -pressum, *to check, curb, restrain*
repugno 1, *to oppose, resist*
res rei f, *a thing, circumstance, fact*
resipisco 3 - sipii and - sipui, *to recover one's senses*
resisto 3 - stiti, *to stand against, oppose*
respicio 3 - spexi - spectum, *to look upon, have a regard for*
respondeo 2 - spondi - sponsum, *to answer*
respublica - ae f, *commonwealth; also, administration*
restauro 1, *to restore, rebuild*
restituo 3 - ui - utum, *to restore*
resurgo 3, *to rise again*
resurrectio - onis f, *resurrection*
reticeo 2, *to keep silent about, give no answer about*
retineo 2 (**teneo**), *to hold back, hold fast, keep back*
retundo 3, retudi retusum, *to check, restrain*
revelo 1, *to reveal, make known*
reverenter, adv., *reverently*
reverentia - ae f, *reverence, respect*
revertor 3 dep., *to turn back, return*
revoco 1, *to call back, recall*
rex regis m, *a prince, king*
rigeo 2, *to be stiff, frozen*
rigor - oris m, *severity, hardness*
rite, adv., *properly, rightly*

ritus - us m, *a rite, ceremony*
roboro 1, *to strengthen, make strong*
robur - oris n, *strength, firmness*
rogatu, abl, *at the request of*
rogo 1, *to ask, request*
rosa - ae f, *a rose*
rosarium - i n, *a rosary*
rudimentum - i n, *the first attempt, beginning*
rugio 4 - ivi - itum, *to roar*
rupes - is f, *a rock*
rursum and rursus, adv., *again*
rus ruris n, *the country;* ruri, *in the country*

Sabbatum - i n, *the Sabbath, Saturday*
sacellum - i n, *a small shrine, chapel, oratory*
sacer - cra - crum, *sacred, holy*
sacerdotalis - e, *pertaining to a priest, priestly*
sacerdos, otis m, *a priest*
sacerdotium - i n, *the priesthood*
sacramentum - i n, *a mystery; a sacrament*
sacrificium - i n, *a sacrifice*
sacrifico 1, *to offer sacrifice*
sacrum - i and sacra - orum n, *the Mass*
saecularis - e, *worldly, profane*
saeculum - i n, *a period of time; the world, the present age; a century*
saepe, adv., *often*
saepenumero, adv., *repeatedly, again and again*

saepio 4 saepsi saeptum, *to hedge in, wall in*
saevio 4 - ii - itum, *to rage, be violent, angry*
saevus - a - um, *cruel, savage*
saltem, adv., *at least*
salus - utis f, *health; salvation*
salutaris - e, *beneficial, salutary*
salutatio - onis f, *a greeting*
salvator - oris m, *a savior*
salvo 1, *to save*
sancio 4 sanxi sanctum, *to decree, forbid on pain of punishment*
sanctimonia - ae f, *virtue, sanctity*
sanctitas - atis f, *holiness*
sanctus - a - um, *sacred, holy*
sané, adv., *to be sure, indeed*
sanguineus - a - um *bloody, of blood*
sanguis - inis n, *blood*
sanitas - atis f, *health*
sano 1, *to heal, cure*
sapiens - entis, *wise*
sapientia - ae f, *wisdom*
satago 3 (ago) *to have one's hands full*
satelles - itis c, *an accomplice, abettor*
scelus - eris n, *a crime, evil deed, sin*
schisma - atis n, *a split, division, schism*
schola - ae f, *a school*
scholasticus - a - um, *pertaining to Scholasticism, scholastic*
scientia - ae f, *study, learning, knowledge*

scilicet, adv., *of course, to be sure; namely*
scindo 3 scidi scissum, *to rend, tear asunder*
scio 4 scivi or scii scitum, *to know*
scribo 3 scripsi, scriptum, *to write*
scriptio - onis f, *a writing; the act of writing*
scriptum - i n, *a piece of writing, written work*
Scriptura - ae f, *Sacred Scripture*
scrutor 1 dep., *to examine, investigate*
se, acc., reflexive of third person
secessus - us m, *retirement, withdrawal*
secta - ae f, *a sect, body, group*
sectator - oris m, *a follower*
sector 1 dep., *to follow eagerly*
secus, adv., *otherwise;* followed by **atque, ac, quam**, *differently from*
sed, conj., *but*
sedeo 2 sedi sessum, *to sit*
sedes - is f, *a seat, throne, See; a site*
seditio - onis f, *dissension, quarrel*
sedo 1, *to settle, calm, allay*
sedulitas - atis f, *zeal, diligence*
sedulus - a - um, *zealous;* **sedulo**, adv., *zealously*
segmentum - i n, *a shaving, chip*
semel, adv., *once*
semi-mortuus - a - um, *half dead*
seminarium - i n, *a seminary*
semita - ae f, *a path; narrow way*
semi-vivus - a - um, *half-alive*
semper, adv., *always;* sometimes also as almost an adj., *constant*
sempiternus - a - um, *everlasting*
senator - oris m, *a senator*
senatus - us m, *a senate*
senectus - us m, *old age*
senex senis, *old, an old person*
senium - i n, *old age*
sensibilis - e, *perceptible by the senses;* **sensibiliter**, adv., *perceptibly, physically*
sensus - us m, *a feeling, sense, meaning*
sententia - ae f, *an opinion, decision, meaning*
sentio 4 sensi sensum, *to feel, experience, be aware*
sepelio 4 - pelivi and pelii - pultum, *to bury*
septennis - e, *seven years old*
sepulcrum - i n, *a grave, tomb*
sequor sequi secutus sum 3 dep., *to follow*
sermo - onis m, *a discourse, speech, sermon, language*
sero, adv., *late, at a late period*
servilis - e, *servile, of a slave*
servitus - utis f, *servitude, subjection*
servo 1, *to keep, preserve*
servus - i m, *a servant*
severus - a - um, *strict, austere*
sexennalis - e, *of six years*

sexus - us m, *sex*
si, conj., *if*
sic, adv., *in this way, so*
siccus - a - um, *dry*
sicut, adv., *as, just as*
significo 1, *to indicate, signify*
signo 1, *to mark, stamp*
silentium - i n, *silence*
simoniacus - a - um, *simoniacal*
simplicitas - atis f, *simplicity, innocence*
simul, adv., *at the same time, together*
simulo 1, *to pretend*
simulacrum - i n, *an image, likeness*
sine, prep. w. abl., *without*
singularis - e, *unique, extraordinary*
singulus - a - um, *single, separate;* per dies singulos, *each day*
sinus - us m, *a hollow; the bosom*
siquidem, conj., *for, since, because*
societas - atis f, *society, association*
socius - i m, *a companion*
sodalis - is c, *a comrade, companion*
sodalitas - atis f, *company, brotherhood*
sol solis m, *the sun*
solacium - i n, *comfort, consolation*
solemne - is n, *solemn rite*
solemnis - e, *solemn*
solemnitas - atis f, *solemnity, a solemn feast*

soleo 2 solitus sum, *to be wont, be accustomed*
solerter, adv., *wisely, sagely*
solidus - a - um, *firm*
solitudo - inis f, *seclusion, solitude*
solitus - a - um, *usual, habitual*
sollicitudo - inis f, *concern, solicitude*
sollicitus - a - um, *anxious, watchful*
solus - a - um, *alone, only;* solum, adv., *only;* non solum ... sed etiam, *not only ... but also*
solutus - a - um, *free, unfettered*
somnium - i n, *a dream*
somnum - i m, *sleep*
sonitus - us m, *a sound*
soror oris f, *a sister*
sors sortis f, *a lot, portion*
sortior 4 dep., *to receive, obtain*
spatharius - i, m, *a deputy, subordinate*
spatium - i n, *a time, a period*
species ei f, *shape, outward appearance, aspect*
specimen - inis n, *a specimen, example, token*
spectaculum - i n, *a spectacle, show*
spectatus - a - um, *approved, respected*
specus - us m, f, and n., *a cave, grotto*
spelunca - ae f, *a cave*
spero 1, *to hope*
spina - ae f, *a thorn; a fishbone*

spiritualis - e, *spiritual*
spiritus - us m, *a spirit*
spiro 1, *to breathe out, exhale*
splendidus - a - um, *shining, outstanding*
splendor - oris f, *brilliance, brightness*
sponsus - i m, and sponsa - ae f, *a spouse*
sponte, abl., *of one's own accord; by oneself, unaided*
sportula - ae f, *a basket*
stabilio 4, *to make firm, stable*
statuo 3 - ui - utum, *to place, set, decide*
statim adv., *immediately*
status - us m, *condition, state*
sterno 3 stravi stratum, *to stretch out, spread out*
stimulus - i m, *a goad*
sto 1 steti statum, *to stand*
strenuus - a - um, *vigorous, active*
stringo 3 strinxi strictum, *to draw* (of a sword)
studeo 2 - ui, *to be eager, to strive after, take pains* (w. dat.)
studiosos - a - um, *eager, zealous*
studium - i n, *study, zeal, enthusiasm*
stultitia - ae f, *foolishness, folly*
stuprum - i n, *ravishment, rape*
suadeo 2 suasi suasum, *to advise, recommend*
suasor - oris m, *an adviser*
suasus - us m, *an advising, persuading*
suavis - e, *sweet, pleasant*
sub, prep. w. abl., *under*

subdo 3 - didi - ditum, *to subdue, subject; add, append*
subeo, *to undergo, submit to*
subicio 3 (iacio), *to set under, subject*
subito, adv., *suddenly*
sublatus, see tollo
sublevo 1, *to alleviate, lift up, support*
sublimis - e, *lofty, sublime, exalted;* sublimiter, adv., *on high, highly*
sublimo 1, *to lift on high, exalt*
subministro 1, *to help by supplying*
suborno 1, *to induce, suborn*
subsidiarius - a - um, *furnishing aid*
subtraho 3, *to withdraw, remove, set aside*
suburbanus - a - um, *near the city, on the outskirts*
subvenio 4, *to come to the aid of, assist, help*
succedo 3, *to come after, follow, succeed* (w. dat.)
succendo 3 - cendi - censum, *to set on fire, inflame*
successor - oris m, *a successor*
succingo 3, *to bind, gird*
succresco 3 - crevi, *to increase, grow up*
sufficio 3 (facio), *to put in another's place, choose as substitute; be sufficient, adequate*
suffragor 1 dep., *to support, favor, intercede for*
sugo 3 suxi suctum, *to suck*
suggero 3, *to supply, provide*
sum esse fui futurus, *to be;*

futurus - a - um, *future, about to be*
summa - ae f, *a summary, compendium*
summopere, adv., *utterly, completely*
summus - a - um, *highest, greatest, supreme*
sumo 3 sumpsi sumptum, *to take*
super, prep. w. acc., *above;* w. abl., *over, above, concerning*
superbia - ae f, *pride, arrogance*
superior - ius, *higher, superior to;*
supernaturalis - e, *supernatural*
supernus - a - um, *pertaining to what is above, from above, heavenly*
supero 1, *to overcome, surpass*
superstitio - onis f, *superstition*
superus - a - um, *situated above;* comp., **superior** - ius; superl., **supremus** and **summus**
supplex - plicis, *humbly entreating, suppliant*
supplicatio - onis f, *a supplication, either of request or thanksgiving*
supplicium - i n, *punishment, torture*
suppono 3, *to place under, put under*
supra, prep. w. acc., *above*
supremus - a - um, *last, final;* superl. of **supernus**
surgo 3 surrexi surrectum, *to rise, get up*

suspicio 3 (capio), *to undertake; to receive, accept*
sustento 1, *to support, sustain*
sustineo 2 (teneo), *to maintain, sustain*
sustuli, see **tollo**
suus - a - um, reflexive pronoun, *his, her, its, their (own)*
synodus - i f, *a synod, council*
systema - atis n, *a system*

tam, adv., *so, much;* non tam ... quam, *not so much... as;* tam ... quam, *both... and*
tamdui, adv., *so long*
tamen, conj., *nevertheless*
tamquam, adv., *just as, like, just as if*
tandem, adv., *finally*
tango 3 tetigi tactum, *to touch*
tantum, adv., *only; so much*
tantus - a - um, *so great, so much*
tempero 1, *to keep from, refrain from* (w. *ab*, or abl. alone)
tempestas - atis f, *a period of time; a storm; attack*
templum - i n, *a temple, church*
tempus - oris n, *time*
tenax - acis, *holding fast to, tenacious of* (w. gen.)
tendo 3 tetendi tentum and tensum, *to stretch out, extend*
tenebricosus - a - um, *dark, gloomy*
teneo 2 tenui, *to hold*
tener - era - erum, *tender,*

soft; youthful, young
tento 1, to test, try
tenuis - e, slight, little
tercenties, adv., three hundred times
terra - ae f, earth, land
terraemotus - us m, an earthquake
terrestris - e, of the earth, earthly
tertius - a - um, third; tertio, adv., for the third time
testimonium - i n, testimony, witness
testis - is m, a witness; t. ocularis, an eye-witness
testor 1 dep., to bear witness, assert
tetigi, see tango
theologia - ae f, theology
theologus - i m, a theologian
thronus - i m, a throne
timeo 2, to fear
timor - oris m, fear
titio - onis f, a burning brand, firebrand
titulus - i m, a title
tolero 1, to bear, carry, endure
tollo 3 sustuli sublatus, to raise up, take away, carry off
tondeo 2 totondi tonsum, to shave, cut
tormentum - i n, torture, torment
torqueo 2 torsi tortum, to twist, torture
tot, indecl. num. adj., so many
toties, adv., so many times
totus - a - um, whole, entire
tractabilis - e, palpable, tangible

trado 3 - didi - ditum, to hand over, hand down to posterity, teach
traduco 3, to lead, bring, carry across
traho 3 traxi tractum, to draw, drag
traicio 3 (iacio), to convey across
trames - itis m, a way, path
tranquillitas - atis f, calm
transeo, to go over, pass over
transfero, to translate; carry to, transfer
transfiguratio - onis f, transfiguration
transigo 3 (ago), to spend, pass
transmissio - onis f, a passage, crossing
transversus - a - um, in an oblique position
tribuo 3 - ui - utum, to assign, give, grant, attribute
triennium - i n, a space of three years; singulis trienniis, every three years
triumpho 1, to triumph
truncus - a - um, cut off, truncated
tueor tueri tuitus sum 2 dep., to safeguard, protect
tum, adv., then; tum ... tum, both ... and
tumultus - us m, uproar, disturbance
tunc, adv., then, at that time
tunica - ae f, a tunic
turba - ae f, a throng, crowd
tutela - ae f, charge, custody, guardianship

tuto 1, *to protect, guard*
tuus - a - um, *your*
tyrannus - i m, *a tyrant*

¹ uber - eris, *rich, fertile*
² uber - eris n, *the breast*
ubi, conj., *where*
ubique, adv., *everywhere;* ubique terrarum, *everywhere in the world*
ullus - a - um, *any*
ultimus - a - um, *last*
ultra, adv., *besides, moreover;* prep. w. acc., *beyond, more than*
ultro, adv., *of one's own accord, voluntarily*
umerus - i m, *the shoulder*
umquam, adv., *ever, at any time*
unanimis - e, *unanimous*
unde, adv., *whence, from where*
undique, adv., *from all sides, from everywhere*
unguentum - i n, *ointment*
unicus - a - um, *one, only, sole;* unice, adv., *solely, particularly, one only*
unitas - atis f, *unity*
universalis - e, *universal*
universitas - atis, f, *a university*
universus - a - um, *whole, entire, all*
unus - a - um, *one, only one, one alone;*
una, adv., *together*
urbanus - a - um, *of a city, urban*

urbs urbis f, *a city; Rome*
urgeo 2 ursi, *to drive on, press on*
uro 3 ussi ustum, *to burn*
usque, adv., *as far as, all the way to*
usurpo 1, *to take possession of, appropriate*
usus - us m, *use, familiarity*
ut, conj., *in order that; that as a result; as;* ut ... ita or sic, *as ... so*
uterque utraque utrumque *both*
uti = ut
utilis - e, *useful, profitable* (w. dat.)
utilitas - atis f, *profit, advantage*
utinam, adv., *would that!*
utor uti usus sum 3 dep., *to use, employ* (w. abl.)
utpote, adv., *as, as being*
uxor - oris f, *a wife*

vacca ae f, *a cow*
vaco 1, *to have time for* (w. dat.), *devote oneself to*
valde, adv., *very much, greatly*
valeo 2, *to be strong, to have strength for, to be able to*
valetudo - inis f, *state of health*
validus - a - um, *strong, powerful*
varietas - atis f, *variety, diversity*
varius - a - um, *different, various*
vas vasis n, *a receptacle, cup, vessel*

vastatio - onis f, *devastation*
vehemens - entis, *violent, strong, ardent;* **vehementer,** adv., *violently*
vel, conj., *or;* adv., *especially, even;* **vel ... vel,** *either ... or*
velamen - inis n, *a covering, veil*
velo 1, *to cover, veil*
velox - ocis, *quick, swift*
veluti, adv., *as it were, just as, as if*
venditio - onis f, *a selling, sale*
vendito 1, *to sell, offer repeatedly for sale*
vendo 3 - didi - ditum, *to sell*
veneno 1, *to poison;* **venenatus** - a - um, *poisoned*
venenum - i n, *poison*
venerabilis - e, *venerable*
veneratio - onis f, *veneration, honor*
veneror 1 dep., *to worship, venerate;* **venerandus** - a - um, *venerable*
venio 4 veni ventum, *to come;* **venturus** - a - um, *pertaining to the future, coming*
venor 1 dep., *to hunt*
vepres - is m, *a thorn-bush, bramble*
verber - eris n, *a lash, scourge*
verberatio - onis f, *a flogging, lashing*
verbum - i n, *a word*
vereor - eri - itus sum 2 dep., *to fear*
veritas - atis f, *truth*
vernaculus - a - um, *native*
vero, adv., *indeed; but*

versor 1 dep., *to be engaged in, be employed in*
verto 3 verti versum, *to turn; to translate;* **anno vertente,** *in the course of a year*
verum, adv., *nevertheless, but*
verus - a - um, *true, real;* **vere,** adv., *truly, rightly*
vester - tra - trum, *your, yours*
vestimentum - i n, *a garment*
vestis - is f, *clothing, dress*
vestitus - us m, *clothing, clothes*
veto 1, *to forbid*
vetus - eris, *old, ancient;* **veteres** - um m, *elders, ancients*
vexatio - onis f, *vexation, agitation*
vexillum - i n, *a banner, flag*
vexo 1, *to harass, torment*
via viae f, *a way, road*
vicarius - i m, *a representative, substitute*
vicinus - a - um, *near, neighboring* (w. dat.)
vicissim, adv., *in turn*
victoria - ae f, *victory*
video 2 vidi visum, *to see;* in pass., *to seem*
vidua - ae f, *a widow*
viduitas - atis f, *widowhood*
vigeo 2, *to thrive, flourish*
vigilantia - ae f, *watchfulness*
vigilia - ae f, *a vigil*
vilis - e, *cheap, worth little*
vincio 4 vinxi vinctum, *to bind, fetter;* **vinctus** - a - um, *bound, tied*
vinculum - i n, *a chain, bond, prison*
vindex - icis c, *a vindicator,*

punisher
vindico 1, *to protect, deliver, vindicate; punish*
vinum - i n, *wine*
violo 1, *to violate*
vir viri m, *a man*
virga - ae f, *a rod*
virginitas - atis f, *virginity*
virgo - inis f, *a virgin*
virtus - utis f, *virtue; power*
vis, acc. **vim,** abl. **vi** f, *force; violence;* pl., *strength*
visio - onis f, *a vision*
visito 1, *to visit*
vita - ae f, *life, way of life*
vitium - i n, *a blemish, fault*
vivo 3 **vixi victum,** *to live*
vivus - a - um, *alive, living;* e vivis, *from among the living*
vix, adv., *scarcely, hardly, with difficulty*
vocabulum - i n, *a name, appellation*

vocatio - onis f, *a calling, vocation*
voco 1, *to call, summon*
volito 1, *to fly, hasten*
volo velle volui, *to be willing, wish*
volumen - inis n, *a roll, a book*
voluntarius - a - um, *voluntary*
voluntas - atis f, *will, wish*
voluptas - atis f, *pleasure, sensual delight*
voluto 1, *to roll around*
votum - i n, *a prayer, vow*
vox vocis f, *a voice*
vulgus - i n, *the people, multitude, crowd, mob*
vulnero 1, *to wound*
vulnus - eris n, *a wound*
vultus - us m, *the expression of the face, countenance, look, appearance*

zelus - i m, *zeal*
zona - ae f, *a belt, sash, girdle*